EXPERTS AND ORDINARY READERS ALIKE
RECOMMEND *Uniting Sex, Self, & Spirit*

A fascinating and illuminating study...reminds us of how profoundly our soul experience and our metaphors for the transcendent are rooted in our bodies... A rich and liberating understanding of masculinity and femininity, of the human and divine.

Christine Downing
Author, *The Goddess* and
Journey Through Menopause

This strong and articulate work is one of the founding documents in a new paradigm. It enlarges our definitions of masculine and feminine, and even the archetypal images behind them. Forward-looking...creative...choice!

Claire Douglas, Ph.D.
Jungian analyst and frequent reviewer for
The San Francisco Jung Institute Library Journal
Author, *The Woman in the Mirror* and *Translate This Darkness*

Explores the spiritual in a unique and profound way. Speaks to the connectedness of body and psyche, male and female.

Amber Coverdale Sumrall
Dena Taylor
Editors, *Women of the 14th Moon*

Combines scholarship with insight and offers us—women and men—a model for reclaiming our Selves as embodied expressions of the Sacred.

Bernice Marie-Daly, M.Div.
Author, *Created in Her Image: Models of the Feminine Divine*

Metaphors from the body add concreteness to archetypal psychology, grounding it in here-and-now reality. Haddon's vision enlarges our sense of ourselves as women and men of spirit.

Connie Zweig
Editor, *To Be a Woman*

Ahead of its time. One of those rare books that change forever how one sees the world.

Linda De Marco
Director/Producer, *Yoga for Round Bodies*

⇨⇨ MORE ⇨

A new model of femininity and masculinity... Haddon's 'God-Feminine' transcends both the ancient Goddess religion and the patriarchal God concept. This book belongs to the emergent tradition of female-centered spirituality and to the most mature efforts of feminism.

Georg Feuerstein, Ph. D.
Authority on yogic spirituality
Author, *Sacred Sexuality*

Valuable for anyone who is striving to grow toward a more holistic consciousness. Illustrating her four-fold model in clinical, cultural, and ritual settings, Haddon offers practical down-to-earth applications of her vision. **Kathie Carlson**
Jungian Analyst and author of
In Her Image: the Unhealed Daughter's Search for her Mother

Highly readable and easily grasped, with inventive illustrations. Exciting, nurturing, and expansive. **Jeanne Grandy**
West Hartford, CT

This remarkable book opens up new vistas of spirituality... Skillfully weaves between body and psyche, female and male. Unique, breaking new ground. **Maura Kelsea**, R.N.
Contributing author, *Women of the 14th Moon*

Striking common-sense symmetry... Even-handed treatment. A timely contribution. **Ann Blessing**
Columbus, OH

I especially appreciate the cross-disciplinary approach.

Myrka Hall-Beyer
Quebec, Canada

One of the three essential books I recommend to everyone. Your analysis of "Alien" is a classic. Genius. Wonderful.

Gay Mallon-Frank, M.A.
Psychotherapist, Dallas, TX

Absolutely inspired! The most exciting approach I've ever read. Beautifully illustrated. **Therese Ridgeway**
Chaplin, CT

As I read *Uniting Sex, Self, & Spirit,* a chord deep inside seemed to awaken and I felt set free. Why hasn't anyone ever said these things before?   **Marsha Pancsofar**
Columbia, OH

Insightful analysis, both outrageous and true. The body metaphors are fascinating and revelatory. A book I expect to go back to for the sake of its sensitive insights.   The Rev. **Rob Fichter**
in *The Loose Leaf*

Uniting Sex, Self, & Spirit

•*Easy to read*   •*Inspiring*   •*Life-changing*

You, too, will intuitively recognize Truth in these pages, and likely be changed forever by this visionary book, as you gain a deeper, richer sense of how sex, self, and spirit are interconnected.

Our own bodies, male and female, reveal four distinct templates shaping our every experience of both the seen and unseen dimensions of the Universe.

Understanding these four metaphors can radically change your relationships to other people, to the Earth, to the Divine, and to yourself. Fresh solutions to hard everyday problems may suddenly seem obvious as you look at life through the lens of the body metaphors.

Living with these new perspectives, you'll grow to appreciate your personal role in the cultural, spiritual, archetypal shift now underway as a New Age dawns.

Uniting
SEX, SELF, & SPIRIT

Let the Body be your Guide to
New Consciousness and
Deeper Spirituality
in a changing Age.

Written and Illustrated by
Genia Pauli Haddon

Foreword by
Georg Feuerstein

PLUS
Publications

Dedication

For Ren,
my life partner in work and play.
We see God in each other.

1993

Published by PLUS Publications
Box 265, Suite 93
Scotland, Connecticut 06264 U.S.A.

Portions of this book were previously published as *Body Metaphors:
Releasing God-Feminine in Us All*, copyright © 1988 by Genia Pauli Haddon.
Segments have been published as:
"Delivering Yang Femininity," *Spring 1987 Annual of Archetypal Psychology and Jungian
Thought* (Dallas: Spring Publications, 1987) James Hillman, ed.
"The Personal and Cultural Emergence of Yang-Femininity," *To Be a Woman* (Los
Angeles: Tarcher, 1990) Connie Zweig, ed.
"Body Metaphors," *Women of the 14th Moon* (Freedom, CA: Crossing Press, 1991) Dena
Taylor & Amber Coverdale Sumrall, eds.

Printed and bound in the United States of America.
10 9 8 7 6 5 4 3 2 1

Cataloging-in-Publication Data
Haddon, Genia Pauli.
    Uniting sex, self, & spirit: let the body be your guide to new consciousness
and deeper spirituality in a changing age.

    Bibliographical references: p.
    Includes index.
    1. Self-actualization—psychological and spiritual.   2. Psychology, religious
3. Spiritual life.   4. Women's studies—femininity of God.   5. New Age—cultural
and spiritual features.   I. Title.
        155.7   Library of Congress Catalog Card Number 92-61120

ISBN 1-881311-13-9

Contents

Foreword

by Georg Feuerstein

Since the creation of cities in the neolithic age, the destiny of our human species has been rigorously shaped by what can be called the "phallic principle." Earlier, the invention of agriculture had led to a more marked division of labor, and women came to be regarded as a precious tribal commodity to be exploited by men. The patriarchal mind-set was born—one of the most fateful events in human history.

The metaphor of the phallus, the penetrating male force, became the dominant energizing idea in almost all cultures of the world, both East and West. Men ruled, went to war, made slaves of the vanquished, formulated laws, meted out punishment, invented, explored, competed, controlled, and generally despoiled and interfered with Nature—for the most part unaware that they had fallen under the hypnotic spell of a potent "masculine" metaphor, paradigm, or mind-set. Soon no one remembered the old ways, the collaborative lifestyle of the eons prior to the neolithic revolution; no one knew things could be different.

Even the ultimate reality, the Divine, was conceived in phallic terms. No longer was it the Ancestral Mother whose presence stirred the hearts of men and women alike. Rather, people's emotions were captured by the male deities, who were often little more than supermen displaying all the weaknesses of ordinary mortal men—provoking and punishing, pillaging and raping. Or, as in the Judeo-Christian tradition, God was the Supreme Male, remote, unapproachable, and in charge.

Despite its demonstrable failures (including countless wars and the gradual destruction of the earth environment), the patriarchal mind-set has proven incredibly resilient. It has inexorably pushed human civilization into the modern cul-

3

de-sac, which is now threatening not only the survival of our sprawling species but of numerous other species, and possibly of all life on our planet.

Fortunately, today a new orientation is coming to the fore, and womankind is slowly emerging from beneath the millennia-long yoke of patriarchy. Long ago, women had been the bearers not only of offspring but also of extraordinary wisdom. Now they are rediscovering and reclaiming that role. Thanks to this hopeful development, a fresh vivifying intelligence is entering the murky waters of our postindustrial civilization. The present work is a powerful expression of that emergent trend.

Dr. Haddon, who is a depth psychologist and a Christian minister, goes straight to the heart of our modern malaise. What we are experiencing is not merely economic uncertainty, political confusion, social unrest, or environmental stress, but a global crisis requiring a profound shift, a spiritual rebirth of our civilization. In all the confusion of this upheaval, the present work can serve as an invaluable compass to determine where we are, both collectively and as individuals.

As Dr. Haddon explains so well, the shift can be understood as a transition from phallus to birthing-womb. However, she is no apostle for a return to matriarchy, if ever such a thing existed. The "God-Feminine" of whom she speaks so eloquently and passionately is no primitive Goddess, but ultimate reality—the Divine Itself—in its feminine aspect. This metaphor seeks to counterbalance the traditional masculine God image, which has been so one-sidedly championed for millennia. It serves as a rallying point for a body- and sex-positive spirituality.

Genia Pauli Haddon's work belongs, in my opinion, to the most mature efforts of feminism to articulate a new life philosophy. Her views are balanced, and her orientation is integrative, synergetically combining elements from traditional Christianity, Eastern Taoism, and Yoga with post-Jungian psychology. Although her approach to spiritual practice is essentially Christian, her ideas and suggestions can readily be applied by non-Christian practitioners as well.

Dr. Haddon helps us understand the "grammar" of our civilization: how we experience ourselves as men and women, and how that experience shapes our thinking about everything, including our conception of the Divine. She takes her cue not from prevailing preconceptions, or stereotypes, but from the raw material of sexual physiology. It is in our physical bodies that we find encoded gender differences that correlate with psychological, cultural, and spiritual aspects. To discover our true identity, as men or women, we must learn and live the fundamental language of embodiment.

This includes learning and accepting that sexuality and spirituality are by no means antithetical. Rather, they are complementary manifestations of our polarized human nature. The new orientation, or consciousness, understands body and spirit to be eternally linked. The new orientation is, as Dr. Haddon explains, thoroughly holographic. Every part contains the whole, and therefore the ultimate reality, the Holy, is present in every facet of our being, including our sexuality.

This is a visionary book, which boldly leaps over established boundaries between discipines of knowledge. It is also an eminently practical book, which, through examples and exercises, seeks to encourage the reader to venture forth into the territory of actual spiritual experience, which alone transcends the limitations of language and the human mind.

I do not know Dr. Haddon personally, but I find that her integrity speaks from every page of this book. She writes with the strength of conviction that springs from personal experience—her experience of the pain and joy of her clients looking for wholeness, and her experience of the sacred through prayer, meditation, and ceremony. At the same time, her words also flow from the fullness of her wide-ranging research. This work combines theory and practice, head and heart, explanation and exhortation, in a felicitous manner.

I feel both delighted and privileged to introduce this book, with the hope that it will serve readers in their quest for self-understanding and spiritual fulfillment.

Georg Feuerstein, Ph.D., is a historian of religion, specializing in the Hindu spiritual heritage. He is the author of over twenty books, including the award-winning *Encyclopedic Dictionary of Yoga*, and *Sacred Sexuality*.

Acknowledgments

The most important resource for this work has been my own soul's ongoing growth toward authentic meanings, symbols, and models supporting fuller consciousness and spirituality. Such unfoldment is never one's own accomplishment. By the grace of the Holy One just the right balance of nurturing and challenging conditions comes together. In this sense, it is inappropriate to single out a certain few for special acknowledgment. Nevertheless, the heart does make such distinctions. I gratefully acknowledge my husband, Ren, as foremost channel of that grace. He, more than any other person, sees and affirms who I am "in God's image," encouraging me to become that in actuality.

Thank you to the many people who read and critiqued portions of the manuscript at various stages: Therese Ridgeway, Barbara Grant, Lyn Haddon, Carmen Maciarello, John Blackley, Joann Kidd, Betsy Skinner, Marie Pauli, Carl Pauli, Jessie Kessler, James Hillman, Holly Hamlet Smith, Dave Lindorff, Kitty Overall, Jim Overall, Maura Kelsea, Ann Voda, Marsha Pancsofar, Janet Goldstein of Harper & Row, Frank Oveis of Crossroad, Connie Zweig of Tarcher, Maria Doubleday of Plus Publications.

Although *Uniting Sex, Self, & Spirit* is for people of both sexes, because of the gender-based subject matter it is not in all instances feasible simply to use inclusive language forms. Where citing both masculine and feminine pronouns simultaneously would be awkward I tend to give precedence to the feminine, followed by parenthetical reference to the masculine. This is in keeping with my natural orientation as a woman and also intentionally counter to cultural assumptions of masculine normacy.

Biblical references are mostly from the Revised Standard Version (1952). I have preferred the Jerusalem Bible (1966) for a few passages where the language of that translation harmonizes especially well with the body metaphor under consideration. Those instances are labeled *JB*. Wherever the exclusively masculine language of traditional translations seemed jarring, I have taken the liberty of rewording to include both genders, in several instances substituting the word *God* for *Lord*.

Uniting Sex, Self, & Spirit

Chapter One

Departing from the Patriarchal Story

Every person reading this book has grown up within a world determined by patriarchy: the rule of the Fathers and the Lord. Even in families where a woman is the "head of the household," that very description reflects a design in which one person is overseer, legal guardian, breadwinner, and orderkeeper on behalf of the rest. This and related designs for living, which until recent decades were assumed innate to human culture, are based on a valid but *partial* foundation that takes as its metaphor a portion of a man's most fundamental experiences of his bodily nature as a male. A culture founded on women's most basic experiences as female bodies would be another story altogether.

Patriarchal patterns reflect at the social and cultural level the experience of the individual male, for whom the question "Who am I?" is first answered with the awareness "I am different than the mother who gave me birth." To assert that difference implies a struggle to overcome the original state of oneness with the maternal source. For the female, this crisis of differentiation is less relevant, for her identity is rooted in awareness of likeness to her source.

The patriarchal story is that humankind develops contrary to nature. Whereas nature delivers each new generation from maternal wombs, in patriarchy this natural identity is superseded by paternal lineage, legally defined and recorded. This development entails the separating of mankind from nature, of the son from the mother, of ego from unconscious, of the sacred from the profane. In this view, human maturity is earned by slaying the dragon and winning one's independence. Both socially and intrapsychically, differentiation is the theme. To differentiate is to distinguish one from another. The subject object split is the most fundamental differentiation, wherein the "I" knows itself as radically distinct from all others or objects.

Patriarchally toned consciousness is founded on the differentiation of pairs of opposites, such as masculine and feminine, life and death, mind and body, heights and depths, good and bad, heaven and earth, light and dark, God and Satan. Both internally and at large, the opposites typically are experienced as in conflict, requiring either-or choices. Competition, with the eventual assertion of dominance of one over the other, is the pattern. Thus God triumphs over Satan, light overcomes darkness, heaven is superior to earth, mind over matter, and so forth. Accordingly, it is through competitive endeavor that both persons and states develop their sense of individual identity. Superior worth and power are the basis for asserting one's identity in contradistinction to an "other," whose primary value then lies in being that "other" against whom the victor contrasts, measures, and thus knows himself.

Within patriarchy, it is inevitable and correct that masculine triumphs over feminine. (In fact, humankind is identified as mankind.) Lordship and dominion of man is the order of the day. Power means power *over*. Thus, mankind "masters" the forces of nature; the individual man gains mastery over his instinctual life or his own fate. Both society and the natural order are envisioned hierarchically. Humans are deemed superior to other life forms. One sex is subordinated to the other. One race or nation is superior or subordinate to another. Subordinate groups and individuals are essential to this way of life, literally just as important as their superiors, for they hold down one end of that necessary polarity. Territoriality and ownership of objects, animals, or other humans naturally follows.

In the patriarchal view, progress is defined in terms of penetrating new frontiers, claiming new territories. A linear view prevails, in which movement toward goals is the pattern and morality consists of "hitting the mark" in terms of ethical goals. Successively upward progress is the ideal. This ideal is projected onto nature, in the theory that evolution has culminated in the creation of man as the superior being. It is projected onto history in the beliefs that modern culture is superior to earlier forms and that superiority is assured by becoming progressively bigger and better than before. In the religious realm, this pattern results in spirit being conceived as masculine and lofty. God is experienced as masculine, up in heaven and Lord over all. A spiritual "high" is called a "mountaintop experience."

Before the development of patriarchy, when "god was a woman,"[1] a different pattern pertained. Anthropologists theorize that in the early stages of human culture, before the male role in reproduction was understood, the mother alone was seen as the parent of her family, "the lone producer of the next generation." [2] Lineage was naturally traced from mother to daughter, and the revered Original Ancestor was of course the first mother, the divine source of all life. Iconic female figurines dating as far back as 25,000 B.C.E. are abundant and widespread. Typically, these picture a pregnant woman. By around 7,000 B.C.E. such carvings have evolved to represent the Goddess as supreme deity in her three aspects as young woman, birther, and old crone. Not until 6,000 B.C.E. does a male divinity appear at her side, and then as a satellite, often her son or paramour.

Prepatriarchal culture generally is called matriarchal. This term was coined by twentieth-century minds thoroughly identified with patriarchal concepts and constructs, and it misleadingly suggests that matriarchy is like patriarchy, except that the "father-king" is a "mother-queen." Although in later times there were female rulers, queens, pharaohs, the hierarchical pattern of a supreme leader is alien to early prepatriarchal experience. For this prehistoric period perhaps the term "matrical" would be a more fitting name.

The word *matrix* derives from the same root as *mother* and *matriarch*, but emphasizes that the individual identity is embedded in that of the surrounding group. This cultural pattern corresponds to the experience of the individual female, for whom the question "Who am I?" is most fundamentally answered with the awareness "I am like my source." During prehistoric periods (25,000-3,000 B.C.E. it appears that identity was by inclusion rather than differentiation, the clan or tribal group being the fundamental human unit. Property was communally held. A style of participational consciousness (which has sometimes been called "participation mystique") probably predominated, the process of mental differentiation, objectivity, and division of opposites not yet having become the dominant mode of cognition. Beginning around 2,500 B.C.E the patriarchal pattern emerged, and by 500 C.E the last goddess-temple in the Western world was closed. The patriarchal story had become our script.

Thus, for many centuries now, the patriarchal world view has been humankind's collective story, told and retold in hundreds of variations. Its motifs resound in old fairy tales, in religious myths and institutions, in the scientific attitude and method, in sociopolitical patterns, in family structures, in countless personal life scripts, and in all the major psychological theories.

Creating and living this story has benefited humankind in the development of discriminating consciousness and all that follows from it.

This patriarchal system holds together with great integrity and "works," so long as one remains contained within that story line. Its eventual disintegration is guaranteed, however, by the fuller development of the very sort of objective consciousness it fosters. When we become able to look objectively at the patriarchal system, we realize that patriarchal is not synonymous with human. Then alternative norms and values for individual development, cultural organization, and spiritual life become viable.

When we begin to see the patriarchal pattern as optional rather than normative, there is a tendency to overemphasize its faults and dangers. Such temporary denigration may be necessary in order to break free of its spell. One thesis of this book is that the development of patriarchally toned, "masculine"style consciousness is a necessary and valuable stage of human development, at both the species and individual level, for both men and women. When elevated as the exclusive norm of human consciousness and culture, however, the patriarchal pattern becomes destructive. The remedy lies not in exterminating, but in relativizing patriarchal consciousness.

Our cultural definitions of human nature, of masculinity, and of femininity are patriarchally toned; that is, they define the nature and role of men and of women *as they function in the patriarchal story,* where the dominant voice is masculine and where womankind functions as the nearest "other," the eternal subordinate. Within an intact patriarchy, woman's subordinate role is indeed her glory, for the continuance of patriarchy depends on her filling that place. Sometimes the woman seemingly usurps the place of dominance, as in so-called matriarchal families. However, regardless of which gender is dominant, which diminished, the *pattern* of superior-subordinate relationship remains patriarchal and is based on the fundamental male experience, "I am different from my source," with its corollary, "I am better (or worse) than the other." So important are women as the "subordinate other" that the male sex is pictured as protecting (and even idolizing) the female sex. Although individual women may escape this role by becoming "honorary men"[3] and distinguishing themselves from womankind, so long as the patriarchy continues intact, women-as-a-class must continue to function as the subordinate "other" to men-as-a-class.[4]

The cultural revolution known as the Women's Movement (and the more recent "wild man" drumming and sharing circles gaining popularity with men) show that established cultural definitions of masculinity and femininity are undergoing revision in the popular imagination. Women and men no longer find the old stories about gender identity satisfying, true to their experience, and evocative of wholesome self-development. It may be that new aspects of the eternal masculine and feminine archetypes are coming to the fore as the patriarchal system cracks open[5]

Although C. G. Jung, the originator of archetypal psychology, assumed that the cultural stereotypes of his day adequately defined masculinity and femininity,[6] he took seriously the fact that actual men and women often did not conform to these definitions. Through observations of himself and his patients, he saw that men commonly display so-called feminine characteristics, and women so-called masculine ones—if not in their outer lives then at least symbolically within their dreams. Jung attempted to account for these observations through his theory of the anima and animus.

He proposed that although a man's primary and conscious makeup corresponds to the masculine stereotype, his psyche also has a recessive "feminine" side, called by Jung the anima, or feminine-soul. Jung felt that female figures in a man's dreams represent this unconscious other side of his psyche, and that "nonmasculine" behavior such as moodiness, emotionality, and sensitivity originate there. The man might even be "possessed" by the anima, believing that females are the more valuable sex, in which case his masculine ego nature would be eclipsed and his manner imitative of the female stereotype. The Jungian ideal is that a man become consciously aware of the existence of his "inner woman" as a subpersonality and thenceforth depend on her to provide him indirect access to feminine attributes otherwise alien to him as a male.

The realm of the anima is said to include the unconscious, the earthy, receptivity, and passivity; the world of affect, relationships, and eros. The anima personifies the *generalized* archetype of femininity. While in a woman, femininity is expressed individually through her ego, femininity in a man remains archetypal. Curiously, according to this theory, if we want to know about the "pure," universal feminine archetype, without the idiosyncrasies introduced by a personal ego, the place to look is not at the woman's life and experiences, but at the man's unconscious![7]

Jung began with the theory of the anima; then, operating on the principle that what is true for the gander should hold true for the goose, he simply transposed the same structure, in reverse, to describe women's psyches.[8] Jung theorized that "masculine" traits sometimes witnessed in a woman are not part of the woman's conscious personality, but rather operate on her from their place in the unconscious psyche. As the impersonal archetype of masculinity, the animus is said to function in a generalized way, often not quite pertinent to the actual situation at hand. Among the qualities attributed to the animus, or masculine-spirit, are clear thinking, assertiveness, initiative, spirituality, creativity, and the world of linguistic expression. The theory is that so long as women imagine themselves personally capable in any of those areas, they are actually identified with the animus. To become womanly, they are to disidentify from those masculine attributes, recognizing that it is really the unconscious animus operating through them rather than they themselves who exhibit these qualities.

In this view, the conscious orientation of males must be thoroughly masculine (as defined by traditional stereotypes); of females, thoroughly feminine. Qualities that fall outside one's gender stereotype are recognized as part of the personality, but held to be permanently distinct from the correctly developed ego-personality. Even such roundabout recognition of a man's "feminine" and a woman's "masculine" nature has been helpful in paving the way for subsequent observers of human nature to depart further from old stereotypes.

Until recently virtually all psychological theory has been developed from the male perspective. Men (or, rather, men as they function within the patriarchal story) have been the norm. Much so-called feminine psychology really tells us more about the anima, as experienced by a man and projected on womanhood, than about femininity as experienced by women themselves. So it is revolutionary when Carol Gilligan of Harvard University reports on hearing a "different voice" in her research interviews with women on the subject of ethical development, suggesting the value and dignity of alternative styles of maturing and of moral sensitivity.[9] Gilligan interviewed both women and men and noted contrasting patterns of development. As she is careful to point out, this "different voice," although heard in *women's* descriptions of their experience, may not be exclusively women's own. Rather, within patriarchy this is the way the polarization has become established.

If we could get free of the contingencies of socialization and cultural biases, what would be the self-defined nature of femininity and masculinity? To look at masculine and feminine in themselves, we need a disentangled vantage point.[10] Jungians traditionally have turned to ancient myths and tales, believing that these provided the needed distance for objective analysis. It was assumed that the blueprint of the psyche itself, independent of cultural and social accretions, could be glimpsed through analysis of these collective materials, and that what was uncovered were universal archetypes.

In *Lost Goddesses of Early Greece*, Charlene Spretnak calls attention to a foundational problem within such Jungian research, namely that much archetypal analysis is carried out on materials that bear the imprint of patriarchal values and symbolism. She writes: "The concept of elucidating the nature of the modern female psyche by drawing on expressions of the female in myth is a creative and potentially profound approach. ...[However] the portraits of the Goddess in patriarchal mythology are...stories told by men of how women react under patriarchy. As such, they are two steps removed from being natural expressions of the female mode of being."[11]

As Jean Shinoda Bolen acknowledges in her description of the "goddesses in everywoman," characterizations from Greek mythology may have little to do with the nature of the eternal feminine, being rather descriptions of how the feminine expresses itself within patriarchy.[12]

A number of researchers have begun to seek out and analyze prepatriarchal versions of myths and goddesses.[13] Their work is exciting and promises to shed light on nonpatriarchal manifestations of archetypes normally seen only in their patriarchal expression.

My own search for an Archimedean point from which to seek a nonpatriarchal view of masculine and feminine has taken me in a different direction. My starting point is sexual physiology. I assume that the bodily dissimilarities between males and females *mirror a corresponding differentiation* between masculinity and femininity as qualities of the human psyche, and between the Great Masculine and the Great Feminine as preexistent archetypal poles underlying all concrete genderlike expressions, whether physiological, psychological, cultural, behavioral, instinctual, mental, or spiritual.

The expression of this polarity in the lives of men and women is not adequately accounted for by traditional stereotypes. Bodily differences provide metaphors through which to envision a fuller femininity and masculinity, which effectively counters both Freud's reductive and patriarchally determined view of anatomy as destiny and the abstract notion of "unisex" as an ideal.

We might prefer to free ourselves of oppressive sex stereotypes by claiming that we are all human beings first, and only incidentally male or female. Whatever we might wish, the actuality is that as early as one and a half years and certainly by three years, a child already identifies her/himself as a sexed person, not a generic person. "We come to link our sense of existence with a sexed existence so early that we cannot...think of ourselves as simply a 'person,' " says Jean Baker Miller.[14]

Insofar as a man's or woman's fundamental sense of self includes a body image and bodily experiences, the organic differences between male and female bodies do build toward differing self-identities for the two sexes. Sex stereotypes reflect an attempt to define these differences. They have a grain of truth, but fail to take into consideration the breadth of the organic basis.

"Female" and "male" are terms concerned first of all with *bodily* sexuality, female designating the sex that produces ova (eggs) and bears offspring, in contrast to the male sex, which fertilizes the ovum and begets offspring. Originally tied to these essential physiological distinctions between the sexes, the terms "female" and "male" have come to be applied to any characteristics suitable by implication to members of each sex. For example, as the uterus *receives* sperm and fertilized egg, and *encloses* and *nurtures* the fetus, so nurturance, receptivity, and similar qualities are designated as female, or more commonly as feminine. This is a valid derivation as far as it goes. However, because only certain genital features are considered, and others ignored, an incomplete inventory of associated psychological, mental, and behavioral cognates results. Sex stereotypes arise when such a truncated image is accepted as a definitive norm of femininity or masculinity. Such stereotypes can best be corrected by rediscovering the fullness of the underlying bodily sexuality from which they have been selectively abstracted. Comprehensive knowledge of the biosexual distinctions between males and females can be the basis of fuller awareness of the breadth of characteristics constituting authentic femininity or masculinity, thus counteracting the stereotypes at their point of origin.

I propose that physical gender differences be viewed as *symbolic* of the ontologic polarity of masculinity and femininity; that is, as ciphers or code language suggestive of matters about which we can in no way acquire all-inclusive direct knowledge. A symbol expresses a relatively unknown fact that is nevertheless postulated or intuited as existing. For example, the Valentine heart and the swastika symbolically imply meanings that permanently exceed direct definition and empirical verification.

Archetypal masculinity and femininity are the "unknown facts" with which this book is concerned; they are postulated as existing and are knowable symbolically rather than directly. The ultimate essence of masculinity and femininity *remains unknown*, but is inferred from the symbolic ciphers of male and female bodies. This book is about deciphering some metaphorical meanings from bodily forms.

Implicit in my efforts to correlate biological with psychocultural and spiritual phenomena is my belief in the underlying singleness or wholeness of the universe. It would surprise me if the realms of psyche and spirit bore no relationship to biological patterns. In drawing parallels between physiological and psychocultural patterns I am not suggesting a cause-and-effect connection; rather that the two are distinct manifestations of a common life pattern that can express itself in either manner.

"KNOWN"
BIOLOGICAL FACTS
AND FACTORS

metaphorical correspondence →

PARTLY "UNKNOWN"
SPIRITUAL AND
PSYCHOCULTURAL
PHENOMENA

UNDERLYING ARCHETYPAL PATTERNS OF
FEMININITY AND MASCULINITY

Symbolic meanings attached to the sexual organs and functions reflect metaphorical correspondences between these known biological facts and the (relatively) unknown psychological/spiritual processes to which they point. These symbolic connections show themselves in bodily experiences, ancient myths, fairy tales, the dreams and visions of women and men today, and etymological connections between words. Contributions from all of these sources will be considered in presenting a vision of femininity and masculinity that neutralizes traditional gender stereotypes by returning to foundational biological metaphors.

Letting the body guide us to new self-awareness builds a trustworthy foundation, which will hold secure even as old Patriarchal structures crumble away. At stake is our readiness to make the transition to a New Age.

Chapter Two

Letting the Body
Be Your Guide

In Chinese Taoist philosophy, the two great primal powers are yang and yin. Synonyms for yang include creative, expansive, radiating, bright; for yin, receptive, containing, consolidating, dark. All of life is said to reflect the interplay of these two principles. Stereotypes of masculinity and femininity identify the former as yang, the latter as yin.

To be masculine traditionally has been defined as to be like the penis, or phallus: potent, penetrating, outward thrusting, initiating, probing, forging ahead into virgin territory, opening the way, swordlike, able to cut through, able to cleave or differentiate, goal oriented, to the point, focused, directive, effective, aimed, hitting the mark, strong, firm, erect. All such characterizations are yang-like, expansive, assertive. Once the equivalence of penis, masculinity, and yang has been drawn, any human impulse or behavior having yang-like characteristics is said to be masculine. Thus courage, leadership, an adventuresome spirit, conquest of all kinds, exploration (whether geographical or mental), powers of discrimination, and mental objectivity all are considered masculine, and women who display such qualities are considered mannish. In the event a woman's personality evidences expansive yang potency, she is likely to be looked upon as both unnatural and dangerous.

Femininity customarily is said to be receptive and nurturing, as exemplified by the receiving and gestating function of vagina and womb. If follows that to be feminine is to be like a vessel: receiving, encompassing, enclosing, global, wholistic, welcoming, sustaining, protecting, nourishing, conserving, embracing, containing, centripetal, stable, holding together, inclusive—in other words, yin. Because

all yin-like behaviors are considered feminine, for a man to demonstrate a marked capacity for comforting, supportive, yin qualities is
considered pathological or at least undesirable.

Such a view does not take into account that along with the penis
a man's physical genitals include testicles. The testicular[1] component of a man's sexuality has very different qualities than the penis
or phallus. Physiologically, the testicle is a reservoir, a holding place,
where seed is nurtured to maturation. Unlike the penis, whose
power acts through intermittent erection and ejaculation, the
testicle is stable and abiding. It quietly and steadily undergirds the
man's sexuality. It "hangs in there." The testicle is the germinal
source, the vessel from which is poured forth the sap or water of life.

If our cultural and psychological definitions of masculinity were
based solely on the qualities evident in the testicles, we would
conclude that the archetypal Great Masculine has a yin nature. We
would describe it as the eternal Source, vessel-like, containing,
patient, steadfast, nurturing. And we would expect men to embody
in their personalities concomitant qualities.

Just as physical masculinity includes both the phallic and
testicular components, so will a fuller understanding of the Great
Masculine and of manhood include both the phallic (yang) and
testicular (yin) qualities, as two distinct components, *both thoroughly masculine and of equal value.*

Vagina and womb have a similar lesson for us.[2] The receptive
and gestating (yin) function is only half of their story. The womb is
also the organ that pushes mightily in birthing. Our understanding
of the nature of femininity needs to be revised to take into account
the birth-pushing, yang, assertive function of the womb.

One woman told me she came to this realization during the birth
of her first child. Fully conscious throughout delivery, she experienced herself as participating in an act of ejaculation: the culmination
of a nine-month erection. The fact that she resorted to describing
this most womanly of experiences in terms of male physiology is a
commentary on how little our culture appreciates this dimension of
femininity in its own terms.

Numerous women have described their awe and joy at the
immense power of the ejaculating womb. Anyone who has assisted
with the birth of larger animals such as sheep or cows will attest the
enormous thrusting power of the womb pushing-toward-birth. If we
were to define femininity solely in accordance with the womb's
birthing power, we would speak of it as the great opener of what has
been sealed, the initiator of all going forth, the out-thrusting power

at the heart of being. As the birthing womb brings forth new life, so yang-femininity is concerned with transformative processes and the experience of self-transcendence.

The word *ejaculate* comes from roots meaning "out" and "to throw." Womb power might better be described as *exertive* ("out" and "to join together"). An old meaning of the word *exert* is "to thrust forth, to reveal." To name this mode of the womb's functioning as exertive brings to mind also that the birthing process is commonly called labor, signifying great exertion.

If our ideas about femininity were based solely on the birth-pushing function of the womb rather than solely on its containing function, women would be expected to be initiators and movers; then, to call a woman "pushy" would be to compliment her on her femininity.

Although existing stereotypes assign yang qualities exclusively to men (and Jungians would say also to the woman's animus) and yin qualities exclusively to women (and the man's anima), there is nothing to indicate such an equation in the original meaning of the words *yin* and *yang*. In its primary meaning yin is "the cloudy," "the overcast," and yang actually means "banners waving in the sun," that is, something "shone upon" or bright.[3]

That these primal opposites are qualities that can color aspects of both masculine and feminine is suggested by the classic Taoist analogy in which yang is associated with the bright side of both mountain and river, yin with the shaded side of both. In a landscape where the south side of the mountain receives sunlight, it is the north bank of the river that is illuminated and warmed. Both yang and yin are manifested in both river and mountain, although *differently* in each. In terms of this analogy, we might say that the masculine is like the mountain, having both yang and yin sides; the feminine like the river, also both yang and yin. These four modes of human experience correspond metaphorically to the penis/phallus (yang-masculine), testicles (yin-masculine), gestating womb (yin-feminine) and exertive womb (yang-feminine).

The original meanings of the words yang and yin underlie the various alternative words frequently used to describe each. The side of an object, mountain, or river that is "shone upon" also appears to shine forth, to be bright. It becomes warm, and both heat energy and reflected light literally move outward from it. Hence, yang is associated with light, warmth, expansion, outward movement. On the other hand, the side not shone upon does not shine forth. Literally, both light and heat energy are more at rest there, and contained. It follows that sometimes yang and yin are described as bright and dark, radiating and unifying, creative and

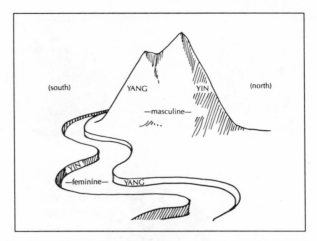

Figure 1 - Classic Taoist landscape analogy of yin and yang

receptive, warm and cool, fiery and moist, assertive and quietive. Yang associates with activity and movement, yin with substance and form. Traditional ideas about masculinity have ignored its yin half, associated with form. Appropriately, in this metaphorical model the missing yin half is recovered by acknowledging the importance of a second male organ, or form. And the missing yang half of femininity, associated with movement, is supplied not by an additional organ, but by recognizing a second function, or kind of movement, of the same female organ as that on which the stereotype is based.

The centerfold chart on pages 24-25 is a further elaboration of this quaternity, representing schematically the yin-yang differentiation of both feminine and masculine, and suggesting various manners in which each might function. Each of the four main nodes of the chart is labeled with the appropriate physical sex organ[4] along with a phrase characterizing its style of functioning.

Each of these four modes of human experience might be wholesomely developed, overdeveloped, or underdeveloped. Using the physiological characteristics of each genital symbol, the chart elaborates qualities that characterize ideal (heavy solid lines on chart), exaggerated (dotted double lines), and atrophied (single dotted line) manifestations in each quadrant.

The yin-feminine mode (upper left) is represented by the gestating womb and vagina, characterized by their receiving and gestating functions. The bold line leading from this quadrant to the center represents the ideal functioning of the gestating womb: nurturant, enclosing, receptive. This list might be expanded to include other adjectives

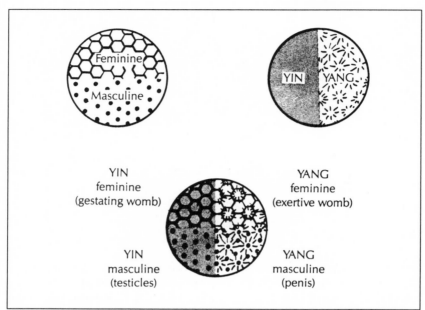

Figure 2 - Intersecting polarities produce quaternity of four sexual modes.

that appropriately describe both the physiological and psychological style of this quadrant, such as gestative, inclusive, containing, gentle, safekeeping. Excessive development of such qualities (dotted double line) results in a style of functioning that is devouring, stifling, overprotective. Thus a person whose yin-feminine side is overemphasized can be expected to relate to others in a smothering, deadly way, behaving possessively, snaring and trapping the love object. On the other hand, if the receiving and nurturing qualities represented by the gestating womb are underdeveloped (single dotted line), we can expect the person to seem aloof, cold, closed off, and impenetrable.

In the upper right quadrant of the chart, the yang-feminine mode of human experience is represented by the exertive womb, with its pushing and birthing functions. Optimum expression of the exertive womb (heavy solid line) results in such effects as pushing that is rooted in the context, organic transformation, intrinsic timing, moving with, birthing, becoming, developing, initiating growth, urging toward completion, ecstasy. Exaggeration of this mode (dotted double line) manifests as rejecting, refusing, abandoning, aborting, premature timing, meddling, forcing. Conversely, atrophy of the yang-feminine mode shows in fear of development and change, grasping for security, going past term, hesitating, missing the wave.

At the lower right corner, the yang-masculine is represented by the penis, with its expanding and penetrating function. Its beneficial expression is out-moving, initiating, goal targeted, adventuring, linear, objective, progressive, to the point. Overemphasis results in a driving, rapacious, coercive, argumentative style. We can expect such a person to be intrusive, rigid, deprecating, punitive, cutting, undercutting, judgmental, exhibitionist. Conversely, lack of development of the yang-masculine quarter results in aimlessness, indecisiveness, fear of going forth, and lack of discrimination.

Finally, the testicles, as self-generating source and place of ripening, represent the yin-masculine mode of experience. Effective development, characterized by resourcefulness, relates to staying power, patience, steadiness, steadfastness, abiding presence, and the providing of an undergirding, supportive base. Overemphasis shows in stagnation, procrastination, festering, sentimentality, grudges, staleness, inertia, stupor. Atrophy of the testicular nature is characterized by instability, testiness, impatience, fickleness, lack of conviction, vacuousness, or overimpressionability.

Although neither atrophy nor habitual exaggeration of a quadrant is wholesome, the ideal is not constant exercise of all four at once. Rather, a person becomes able to call upon or to temporarily suspend functioning in each mode, depending on the situation at hand. The solid lines represent the discretionary availability of optimum functioning in the four modes. These four main lines lead toward the center, where together the quadrants constitute a full circle representing the ideal fullness of human development. This ideal is the image of God upon whom major religions say humankind is patterned. Although real people may not fulfill their God-identities in roundness, this circle represents the full, optimal design.

Where a quadrant is largely undeveloped, repressed, or unconscious in its functioning, abrupt reversals between under- and over-energizing of that mode are likely. This is because rejected aspects of human nature do not go away. On the contrary, when banished from conscious inclusion they continue to operate in the larger, nonconscious psyche, secretly gathering to themselves life energy (libido). Periodically, this energy builds to the point of discharge, temporarily overwhelming the conscious personality with the rejected content, until it again falls to the background of the psyche. In religious terms, these are the demonic forces that disrupt us. Fulfillment requires conscious integration and development (redemption) of the heretofore banished elements. In our culture this means especially the quietive yin-masculine and assertive yang-feminine potentials.

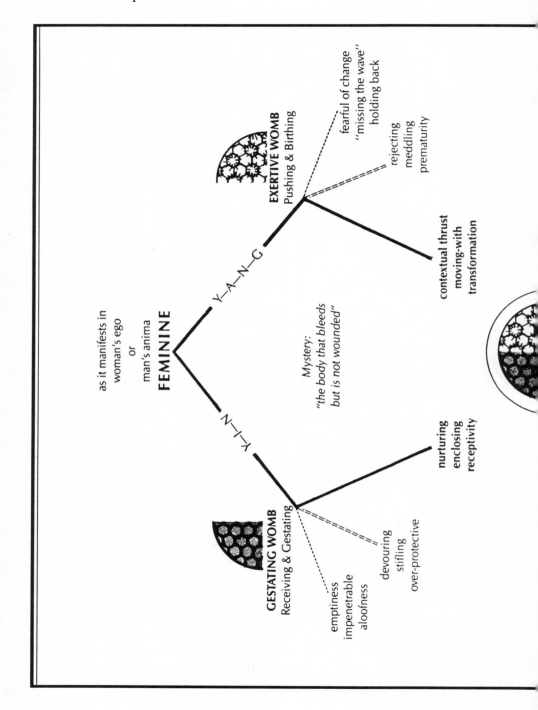

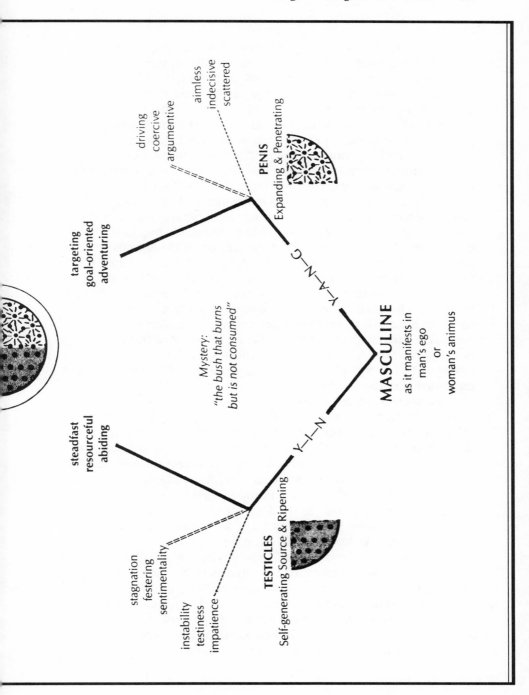

driving
coercive
argumentive

aimless
indecisive
scattered

PENIS
Expanding & Penetrating

targeting
goal-oriented
adventuring

Y—A—N—G

MASCULINE
as it manifests in
man's ego
or
woman's animus

Mystery:
"the bush that burns
but is not consumed"

steadfast
resourceful
abiding

Y—I—N

TESTICLES
Self-generating Source & Ripening

stagnation
festering
sentimentality

instability
testiness
impatience

Developmentally, both sorts of distortion play important roles in the larger economy of the psyche. Picture an automobile, with its four tires representing the cardinal points of the chart. In this analogy, gross underdevelopment of any quarter is represented by a flat tire. An overinflated tire is analogous to buildup of libido that is not integrated into the larger balance. In an actual vehicle, such imbalances automatically cause a compensatory veering of the vehicle toward an underdeveloped quarter, away from an over emphasized quarter. In a similar way, the psyche regulates and re-balances itself, the neurosis bearing within itself seeds of the cure.

The same principle applies to imbalances within cultures. Such compensatory shifts are responsible for the turning of the Ages. When sufficient potential energy builds up within the collective species' psyche, a movement counter to the predominant forces of the Age ensues. The emerging Age supplies what was lacking, repressed, undeveloped in the former Age. That Age in turn must come to an end when the health of the species requires a new balance. It appears that the human species may be at an evolutionary turning point where the patriarchal emphasis on yang-phallic (and its subordinate counterpart, yin feminine) has become overemphasized to the point that either replacement or transformation is inevitable. The fourfold body metaphor provides a framework for discerning what sort of new story might next unfold, in place of that patterned after the phallus.

The stories we tell ourselves about the nature of life and the world (whether fairy tales, religious myths, personal life scripts, scientific principles and paradigms, or psychological theories) not only reflect our current views, but also shape our evolving con-sciousness. To envision that the Great Feminine principle, like the womb, has both gestative and exertive attributes helps women and men to recognize and value womanly assertiveness as a *feminine* virtue and become able to distinguish between an animus-pos-sessed woman who is "wearing the pants" and a fully feminine woman who knows how to "push from her womb" as well as how to nurture. To literally "re-member" that the Great Masculine principle has testicular as well as phallic attributes helps men and women appreciate *as masculine* the supportive, patient, faithful attributes of the masculine principle, instead of labeling them feminine or effeminate. These realizations promote deeper self-understanding and call into question established cultural values, preparing the way for new cultural patterns and even new images of God.

Chapter Three

Body Clues to
Fuller Manhood

The predominantly phallic emphasis in Western culture manifests itself in many positive ways. Think of the development of allopathic medicine and surgery, objective scientific methodology and technology, religious and legal systems that clearly codify and spell out distinctions among things. Penis power is visible as the rocket probing outer space, the scalpel dissecting the body, the electron microscope differentiating the component parts at subcellular levels, the electron accelerator splitting the atom. Such phallic expressions become problematic only when they are carried too far, too exclusively.

Patriarchal culture greatly elevates the phallic masculine qualities, expecting a subordinate all-yin feminine to provide sufficient counterbalance. But unless balanced by the presence of testicular masculinity, plus both the gestative feminine and the exertive feminine, eventually the phallic masculine turns pernicious. The exaggerated phallus becomes intrusive, rigidly erect, unbending, hard, harsh, domineering, coercive, invasive, exploitive. It results in the raping of the planet for her natural resources, questionably intrusive medical procedures, the proliferation of penis-like instruments that shoot bullets and missiles, perpetual striving for dominance by powers and superpowers, dependence on rigid doctrine in religion, absence of contextual compassion in the legal system, and so on.

At the individual level, either a man's ego or a woman's animus[1] might manifest the phallic as the primary masculine component of the personality. In fact, most of what has been written about masculine ego consciousness and about the positive side of the animus refers to the wholesome expression of the phallic half of masculinity. However, if the testicular masculine character has not developed, all yin libido must be carried by the feminine side, leaving the way open for destructive expression of the phallic nature. This may result in the "macho" personality, the excessive drivenness of the workaholic, sterile intellectualism, rigidity, rapaciousness, co-erciveness. Exaggeration of the phallic dimension may give rise to a punitive inner voice that drives and deprecates. Opinionated statements perhaps punctuated by stabbing gestures of a phallic forefinger; slogans, often just off the mark; cold intellectualism; and merciless judgments toward both self and others characterize the man or woman whose psyche is dominated by the phallic pattern. Cut off from the testicular masculine, the exaggerated phallus becomes an *empty* penis. Whether wielded by the macho man, the dried-up intellectual, or the animus-y woman, this empty penis is sterile and destructive. It is sterile not simply because it fails to connect with the feminine counterpart, but because its own testicular qualities have been lost. In street language, it has unknowingly "lost its balls"—by projecting onto the feminine those yin attributes that belong by original design to the testicular masculine. At an earlier stage this projecting was exactly what was needed for growth and development; at a later stage, the projection must be taken back and integrated as part of masculinity if growth is to continue.

Projection is an involuntary psychological process through which an unconscious element of the personality calls attention to itself indirectly by causing the mind to perceive another person (or object or situation) as though it were the unknown element of the personality. The "other" functions as a symbol of some component of the potential personality which is unknown and as yet *unknowable* directly by the person.

Projection happens automatically and unconsciously. When I am projecting I do not realize that the outer object is functioning as a symbol. It seems to me as though I'm simply reacting to the object itself. In reality, I am reacting as well to the hidden inner factor. The projection continues as long as it serves the purpose of indirectly revealing the hidden potential in the projector's own psyche—which often is an element the person would just as soon not own. As soon as conscious ownership is accepted, the projection dissolves.

Even if the projected element seems undesirable, there are benefits in reclaiming it. First, it then becomes possible to see and relate to the actual other person. Projections interfere with genuine human relationships. Even if what is projected is valued and desirable (as in the mutual projections of "falling in love"), if we are attracted to the projection rather than the actual person, we subtly dehumanize him or her. Second, the psychic energy formerly used to maintain the projection is released and released and becomes available for living. Third, despite ego attitudes to the contrary, we are incomplete and unfulfilled if we have refused or denied some parts of ourselves—even if those parts are different than we imagine ourselves to be.

As temporary developmental steps, projections serve a purpose. What matters for growth and health is taking ownership of formerly projected potentials when the time is right to do so.

Collective projections may be generated by members of a group who share similar values and development.[2] It is becoming evident that *man*kind as a whole has projected on *woman*kind as a whole, elements that are part of the masculine potential—and that this, too has been a valuable stage in human evolution, which is now to be outgrown.

Prior to discovering that he has an inner feminine, or anima, a man tends to project his own yin side entirely onto women. His mother, his wife, his sweetheart, his daughter, his secretary, a co-worker, or movie star may incarnate aspects of his inner image of the feminine, as everything he himself is not and cannot be as a real man. As his earliest step in answering the question "Who am I?" was an awareness that he was different from his mother, so again and again he defines who he is by contrasting himself with a woman. She is experienced as fascinating and desirable insofar as he yearns for those unavailable qualities; or as dangerous, reprehensible, disgusting, or demeaned insofar as he devalues and rejects them. In either case, he is disowning a part of himself by experiencing it only as lived by women around him. During Jungian analysis, the man is encouraged to value the yin qualities by cultivating a connection to his anima. In this way the feminine "other" comes to be experienced as part of himself, although still clearly other than his ego personality. Such a step constitutes a major psychological transformation, involving a withdrawing of the outer projection and the opening of new channels for the flow of psychic energy. As the projections are withdrawn from women, his relationships become more authentic. If the qualities of warmth and care are among those that the outer women had been expected to carry, realizing them to be available through an inner helper dramatically changes his capacity for intimacy. A man at this stage of development has a vivid and personal impression of the yin side of human experience, personified in the anima, and accepted as the feminine side of his own nature. However, he still does not acknowledge and experience his own testicular yin-masculine heritage. To do so involves another major transformation.

A man's dilemma is not simply that he projects his inner image of the feminine (or anima) onto an outer woman, but that he has established his fundamental sense of masculine ego identity by projecting part of his authentic ego-potential onto the Great Feminine, personified in the anima. To call "feminine" attributes that are actually part of his *masculine* heritage serves the purpose of promoting the unhindered development of his phallic masculinity. But just as he can learn to take back outer projections of the anima without jeopardizing his hard-won masculinity, at a later stage of development he may become ready to redefine the parameters of his masculine identity to include the testicular yin qualities.

A significant issue for men is to value their genitals *the way they are most of the time*, rather than glorifying the relatively brief periods of erection as the only proper image for masculine identity.

BAGGY LADIES [3]
or From Under His Steel Fig Leaf

females have been seen as vulnerable
soft
spontaneous
limp ladies

rejected as   wrinkled
baggy
irrational
hairy witches

from primitive hiddenness projected.

males have known themselves as
hard
driving
productive
competent Monuments

from occasional moments of potent actuality.

As he begins to take ownership of the yin energies symbolized by the testicles, both his ego and his anima are transformed. Freed of carrying all the yin, the anima begins to fulfill her exertive yang potential in a positive way, rather than through periodic witchlike rampages or devastating moods. The man becomes able to experience directly (rather than through the mediation of his anima) testicular qualities such as self-containment, steadfastness, patient ripening, rootedness—and to know that they are components of his full masculinity.

Kathy and Bob[4] have been married fifteen years. Several years ago, following the birth of a severely deformed and retarded baby who survived more than a year, they found their marriage disintegrating under the strain of grief and guilt precipitated by that crisis. Depth psychotherapy begun at that time not only helped them come through the crisis, but opened the way for profound growth and change for them both.

After several months of intensive therapy Bob, an esteemed leader in a high-pressure profession, had discovered his "inner feminine" and was beginning to cultivate it by making space for non-goal-oriented activity in his life. He still named as "feminine" all yin qualities, defining his ego-identity exclusively in phallic terms, as does our culture. Meanwhile his wife had been developing in many areas of her life personal strength and assertiveness, which they both called her "masculine" side. They applauded and supported each other's efforts to discover and make room for their contrasexual sides. Of course, neither expected Kathy to develop more than token assertiveness, to be drawn on in particular settings through the mediation of her inner masculine helper; and both imagined that Bob's phallic identity would be tempered but not fundamentally altered by his cultivating of the anima.

At this time Kathy went by herself to a three-day workshop on healing and inner power at which for the first time she consciously connected with her own yang side, not as animus, but in its feminine mode. She returned home radiant with the discovery and feeling both more feminine and more assertive than ever before.

Up until that time Bob and Kathy had had a satisfactory sexual relationship, in which both expected that Bob would be the active, initiating, penetrating, one-on-top in physical lovemaking. Neither was prepared for the outflowing of yang-feminine energy that the workshop released in Kathy. Bob described later that he felt frightened as Kathy spontaneously mounted his pelvis, allowing her exuberant feminine-yang energy to express itself physically. According to the old guidelines, it was okay for Kathy to dabble in assertiveness, so long as Bob remained consistently more yang than she; similarly, befriending the inner "feminine" was not threatening so long as all yin qualities were clearly marked off from his masculine ego. But if Kathy had this much yang energy, how could he possibly have even more? Imbued with the cultural ideal that a man knows and shows he is a man by asserting himself sexually, Bob at first felt overwhelmed, defeated, afraid. He might have protected himself by dismissing Kathy's behavior as unfeminine and by refusing to engage with her. But as his inner being began to respond to Kathy's authentic feminine initiative, he found that what was called forth instead of yet more yang energy was his own dormant testicular potential. He began to experience himself as a firm foundation lying beneath Kathy, providing a steady, solid grounding upon which grew the tree of his own phallic erection, and which was equal to supporting and sustaining all of Kathy's yang-feminine energy.

Contrary to the popularized notion that women prefer extremely phallic "Supermen types" is the response of American women to Ann Lander's 1985 public opinion poll in which she asked her women readers whether they would be content to be held close and treated tenderly and forget about the act of intercourse.[5] She was astonished that some one hundred thousand responded with cards or letters—more respondents than for any other question ever put to her readers. Moreover, she reported than an overwhelming 72 percent indicated that if they must choose, they prefer cuddling to sexual intercourse.

Perhaps these women were not voting against intercourse, but *for* more tenderness. Perhaps they share in common a yearning to experience the testicular-yin qualities of the masculine and have thus far found typical experiences of intercourse to be so phallic (both physically and psychologically) as to seem incompatible with testicular ambience. As the example of Bob and Kathy shows, connection to the testicular does not after all interfere with good sex. As he and other men have found, once accepted as his own, a man's testicular qualities undergird rather than undermine phallic masculinity.

Preferred positions for intercourse are expressive of attitudes about masculinity and femininity. The pattern of man above, woman beneath has long been favored by patriarchal societies. Not only does it reflect the pattern of male dominance, female subordination, but also enacts the story that the male is active-yang, the female passive-yin; the male related to God-up-in-heaven, the female more earth-bound and less spiritual. So important are these symbolic meanings that Christian missionaries taught their heathen charges that any other way of coming together sexually was sinful (*see Fig. 4*).[6] Moslems likewise insist upon this as the only proper position: "Accursed be the man who maketh woman heaven and himself earth."[7]

Figure 3 - The tree-like phallus (left) from a fourteenth-century alchemical manuscript and (right) in a drawing of a dream by a counselee.

There are psychotherapists today who continue to view the "missionary position" as the only one reflective of good psychological health. Without having ever been told they should prefer that position, given Bob's and Kathy's earlier orientation, it was natural and authentic for them. In breaking with this pattern, they symbolically moved out of the exclusively patriarchal orientation and toward new ways of relating. It marks not a simple reversal of male-female dominance, but the emergence of a new dimension of masculinity, which authentically expresses itself in an undergirding position. Thereafter both sorts of orientation were comfortable and delightful to Bob and Kathy, greatly enhancing their sexual relationship.

Accustomed as we are to thinking of masculinity exclusively in phallic terms, how startling it is to recover what may well be the root meanings of the word *testicle* and to realize that the male gonad is named not in accordance with the familiar phallic hallmarks of masculinity, but as a "little earthen vessel" in which grain or seed is stored.

Some sources state that *testicle* is the diminutive of Latin *testis*, meaning "witness." One explanation given is that the testicle "witnesses to" the man's virility. A similar root is *testum*,[8] meaning a little baked clay pot or earthen vessel. A fragment or shard of such a pot is a *testa.* In the Greek, the equivalent word is *ostrakan* (earthen vessel, tile, tablet, potsherd, shell), from which comes *ostracize,* a method of temporary banishment practiced in ancient Athens, whereby a too-popular or powerful citizen could be sent into exile for a period of time. Each male citizen bore witness (Latin *testis*) by writing the name of the person proposed for exile on a potsherd or *ostrakan.* So a clay tablet (Latin *testa,* Greek *ostrakan*) with markings on it is the instrument for witnessing or giving *testi*mony (*testis*). This connection suggests that although *testicle* may derive from *testimony,* both words are ultimately related to Latin *testum,* a baked clay pot or earthen vessel, from which comes the idea of any encasing shell.

The testicles produce the semen, or seed. Botanically, the outer covering or shell of a seed is called the testa. It is the protective covering, encasing and enclosing, keeping safe the kernel as it ripens and matures. A man (or a woman's animus) functioning out of his testicular nature will be in touch with slow maturational processes. The testicular aspect of masculinity is characterized by patience and a capacity for self-containment and endurance. Men who develop their testicular masculinity become comfortable with the experience of being filled—filled with emotion, for example, or with feelings of spiritual satiety—in ways unfamiliar to the purely phallic man, who must "travel light" toward the goals for which he lives.

The ancient tale of the hare and the tortoise[9] is suggestive of the contrast in style between phallic and testicular libido, respectively. The surprise twist in this fable is that, contrary to popular wisdom, the testicular mode is not inferior to the phallic after all.

Although not so bold and dramatic as the erection of the penis, the abiding faithfulness of the testicular masculine is of great value. We see its effects in the steady patience of the careful craftsperson; the unfailing, supportive backing provided by the spouse or bene-

Figure 4 - As in this fragment of a Hellenistic relief, assertive feminine sexuality has commonly been depicted as evil. Here a feminine figure astride the man is pictured as a demonic being with taloned feet.

factor (of either gender) who stands behind the flashier creativity of the more phallic partner (of either gender); the resourceful depth of the "natural born" teacher or of the true practitioner of animal husbandry. Our earth desperately needs men who know themselves as "husbands" in the sense of good stewards, skilled at careful use of resources.

Zoologically, land tortoises and turtles are classifed in the genus *Testudo*—from the familiar root *test*. Tortoises are known not only for their slowness of movement, but also for their longevity: they live longer than any other extant animal. According to the mythologies of the Iroquois, Delaware, and Algonquin Indians, the tortoise is the faithful foundation on which the earth itself rests. Its steady, earthy, self-contained style makes the land tortoise an apt symbol of the testicular mode of experience.[10]

Masculine-yin and feminine-yin function in differing ways. Whereas the womblike feminine-yin style of nurturance enfolds, accepts, comforts, and builds up, testicular masculine-yin provides a perpetually stable point of departure and grounding. It is like the solid earth on which one can reliably stand, the starting block from which to "shove off," the unmoving fulcrum upon which to base one's leverage, the unfailingly trustworthy and faithful foundation on which to rely.

If the testicular side of man or animus is impoverished, all the yin must be carried by the feminine aspect of the psyche. Since feminine-yin is not the same as masculine-yin, the psyche remains deficient in the direct manifestation of one component of human experience. The person may lack the patience and fortitude to follow through faithfully. The man or animus may have lots of phallic "get up and go," but no solid foundation. He may seem fickle, impressionable, shallow of conviction, easily bored with the familiar.

If the testicular side is not developed with conscious assent and connection, libido may secretly build up in the testicular configuration—resulting in unconscious exaggeration of testicular qualities,which periodically possess the personality. This is dramatized in the fable when the superphallic hare is temporarily overwhelmed by exaggerated testicular behavior, which roots him to the spot in a stagnating way. Periods of stagnation, inertia, holding of grudges, festering of old wounds without movement toward healing may indicate a problem in this mode. *Test*iness of the sort often attributed to "anima moods" might better be understood as the backlash of the neglected testicular-masculine, which cannot be carried adequately by the anima.

In our culture, most men work at developing those attributes symbolized by the phallus. Like Bob, even men who have come into relationship with the anima through significant "inner work" often continue to feel uncomfortable about their own yin potentialities. Whenever they experience what I call the testicular side of their masculinity they hastily attribute it to the feminine, or anima.

Samuel, a psychologically sophisticated man in his sixties who fits this description, dreamed:

> He and his wife entered a shop. There his attention was attracted by some unusual swimming trunks of a brown or green loosely woven material. The storekeeper, who seemed to be a sort of magician, pointed out that this loose weave would absorb a lot of water—a valuable feature. Sam went to a dressing room across the street, put on the trunks, and looked in the mirror. To his surprise and dismay, these trunks left his testicles fully exposed. Feeling uncomfortable about this part of his body being uncovered, he readjusted the trunks to cover the testicles. Then he saw that his buttocks were exposed instead.

Samuel probably feels as uncomfortable in everyday life when his own testicular nature begins to show as he did in the dream when those physical organs were exposed. The classical solution of projecting the testicular-yin energy onto the feminine is pictured in the dream.

Another name for the naked buttocks is "moon." Flashing the buttocks in public is called "mooning." A generation ago, boys swimming nude together in the river would do porpoiselike leaps of two kinds: "shooting the sun" meant flipping over so the front of the body and the penis were exposed; "doing the moon" meant flipping in the opposite way, so that the buttocks were exposed. In patriarchally toned mythologies, sun and moon often symbolize masculine and feminine, respectively. In the dream what is really designed to show forth as testicular masculine libido is shifted by ego preference to the "moon" (buttocks) or feminine side of the psyche. Formerly, this shift was entirely unconscious. The dream suggests that through conscious reflection (the mirror) Sam now can choose to withdraw the longstanding projection.

Several features in the dream hint at the potential value of becoming comfortably testicular. Swimming trunks are for immersing oneself in the watery realm and probably have more to do with one's relationship to the unconscious than to one's outer "persona" garb. If Sam were to wear the new trunks as designed, his testicles would be in direct contact with the watery realm of the unconscious. When he alters the design, the means of connecting with the unconscious is shifted onto the "moon" (feminine). Samuel associates green and brown with vegetative growth and earthiness, both attributes traditionally associated with the feminine, but also characteristic of the testicular masculine. The word *trunks* has a double meaning, one of which suggests the testicular capacity for storage. Furthermore, it is the *store*keeper who offers these to him. Sam is attracted to this new style, but to make it his own he must "make a crossing," reflect consciously on the new configuration offered him, and absorb it.

Despite the Western emphasis on the phallic style, either a man's ego or a woman's animus may be predisposed toward testicular expression as the primary masculine component of the personality. Men who have not identified with the phallic qualities, who have early-on openly valued their yin side and developed healthy personalities around that keystone, are in the minority in our society. Fred Rogers, creator of the award-winning children's program *Mister Rogers' Neighborhood*, is one of the few positive public figures who are openly testicular.

I have worked in depth with three men whose primary orientation is testicular, ranging in age from thirty to fifty years. Vincent, Jerry, and Henry each began therapy to work on a specific issue, which led to depth-transformational attention to their underlying personality structures. As do phallic-dominant men, so too men with testicular orientation face the challenge of developing and coordinating both halves of masculinity.

As might be expected, these men sometimes have been considered unmanly because they do not fit the phallic ideal. Yet all are admired and liked by many women. All three married strongly yang-oriented women, and for two out of three this complementarity has resulted in a creative and satisfying relationship—though not without some uneasiness in both partners about their joint deviation from the collective norm. None has ever had a problem with sexual impotence. To say these men's personalities are testicular rather than phallic in orientation does not imply physical inertness of the penis, any more than a phallic cast to the personality implies non-functioning of the testicles.

All three men are successful in their occupations. Vincent works for a large company in a position blending professional, technical, and personnel skills. Jerry teaches music at a private secondary school for artistically gifted youths. Henry is successfully self-employed as a stonemason. All three highly value the testicular qualities of stability and faithfulness. They tend to be patient and steadfast to a fault.

All three have needed help becoming comfortable with the phallic side of masculinity. Fearing that to do so would mean abdicating their allegiance to testicular values, they tended to avoid experiencing and developing those psychological qualities associated with the phallic style. They needed to integrate their own phallic libido, but with good reason feared that to do so they must renounce as unmanly the testicular attributes—which are, for them, authentically the dominant masculine configuration in the psyche. Within classical analysis, it is likely that such a man will be prompted to differentiate his ego from an anima conceived as all-yin, at the cost of losing direct contact with half of his masculine birthright, which the analyst encourages him to think of as feminine. The unfortunate result is that he feels thenceforth he can be in touch with the yin half of human experience only through the anima, and that his direct experiencing of his own testicular nature is somehow wrong or pathological. Simply being able to picture that both the testicular and the phallic halves are masculine has helped these men redeem the latent phallic libido without losing their testicular orientation.

Henry had long been frightened of the aggressive energies associated with the phallic side of his personality. Partly because of traumatic early life experiences, partly because of an authentic devotion to a nurturant, supportive, steady style of relating to others, he had consistently relegated the phallic masculine energies to the shadows. He found that the women in his life—mother, wife, teachers, female friends—took a dominant role, as though the patriarchal pattern had been turned upside down. He considered males to be insignificant compared to women. Women seemed great and wonderful, first, because his own highest personal values are assigned by the stereotype to the Ideal Woman. At the same time, any yang-oriented women around him called forth projections of his own unrealized yang-masculinity, which in the patriarchal story is personified in the phallic patriarch. Thus Henry often experienced women as larger-than-life "matriarchs"—kings-in-skirts—ruling in place of the phallic patriarch. When he entered therapy, he was often hounded in dreams by animuslike figures typical of the dreams of women who are not yet on good terms with their inner masculine side. As he began to accept and value the heretofore feared phallic energies, his dreams reflected this transformation. A threatening male dream figure named Knife Man became a valued companion, and a female dream figure formerly pictured with a phallus told him she was being healed through medical removal of the penis, and that the process was half completed. At about this time he had the following dream:

A sort of turtle or turtle shell on the ground. A small brown dog comes over and a sort of tapeworm [but unsegmented and on its edge, rather than flat] comes out of the shell and into the dog's mouth. This takes awhile. Then the dog comes over to me and tries to put its mouth near mine so that the worm can come into my mouth. I feel upset and try to stop it. I grab him by the lower jaw and break it off. I can feel his teeth.

Henry recognized the long, wormlike form to be like a penis and associated the entry into the mouth with sexual penetration. Upon discussion, he further associated this phallic symbol with his father's belt: being whipped as a boy was an early experience of the aggressive expression of intrusive phallic energy by his father. Partly as a result of such childhood experiences Henry has been unable to stomach his own phallic potentialities, fearing their possible aggressive expression. Of course, paradoxically, he intermittently has been overwhelmed by unintegrated phallic energy. For example, under the influence of a hallucinogenic drug, he was shocked and frightened to hear a voice urging him to get a knife and stab someone. The dream shows that in his intention to protect himself from participating in the dreaded phallic aggression, he commits an aggressive act, tearing off the dog's jaw. There is no way any longer to avoid "feeling the teeth" of this side of himself. In this dream the turtle shell (*test, Testudo*) and the worm/belt resemble testicles and penis. His healing process seems intent on his taking in and assimilating the phallus, which is still experienced by the ego as disgusting and threatening.

The dog is associated with loyalty, a testicular quality. Here the dog mediates the elemental phallus for Henry to take in. In real-life time, that process took the better part of a year, during which Henry experimented with various expressions of his phallic heritage. This involved such things as cultivating a place for himself among the macho men at local hangouts, going on a hunting trip, entertaining fantasies of punching out an aggressive adversary who then became a buddy, standing up for himself and his son to "the matriarch" (really a parody of the rejected phallic patriarch) as embodied in various women around him. A very important series of therapy sessions during this time concerned reliving traumatic childhood events, alternately being himself-as-a-child and himself-as-an-adult standing up to the long-ago abusers.

Whether in imagination or in everyday life, his task was to become able to draw upon the feared aggressive dimension of phallic energy, experiencing its value and its place within the larger economy of his psyche. This entailed a *temporary* deemphasis of testicular values. When he resumed his native testicular mode, it was with an adequately developed phallic complement available to call on as appropriate. As this reaffirmation of his naturally testicular nature crystallized, he dreamed: "I am a Professor of Turtles." He is a "professor" of the testicular in both senses of the word: one who professes or *has faith* in testicular values and behavior; and one who *has expertise* and outstanding knowledge of the testicular mode.

At a crucial stage in therapy, homosexual motifs entered Henry's and Jerry's dreams and fantasies, including both male-male and female-female couplings. These themes signaled that masculine and feminine components of the psyche each were ready to be reunited with the missing same-gender halves: phallic and testicular coming together as a single masculinity; receptive and exertive modes uniting in the anima. These important psychological changes showed in the men's outer lives, transforming their ways of relating to people and situations. For example, Henry found he could be quietly forceful in promptly ejecting an obnoxious tenant from a rental property. Formerly, he would have avoided the confrontation as long as possible, then acted in a rigidly authoritarian, stiffly righteous manner, because temporarily identifying with the over-hard, exaggerated phallus. All three men had histories of being overtaken briefly by rigidly judgmental and harsh attitudes toward others, whenever the buildup of unconscious phallic libido became strong enough to overshadow the ego-personality. The goal is for the ego to accept and integrate the phallic qualities and so become able to exercise vigorous and purposeful phallic decisiveness without exaggeration. For Jerry this involved visualizing and cultivating his own "inner erectness," including standing up for himself as needed and becoming able to know what his own most personal wants and needs are and to sometimes either ask for them or assertively "go for 'em."

It was very important for these men to visualize that their phallic qualities could be developed without destroying their primary testicular orientation. Faced with situations requiring an assertive, phallic response, at first Vincent would say, "But that's just not me!" In time he learned that he could let it be *part* of him, without abandoning his authentic testicular nature. He became able to take a stand against relatives who tended to take undue advantage of his desire to be helpful and supportive.

The transition was fraught with fear for both Vincent and his wife, Judy. She highly valued Vince's testicular qualities and mistrusted the emergence of his phallic side at least as much as he did. This fear, and its effect on Vincent, was played out one Sunday evening as they drove homeward amid slow, bumper-to-bumper holiday traffic on a multilane highway.

Vince was at the wheel. Suddenly, a short distance ahead, a van from their lane pulled in front of a bus in the lane to the left, the two vehicles crunching against each other. It was apparent that no one was hurt, but the car immediately in front of Vince and Judy stopped and waited, completely blocking traffic in that lane too. After a moment Vincent growled in a soft voice "Let's move it , buddy," and honked the horn. When the other car still didn't move, Vince muttered "Get out of the way, you stupid asshole," leaned on the horn, and began inching forward. Judy felt suddenly frightened. She gasped, braced herself as for a crash, saying, "Vince! No, don't! Take it easy. You can't get through. Don't push it. Wait!"

She told me afterward that she had felt terrified and in great danger. I asked what she was afraid might happen. She said she thought Vincent might actually ram the other car to push it out of his way. Vincent acknowledged that this was exactly what he itched to do. The phallic response to an obstacle in the way of a goal is to push through. The fact was that Vince was inching ahead so slowly that even had he contacted the other car, it would have been but a nudge, doing no damage to either vehicle. Judy's terror was not about the physical danger, but was an unbidden reaction to the psychological danger posed by Vincent's expression of phallic intention. Judy's fearful reaction in turn undermined Vincent's shaky integration of his phallic energy. Had she been more comfortable about him developing his phallic side, her response might have been quite different. She might actually have cheered on his determination to break through the obstacle, trusting that he would have enough control over those energies not to literally plow into the other car's bumper.

As it was, her anxiety undermined what control Vince had. He didn't ram the car ahead; it finally pulled over onto the shoulder, allowing traffic to flow again. However, he did then zoom ahead unnecessarily fast, quickly cutting over into the next lane and nearly colliding with another vehicle, thus seemingly confirming Judy's fear that the emergence of phallic forcefulness is dangerous.

Fortunately, Vincent and Judy were able to gain insight about what had happened. Both acknowledged that there was something appropriate and valuable about Vincent's phallic impulse to push through an obstacle. Judy could see that initially her fearful reaction had more to do with fear of the phallic dimension of masculinity (in both her spouse and her inner animus) than with the actual danger of bashing the other car's bumper. Vincent realized that his reckless driving once the obstacle had been passed was an unwholesome expression of uncontrolled phallic libido, but that this did not mean that every expression of phallic energy is dangerous. On the contrary, in this instance his phallic focus on getting through had literally cleared the way and gotten them past the obstacle.

The successful balancing of phallic and testicular sides of the personality might be likened to integrating the alternative modes represented by Superman and mild-mannered Clark Kent into a single personality, *both halves of which are fully valued.* Such a task is doubly difficult without good role models, which are of course scarce in our phallically determined world.

In response to this need, men have begun gathering in all male groups dedicated to discovering what it means to be a man in fulness, limited neither by old macho stereotypes, nor by the expectations of women. Beginning as early as 1975, gathering momentum through the eighties, and becoming a significant grassroots force in the nineties, the multifaceted Men's Movement is helping men discover that full masculine development includes the opening of the heart to all manner of long-avoided feeling.

Often employing drumming and dancing, poetry and singing as resources, these men's circles provide a safe place where tears can begin to fall as they express truthfully their lonliness, abandonment, grief—for these painful emotions are often the first to surface. Energies long shut away in the testicular "turtle-shell" are becoming accessible, for the good of individual men and the benefit of the collective human psyche, as well.

This work requires phallic courage as great as any on the battlefield or in the corporate race. At the same time, the men practice bearing witness to one another's pain and truth, developing testicular skills of supportiveness. The result is not "soft men", but men in whom testicular and phallic modalities are integrating.

Chapter Four

Womanhood Delivered

Picture a belly-dancer rhythmically rolling her bare torso in rippling undulations. Slowly at first, then more strongly and faster, her belly jumps and quivers, contracting in waves that seem centered just below the navel. She dances with passionate intensity, her entire body resonating with the power of these contractions.

An exploitative performance for a crowd of leering men? On the contrary, the setting for this imagined enactment is the women's quarters of an oriental sultanate: the place where no man enters. The women together have created this dance in sacramental celebration of the birthing power of the womb. It expresses not seductive sexuality, but the assertive feminine power symbolized by the exertive womb. So strong is the yang-feminine power this dance represents that a man's sense of phallic potency could be endangered by exposure to it. Only if reframed as a performance done at the sultan's bidding does it become erotic entertainment rather than sacramental celebration of the womb's power, and thus safe to watch—part of its fascination deriving from its dangerous origins. No wonder the women are shut away in a harem where only eunuchs, symbolically feminized males, dare venture. Such an arrangement keeps assertive femininity safely contained, protecting the jurisdiction of the sultan from disruption.

Both in individual development and culturally, yang-femininity has been kept out of the mainstream of human development, left unnamed, repressed, banished, relegated to the shadow.

The ancient story of the Goddess Lilith[1] tells of casting out the exertive-yang feminine dimension from the psyche in order that the yang-masculine style of consciousness might develop unencumbered. Hearing her story helps us begin to appreciate the missing half of femininity and to picture what it might mean to reclaim the qualities she personifies.

43

Originally known as Belit-ili or Belili, meaning Divine Lady, Lilith was the Sumero-Babylonian Great Goddess.[2] As such she once personified all that was finest and most wonderful about the feminine. As the God-centered religions became dominant, she came to be regarded as a demonic figure, to be feared and hated rather than revered.

Early rabbinical tradition no longer considered Lilith a Goddess at all, merely Adam's first and highly unsatisfactory wife, created simultaneously with him (Genesis 1:26-27). She was replaced later by Eve, created from Adam's rib (Genesis 2:21-23) as the prototype of the subordinate role of the feminine.[3] So to look at Lilith is to glimpse something that was once honored and later discarded.

One ancient source[4] describes her origin as the result of primal Darkness flaming forth with its full, assertive power, and from this dark flame Lilith was created in the guise of the Moon. In the beginning, this yang-feminine Moon had dignity equal to that of the Sun, and both shone with equal splendor. However, a dispute arose, and God took the side of the Sun, causing the Moon to diminish herself and establishing the ascendancy of phallic values in both psyche and culture.

Lilith's nature is depicted in a number of ways. She may be envisioned as a beautiful woman from head to navel and composed of dancing flames below the navel. She may have "unfeminine" hairy legs, sometimes with taloned owl-like feet. The owl, solitary seer-in-the-dark, is her familiar. She is a wild, winged spirit, creature of the night and depths, incompatible with phallic values of light and height as images of holiness, thus fearsome to men and to faithful daughters of the patriarch. She has an active, assertive sexuality which Adam and the rabbis found displeasing. According to the rabbinical account, Lilith refused to lie beneath Adam, claiming equality with him. Rather than relinquishing her original dignity and submitting to the hierarchical mode of relationship, she fled to the wilderness. In her anger at this rejection she went about secretly seducing men and tickling to death or smothering the babies born of Adam-style love-making to other women.[5]

In all these versions, Lilith personifies yang-femininity: flaming darkness, sexual assertiveness, refusal to be submissive and sub-ordinate. Because the initial development of consciousness as a phallic-yang power requires the temporary exile of the feminine-yang power, Lilith and all she represents have been called evil.

Ancient Jewish tradition held that Lilith's dangerous power could be captured under an inverted bowl or pot. In view of the etymological connections between te*stum* (bowl, pot, vessel) and *testicle*, this belief may reflect symbolically the urge to identify all yin (including the testicular) with the feminine—the underlying strategy for the successful development of phallic consciousness on which the elaboration of phallus-modelled culture depends.

If Lilith's exertive yang nature can be encapsulated in the *testum* (representing the composite yin of testicles and containing womb), her threat to the patriarchal equilibrium can be bound. Because Lilith refuses to receive this projection and become wholly yin, she is ostracized: fragments of the refused *testum* are turned against her to effect her banishment.

Prevailing consciousness has good reason to be terrified of Lilith as a personification of part of human heritage, for she is full of rage at the denial and perversion of her true nature. The venom of some proponents of the Women's Movement expresses this rage of Lilith as she begins her return from the wilderness. In her original Goddess form, she governed both birth and death as transformative experiences. Her deadliness is a perverted, blocked expression of her potential creativity as a bringer of transformation, a pusher-to-birth. Her demonic attributes mask the primary gifts of her authentic nature, which her reinstatement promises to reveal anew.

If it has been of value to the species for yang-femininity to have been repressed for a time, it is just as essential now that we develop these very attributes. It seems to be the task of many women and men today to undertake the integration of the long-exiled feminine-yang side of the psyche—both for their own development and for the further evolution of human consciousness. It is no longer sufficient for a woman to be assertive solely through the good graces of her animus. She must come to know that sometimes being assertive is feminine.

Forcefulness from a woman typically is given nasty names. We say she is bitchy, witchy, wearing the pants, a ball-buster, animus-ridden. It is not surprising that many women are at first completely unaware of this force, having learned early to repress and fear it as "unfeminine." For example, when she began depth psychotherapy with me, forty-two-year-old Marcia did not consciously notice when she was being "a bitch" and could have imagined nothing more discrediting than being proved one. As she grew in self-awareness, she developed the ability to recognize when she "acted like a ball-buster." This was a difficult admission, and at first she wanted to be cured of such behavior. Traditional Jungian theory would have said that Marcia's animus had taken over and that her task was to disidentify from the yang energies in order to become nurturing (yin-feminine) again.

Figure 5 - The Goddess Lilith.

Note wings and owl feet, similar to Figure 4 in Chapter 3. From Sumerian terra-cotta relief, ca. 2000 B.C.E.

Different meanings emerge, however, if we ask what *birthing value* Marcia's bitchiness might serve. The man at whom she tended to bitch was stuck in procrastination, a negative expression of poorly integrated testicular masculinity. At its best, testicular masculinity gives one the capacity to "hang in there," hence steadfastness, patience, and stability. In exaggerated form, this becomes stagnation. Like the witch in a fairy tale, she had provided a necessary, though unpleasant, antidote. In this context, the image of busting open the balls suggests not castration but opening the way for the seeds of creativity to come forth. It is a kind of birthing.

Marcia came to see that her task was not to eliminate her feminine force but to become more and more conscious in exercising its birthing function. Marcia finds that as she does so she is able to exercise this womb-function while maintaining a sense of her larger identity. She no longer *becomes* a bitchy witch; instead she plays that part magnificently as needed, with awareness of what she is doing and self-acceptance of her birth-pushing role as part of her authentic femininity. With such awareness comes a sense of intimacy and care, even as she goads the procrastinator. She begins to see her pushing as contextually appropriate, reclaiming a side of femininity that had been repressed and deformed from an early age. Although being pushed to birth is generally not an enjoyable experience, when Marcia operates from her new awareness others usually seem to sense the value of her style of pushing, no longer considering her to be simply bitchy.

Even women who are uncomfortable with feminine assertiveness nevertheless are able to describe childhood experiences of their yang-femininity. With gusto, Tess tells the women in her support group her experience as a ten-year-old when she stopped a big fourteen-year-old bully who was picking on younger children. As she describes the incident, her face is radiant. "I felt so whole!" Then, with a trace of regret in her voice, "I guess that was the last time I did something like that." Jenny, fifty, describes the intensity of her experience of self-birthing when, as a five-year-old, she undertook to pedal her little red tricycle over forbidding terrain. The motive was not to get to the other side of the field or to be the first to do it. She was simply responding to an inner urge to exercise untried strengths and abilities. This was energetic action in harmony with the context of the moment, rather than for the purpose of reaching a goal or winning a contest.

These are yang experiences of girls before they banished that side of themselves as "masculine." A woman's readiness to reconnect with those banished energies may be signaled by a dream of a vigorous little girl of the age at which this aspect of femininity was lost. At such a turning point, Jenny dreamed of a five-year-old "with springs in her legs" running exuberantly and freely to get on the school bus for kindergarten. She weeps as she tells this seemingly trivial dream, so moved is she by this image of her long-dormant yang-femininity announcing its readiness to come forth again in her life.

The woman (or anima) whose exertive yang-feminine side develops well knows how to push herself and others toward new life in harmony with organic processes of transformation. Her style is to *move with* the birthing process in ongoing affirmation of herself and others through the throes of change. Like a womb at full term, she responds to the intrinsic timing of birth labor with contextually harmonious initiative—whether she is a psychotherapist nonjudgmentally reflecting back to someone a clear picture of behavior patterns that are no longer adaptive; or a mother encouraging her five-year-old going off to kindergarten or nudging adult children from the nest; or an artist or writer working through the night, not because of an extrinsic deadline, but in order to catch the wave of creativity. She bears down, demands, pushes, and thrusts forth creatively.

A distinction worth noting is that whereas the thrust of phallic yang energy acts *toward* a focused goal, feminine-yang initiative acts *from* a field of reference.[6] This contrast between goal-oriented and contextual yang styles of energy is illustrated by the experience of Beth, the only woman on the five-person board of directors of a large nonprofit organization. Each year the board draws up a five-year plan, allocating funds and setting priorities accordingly. Beth has noticed, however, that emergencies play a large role in determining how resources are actually applied. Phallic energy goes into planning long-range goals and strategies for reaching them. Exertive energy expresses itself in the emergencies, through which a sense of direction emerges out of the needs and gifts of the moment. When we are heavily invested in the phallic style, emergencies are frightening, distressing, taken as signs of poor planning. If we are comfortable with the ways of the exertive womb, we recognize such emergencies as *emergences*. If we greet them as welcome input urging us to make a timely course adjustment, then the transformational energy they represent need not escalate to full emergency proportions in order to express itself. So Beth continues to make careful five-year plans, but she now values emergencies as well, trusting both ways to move the work of the agency forward.

If yang-femininity becomes overcharged (either directly or through compensatory buildup), a woman's style becomes forced. She pushes prematurely, demanding untimely changes of herself and others, rejecting old patterns without respect for the purposes they may serve, often abandoning tender potentialities before they are mature enough to survive. Figuratively speaking, this is the kind of person who repeatedly opens the oven door while the cake is baking, prematurely exposing what should be left covered, meddling where such "help" is not needed.

In a culture where femininity is defined as yin, women are conditioned to neglect their yang side. When little libido flows in the yang-feminine mode, the woman or anima hangs back, perpetually "in neutral," afraid of initiating, never throwing her weight into what is developing, afraid to push. Long after another person would have "had a bellyful," she continues on the same track, failing to give birth to what might be. The young woman in the fairy tale "The Frog-King, or Iron Henry"[7] is like this. Closer examination of this story reveals a solution, both for individual women and for our culture, which likewise is collectively characterized by lack of yang-femininity. As we shall see, at the behest of her father, the king, who represents the wisdom of the mature patriarchal system, she responds affirmatively to every demand for nurturance, expressing her feminine nature exclusively in the gestative mode, as prescribed for women within patriarchy.

The tale begins when the princess drops the ball that she has been endlessly tossing in the air and catching. This might be taken as an early sign that her seemingly perfect receptivity as nurturing womb no longer suffices. The ball rolls into a deep well, from which a male frog retrieves it. That evening, the frog comes to the castle to claim his reward. The princess would refuse him entry, but her father insists that she invite him in. When the frog wants to sit near her at the table and eat her food, her father insists that she provide nurture from her own plate. When the frog wants to crawl in bed with her—perhaps more like a little child than a suitor—again, the father insists; it is her duty to be receptive. In all of this, the maiden exemplifies the qualities of the idealized gestating womb.

Finally, she has had enough. She becomes furious, snatches the frog from her bed, and throws him with all her strength against the wall. At first glance this seems a destructive act and perhaps reminds us of the dark side of such goddesses as Lilith and Hecate, or the bitchiness of Marcia. However, it also can be understood as a dramatic emergence of the young woman's assertive femininity. In powerfully ejecting the frog, she is pushing-to-birth. The frog is not destroyed after all, but transformed into a youthful king.[8]

One would think that would be the end of the tale, and in some popularized modern versions it is. However, in the original story there is an odd addendum about the simultaneous deliverance of the young king's faithful servant, Henry, who arrives with the king's fine gold carriage drawn by eight white horses to take the couple back to the kingdom. Faithful Henry helps them in, then resumes his place behind the carriage. He had been so unhappy while his master was a frog that he had caused three iron bands to be laid around his heart, lest it should burst with grief. Now he is so full of joy because of this deliverance that the bands spring from his heart one after another with great cracking sounds, which the young king at first interprets with alarm as the breaking apart of the carriage.

Iron Henry typifies the testicular quality of steadfast faithfulness. Like the testicles, he literally "stands behind" the flashy, upfront horsepower of the phallic king. When the maiden breaks free of patriarchal projections, she sets in motion the liberation of the long-bound testicular resources. As has often been pointed out by proponents of the Women's Movement, men suffer as well as women when femininity is not allowed full expression. One feature of the "wild man" men's groups as promoted by Robert Bly and others, is to free men to express what has long been bound in their hearts. In such circles men are discovering that breaking the bonds constricting their testicular nature need not turn them into wimps.

Despite the salutary effects on masculinity, it is important to recognize that a woman who accomplishes this sort of initiative is coming into a new relationship not simply with masculinity but with the assertiveness of her own feminine womb nature, by actively delivering a lost side of herself. Notice that the transformation comes not through kissing the frog but through forcefully ejecting him; not through nurturing warmth but through fiery feminine thrust. If a woman at this stage of development shrinks from her own exertive womb power and reverts to kissing the frog, she may end up with nothing more to show for it than warts.

As the following example shows, delivering forth her own yang-femininity can be a long labor for a woman who has adapted well to the patriarchal ideal of receptive womanhood. Sandra is a thirty-five-year old executive secretary at a Christian college, a good church-woman, wife, and mother of three children. Both her upbringing and these adult roles have urged her to be unendingly nurturing and self-sacrificing. Although intelligent, artistic, articulate, and well educated, her unspoken rule of life was "Don't stand out." Our work with her dreams had helped her realize that this "doormat" orientation was counterbalanced by a secret desire to be the "Queen of England". She often found little ways to set herself above others—although not with any deep or lasting boost in self-esteem. Both inwardly and in the outer world, her life was determined largely by bowing to patriarchal values and structures. She felt stifled and demeaned in her job, which did not allow her to exercise her considerable creative talents.

Sandra had a series of dreams and therapeutic fantasies over the span of three years that trace her progressive discovery and integration of the yang aspect of her "womb-nature." These dreams show how the archetypal pattern dramatized in the Lilith and Frog-King stories comes to the fore when a woman engages to deliver her yang-femininity.

In the first of these dreams, she revolts against the singularly yin mode, but does not yet have access to her own feminine-yang libido, so the only alternative at hand is to appropriate yang energy in the masculine style:

> I am at a celebration at [the college where I work.] I have coffee with [the president of the college, a priest], then go off with W____ [a religion professor and clergyman]. He parks in a parking lot, instructs me to stay in the car, picks up a prostitute, and goes off with her. An ugly old man comes after me in the car. I try to fight him off, but he gets me out of the car and takes me to his tiny house. There is another older, very attractive woman there. There is also his palsied son. The man is threatening to kill me with an ice pick. He throws it at me

and misses. I throw it back; it hits him in the chest and he falls, but has not been badly hurt. I run over to him, realize he is really a sweet and loving person, and fall in love with him. We all go to a celebration. The older woman thinks she is going to announce her marriage to the man, but he intends for her to marry the son. She is repulsed by the son and says so aloud. Suddenly the old man has an attack of some kind, falls to the floor, dying. I go to him, kiss him, and he dies.

This dream depicts Sandra at first as socially responsive and pliantly obedient to the "church fathers," representatives of the wisdom of the mature patriarchy. In reality, once a certain level of conscious development has been reached, a relationship to the masculine (inner or outer) based on obedience rather than mutual responsibility is a kind of prostitution and demeans both partners.

Realizing that such submission to hierarchical patterns results in being raped, Sandra asserts herself by appropriating *phallic* yang energy. This cold, raping phallus is a projectile that allows wounding contact without closeness. In throwing the ice pick she approximates the action of the maiden in the fairy tale, but is unable to sustain the necessary yang orientation because to do so in this form would entail being taken over by yang-*masculinity*, rather than pushing from her exertive womb. So instead she immediately falls back into the familiar yin-feminine style, running over to comfort him. The yang-libido, bound up entirely in the projection onto the animus, is again accessible only through "falling in love" with him. When the older woman openly expresses her repulsion of the patriarchal line (a rejection which according to the fairy tale is what is needed for transformation) instead of the predicted marriage, the dream ends in death—which might be called incomplete transformation. What is needed for the process to complete itself is Sandra's willing exercise of the kind of assertive femininity modeled by the birthing womb.

Another dream, nearly two years later, came after Sandra had made significant progress in recognizing her own gifts and strengths and had begun to take first steps to prepare for a job in a field where her verbal and graphic arts creativity would be exercised and valued. The earlier danger, that she would not be able to "get ahead" or to "stand out" without adopting a masculine-aggressive yang style of presenting herself, seemed largely resolved. However, when job opportunities began coming her way, she found herself making excuses not to act on them, with consequent energy depletion. It was as though she had nurtured herself to full term and now was stuck again. The old ways of relating to the inner and outer patriarchy were outmoded; it was time for a contextually appropriate thrust, of the sort imaged in the fairy tale, time for Sandra's exertive womb power to become conscious.

In the following dream she is much like the maiden at the beginning of the tale, innocuously, vacuously playing with a ball in obedience to the instructions of the church fathers:

> It is Christmas and I am celebrating with a large group of people. We are waiting for my son, who is playing a concert in [a city noted for its parklike model of the Holy Land]. While waiting, I go out for a walk. I am very tired, however, and I lie face-down, on the sidewalk for a rest. Soon B__ [my boss, a clergyman] comes along and helps me up. I tell him I want to keep walking, but he takes me back and tells me that if I want to exercise, I should make balls of newspaper and roll them along a piano. I walk through a dining-room and Nancy D__'s younger daughter is running around. I pick her up and put her in a highchair to eat. Then I see that Nancy and an older woman are sitting in highchairs also.

The dream suggests that Sandra continues to project her creativity onto the masculine. Furthermore, its location in a mock Holy Land indicates that this is a spiritual problem for her. Sandra recalled that Nancy, a member of Sandra's church, had always been shy—until she took on leadership of the annual church bazaar, becoming temporarily "obnoxious," perhaps possessed by masculine-yang libido rather than pushing from her "womb." Sandra fears this for herself if she exercises her pushing power.

Denying one's authentic power is exhausting. The dream acknowledges that she is literally getting tired of this, yet still taking the old doormat posture. The patriarchal representative ostensibly is helping her to get back on her feet, but actually undermines her unfolding by telling her to crumple up the new, "play ball," and not exert herself meaningfully.

What is new in this dream is that she is able to see that the familiar overdevelopment of nurturant femininity is infantilizing, putting three generations of women into highchairs. The fact that a great many women assiduously shave their underarms and legs to babylike smoothness attests to the infantilizing effects of conforming to patriarchal ideals of femininity. In abhorring our natural Lilith-like hairy legs we also symbolically cut ourselves off from exertive womb power, our birthright, which she represents. Daring to leave her legs unshaven sometimes marks a woman's movement toward mature womanhood, which includes her "Lilith" side.

Because there were signs that Sandra was ready to move beyond this impasse, at our next session I suggested that she engage in Active Imagination,[9] picking up where the dream showed her enacting the doormat posture and receiving her marching orders from the church father—to see what would happen if she kept walking her own way.

The fantasy began with a long sequence of walking: off the sidewalk, on a woodland path, down in a gully, into deep woods. In other words, she must depart from the beaten path if she is to actualize a side of her femininity not encouraged in patriarchy. When she stops, a large crow appears as though to encourage her to continue. Mythologically, the crow is the familiar of the witchlike Goddess Hecate, who, like Lilith, is associated with what patriarchy calls the negative aspect of the feminine. According to myth, Hecate is encountered at the crossroads of life during the dark of the moon. Sandra is approaching a crossroads experience having to do with dark, fiery yang-femininity.

She follows the crow. The way goes down, then into a brook, whose current carries her faster and faster, then down a waterfall. Behind the waterfall, she comes to a wooden door with vegetation growing on it:

> I go in the door. It's dark. There is writing on the wall—"This way..." I hear water dripping. A monk comes. About three feet tall, gray robe. Can't see his face under cowl. Leads me through narrow passageway. The sides of the wall are breathing in and out—like I'm inside a big animal. I can hear it breathing very loud now. I'm in a room formed by its ribcage. A red light is glowing. I'm told to sit and wait. The monk leaves. I wait. Now what? I wait. [Pause.] A tray magically appears before me. On it a tiny silver cup with silver liquid in it. I'm unsure what I'm supposed to do. Drink it? Wait some more? Or what? [Pause.] A booming male voice commands, "Drink!" [Pause.] What I really want to do is throw it! [Pause.] But if I don't obey, would something terrible happen? [Pause.] Shall I pretend to drink it? [Long pause.] [Gasp.] I threw it! It hit the wall. A silver streak on the wall where it hit. The beast is groaning; its breathing is very heavy. The room shakes! It's like a shipwreck, a violent upheaval! Now it's black... [Pause.] Where am I? Deep black. Totally alone. No bearings. Stillness. I'm dead. There's

just nothing. [Prolonged silence.] A current is lifting me. It's less dark. I hear a bell—no, it's a triangle. As though someone lightly strikes a silver triangle intermittently. Now I'm on a path again. Walking. The path itself is all lit up, but surroundings are dark gray. Now I'm in a hallway of glass. It is a series of Roman arches. I'm enroute to my wedding! I'm a special, wonderful person. I pause. I'm looking through the glass to my right. I see people in a cathedral. One by one they come up to kiss the foot of a man sitting on a throne, like the pope. This is no longer required of me. I continue down the glass hallway. The light becomes very blue. I'm in a big room with lots of windows of deep blue glass. It's a long, narrow, tall, grand room. A cathedral. I am at the point where the transcept crosses. I stand in the middle. Sunlight streams down on this one spot. I feel really good! I exult, lifting my arms up. I am strong! Now the bell or triangle is playing its heart out. [Laughs.] Ha-ah! The crow flies in, lands on my shoulder, laughing with me.

This imagery signals a drastic upheaval, the beginning of a new age for Sandra, marked by new understandings of herself and of the spiritual significance of her female sexuality. In rejecting the cup, which she associates with the symbolic blood of the communion chalice, she breaks free of the imposed patriarchal wisdom and begins to live out of the womb's own blood mystery. She can relate now to the masculine realm in ways that allow her to feel exultant, assertive, strong. Her readiness for a newly creative relationship with the masculine dimension is represented by the shaft of sunlight—reminiscent of the impregnating shower of gold on Danae in the myth of Perseus, or on the maiden who develops her exertive womb in the fairy tale "Mother Holle."[10]

In her daily life, Sandra has gone on to discover new modes of relating to people, alongside of the familiar role of nurturer. She has had the courage to change jobs, bringing to birth her artistic and leadership potentials. Confrontation had always seemed to her dangerous and destructive of intimacy. She has experientially rediscovered the root meanings, "bring together" and "face." When she is functioning out of the contextually oriented yang-womb, to confront another is literally to come together face to face, intimately. Concurrently, Sandra's dreams and Active Imagination work have given her vital new images of the feminine side of the divine as cat, owl, sculpture of the vulva, crow, helpful spider, kneeling dragon, newly discovered planet in the solar system—profoundly altering her spiritual orientation. As a woman shaped by Western culture, Sandra continues to bear much pressure (intrapsychic as well as outer) to identify exclusively with the *yin* mode of the womb. Having passed the crossroad marking the emergence of her *yang*-identity, she now feels womanly while functioning in either style.

Sandra's story illustrates how the archetypal motifs in the story of the Frog-Prince emerge within individual women's lives. The tale also casts a revealing light on contemporary cultural changes. We could say that, like the princess, cultural femininity has been slow to assert its values against those of the patriarchy. From this perspective, the Women's Movement is long overdue. A woman's awakening to feminist values commonly is marked by a period of outrage and anger: "We're mad as hell, and we're not gonna take it anymore!" Ideally, this energy should express *exertively*, along the lines modeled by the maiden in the story and with equally transforming effects. However, as long as yang and phallic are equated, women's only access to yang energy is to adopt phallic rather than exertive values. Figuratively speaking, some women graft on a phallus but find it doesn't work right for them. Chronic impotent anger is the result.

There is a place in the economy of a woman's psyche for all four gender modes. In some circumstances, phallic energy is just what is needed—but never as an unconscious substitute for yang-femininity. Both for individuals and for the collective culture at large, the solution is for women to differentiate between phallic-yang and exertive-yang styles, claim their exertive feminine birthright, and push the entire culture to rebirth.

In the story, we see that phallic masculinity is dually depicted. On the one hand, it is the king, the patriarch, the ruler of the culture. At the same time, it is an odious frog hidden deep in a well. Despite the great development of phallic consciousness in the human species, there are ways in which phallic masculinity remains very primitive. As the feminine yang values begin to emerge with vehemence and power, we can expect even the seemingly well-developed patriarchal consciousness to be transformed. With the emergence of yang-femininity in a woman's consciousness, yang-masculinity begins to function in new ways in her own personality and in the world around her.

One hallmark of yang-masculine consciousness is the ability to cut through irrelevancies and get straight to the goal. Commonly this gift is exercised with an attitude of mastering and overpowering obstacles. With the emergence of yang-femininity, this phallic talent is found to operate with humor, lightness, and laughter rather than aggressiveness. Ann, a naturally gestative woman, was just emerging from her patriarchally prescribed role as exclusively nurturing and maternal. She sought a new way to engage with an everyday situation in which phallic energy had been expressing itself in a manner she described as "guerrilla warfare." As she said the word *guerrilla*, we were reminded of her recent dream of a gorilla menacing a nun who intended to stab him. Through Active Imagination culminating in physical enactment, Ann had a vivid, transforming experience

As she enacted Gorilla, jumping, scratching, flaring her nostrils, snorting and snuffing, I was repeatedly dissolved in thoroughly unprofessional laughter. She *was* Gorilla; and she was very funny as she danced around the scissors-wielding nun. The hostile nun was disarmed by the laughter that bubbled up, and the two happily embraced instead of either one dominating the other.

Afterward, Ann said she had especially noticed the male organs swinging between her thighs as she danced around. When she subsequently considered the "guerrilla warfare" situation from the perspective of the laughing Gorilla, suddenly she could envision responding a different way: cutting through the bullshit with humor rather than aggression, disarming the situation rather than over-powering the seeming menace. This is not the derogatory, cutting, stabbing sort of humor often seen in both men and women who are expressing yang-masculinity in its more usual mode. It is a joyful and contagious invitation to shared delight in "getting on with it."

Another woman, Gail visualized the transformed role of phallic energy in a different manner. During intense Active Imagination she saw a beautiful, round stained-glass window in the center of her body break into its constituent pieces. These shifted around and came back together in an equally beautiful pattern, leaving out one elongated triangular piece. This piece was then released through the crown of her head "to return to the far distances." Through working with her associations, we recognized that this triangular piece had to do with Gail's customarily experiencing phallic energy (in both the men and the institutions around her) as a thorn in her side. Having at one time identified with yang-masculinity, then subsequently having trans-ferred her allegiance to the exertive feminine style, she was frequently irritated and upset by the predominantly phallic tone of our culture.

Immediately following this vision, Gail developed a significant friendship bearing out its implications. Her new friend, Karl, was a decidedly yang-masculine man seriously engaged in personal growth work, who envisioned his spiritual path in typical phallic manner as a straight and narrow, ever-upward way, requiring heroic exercise of firm will. What struck her most about Karl, however, was the humor and good will with which he homed in on obstacles to growth. She found his low-key laughter a gracious and contagious catalyst to her own continued transformation, pictured from her exertive-womb perspective as a circular, perpetually spiraling process. No longer in danger of falsely identifying with yang-masculine ways or experiencing them as a thorn in her side, Gail found it natural to stay true to her own exertive process without denigrating Karl's phallic approach to spiritual work. And she experienced Karl doing the same vis-a-vis her, respecting her way though unable to comprehend it fully.

It is a fitting irony that in defining ideal womanhood as all yin, patriarchal culture generates a configuration that inevitably calls forth the very monster most feared, represented as the devouring dragon or spider. The perpetually egg-laying monster in the 1986 movie *Aliens* fits this genre. A cross between a dragon, spider, giant crab, and octopus, she snares and entraps all who come within reach of her clawed appendages, twisting tentaclelike tails, or resinous webs. She traps her victims not out of hostility, nor to consume them, but out of urgency to fulfill her exaggerated gestative impulses. Each victim becomes an auxiliary womb within which her hatchlings can be safely gestated.

Annie Wilkes, the ex-nurse in Stephen King's horror novel *Misery*, likewise epitomizes the nightmare of gestative femininity gone berserk. In this story, Paul Sheldon, famous author of a series of gothic novels featuring a typically yin-feminine heroine, regains consciousness after a near fatal automobile crash to find himself in the care of Annie at her isolated farmhouse. The entire plot consists of ever more terrifying enactments of her version of TLC. She "loves" and "protects" him with warped intensity.

Whereas the wholesome gestative womb is characterized by receptivity and beneficent containment, overemphasis of this mode makes a woman or anima secretly devouring and possessive rather that welcoming and receptive. Like the proverbial "Jewish mother" she will snare and hold onto all entering her domain, smothering and stifling even those she "loves." She is likely to be overprotective of both herself and others, with a cramped and cramping style.

Gestative overinvolvement can vary in degree from the hostess who hovers over the dinner guest, mentally noting exactly what is eaten, urging another helping of this, a bit more of that; to spouses who phone each other several times a day to keep abreast of how the day is going; to the mother who secretly rejoices when her son is struck helpless with a grave disease requiring her constant care, because it means now he'll always need her. The spider and its web[11] or octopus with grasping tentacles are typical dream images relative to this sort of misdevelopment in both women and anima.

Women who vehemently refuse to "carry the ball(s)" may reject their own gestative yin nature altogether. Then it is as though the womb remains closed and empty. In some cases, the woman literally either cannot or chooses not to become pregnant for fear that the nurturing aspect of her nature would consume her entire personality. These persons may experience feeling empty and hollow. Others may find them to be aloof, cold, impenetrable. They are unable to nurture themselves, to know what they want, to ask straightforwardly for what they need, or to receive what may be offered. They are never satisied, may whine and complain and criticize without ever getting to the root of what they need, and may be as insensitive to the real needs of others as they are unaware of their own.

All women have both gestative and exertive sides; in each personality, one or the other seems naturally dominant. If, like Gail, a woman's authentic nature is characterized by a preponderance of feminine-yang energy, she faces the difficult predicament of living in a culture that equates yang with masculine and overvalues both. If she eschews her own considerable assertiveness (projecting it onto inner and outer men) in order to be completely "feminine" by cultural standards, her individual femininity is sabotaged. Having a good relationship to a yang-animus does not suffice. She has an intrinsic need and responsibility to fulfill her feminine-yang proclivities. Furthermore, cultural values tell her that the yang mode is "better," so if she values herself, she has that added incentive to develop her "more valuable" yang qualities.

However, if she does begin to fulfill her femininity in the yang mode, she (or others around her) may name as masculine this authentically feminine development.[12] Partly because of this cultural predisposition to call her yang-feminine gifts both "more valuable" and "masculine," she is particularly vulnerable to inauthentic identification with masculinity. If she is familiar with Jung's description of the animus, she may picture her inner man as the exclusive personification of all yang energy. She may feel that in order to develop the yang aspect of her own feminine consciousness, she must wrest it from the animus or become masculinized herself.

Terry, a woman in her early thirties struggling with this dilemma, dreamed that she needed to keep her blouse buttoned up high so that no one would see she had hair on her chest. Her discomfort with the very qualities most central to her natural personality arises in part from not knowing that there are womanly yang expressions as well as masculine ones. She feels both covetous of yang energy and ashamed of owning it. This inner conflict is lived out in her relationships with men. On the one hand, she values the company of males more than that of females. At the same time, she is likely to feel hostilely competitive and resentful toward men. She projects her own yang power on men, then seeks to reclaim it first by affiliation, then by force. Such a woman may feel admiration for strong men of accomplishment, yet choose as a mate an ineffectual man, as though for reassurance that all the yang resources have not been preempted by the male.

Women with natural tendencies toward yang-femininity are especially affronted by the old feminine stereotypes. In their urgency to demonstrate their freedom from those false ideals, they may take on another false identity, expressing their bountiful yang energy in phallic patterns. When this happens yang-femininity remains repressed, and the overburdened phallic channel no longer functions beneficially. It lends a driving and driven intensity to the personality, a brittle hardness, an acidic sharpness. In a caricature of phallic effectivity, these misplaced yang energies generate a powerful canon of "oughts," and "shoulds" which the woman applies without compassion to both herself and others.

When functioning well in either a man or a woman, phallic energy generates goals and fuels purposeful activity toward those goals. When substituted for the woman's exertive-womb energy, the phallic animus instead fixates on abstract, unreachable goals that, although irrelevant to the real concerns of the woman's life, become her taskmaster. She is as though possessed by a frantic energy that operates in the service of this inhuman goal.

In contrast, if her yang-femininity develops, she pushes from *within* her actual life context. Forward movement is oriented toward the flowering of what has been gestating within the situation, rather than toward an extrinsic goal. Preoccupation with authoritarian "oughts" is replaced by a compassionate demand for authenticity rooted in the actual context of each situation. Her womb power, in the service of bringing forth newness in the fulness of time, tends to push *with* what is being birthed rather than insisting that things should be different in accordance with an extrinsic ideal.

These same principles apply collectively as an upwelling of yang-feminine energy now taking place in countless individual lives poises the entire culture for a momentous shift. The time is ripe for deliverance of full womanhood by the power of the yang-womb. This will catalyze a quantum leap for the entire human species to a new order of consciousness and spiritual development.

Chapter Five

Sorting Religious Practices

As I have come to respect and value all four gender modes in myself and others, I have become progressively uncomfortable with religious practices and teachings that ignore or dishonor one or more of them. This dissatisfaction has had the salutary effect of encouraging me to seek out within the riches of my faith tradition elements that encourage me to image and worship the Deity in all four modes. Learning to recognize the phallic, testicular, gestative, and exertive patterns pays spiritual dividends, whether you remain in a traditional faith, begin New Age practices, or even pioneer new paths.

Public worship patterns of most Jewish, Muslim, and Christian communities (my own denomination included[1]) are strongly phallic in orientation. And despite their intentions to leave old, patriarchal ways behind, many New Age teachings, such as the highly popular *A Course in Miracles*, continue to emphasize phallic imagery and values. Yet, just as my religious tradition bears within it unnoticed elements that resonate with the other three gender metaphors, so may other systems of belief. The following account of some of my discoveries and experiments may inspire others to find their own unique ways of unfolding the four body metaphors within their particular belief system.

I first became aware of how the physical shape of a worship space influences our experiences of God when I worshiped in two different outdoor settings at a retreat center in hilly New England. The main outdoor chapel is reached by a long, easy climb on a woodland path to the highest point on the grounds. There, in a clearing at the crest, benches of roughhewn logs have been placed like pews facing an equally rustic pulpit and cross. The vista beyond is breathtaking: across the breadth of a lake-filled valley and ever outward toward the horizon and upward to the open sky. This place-at-the-top calls forth feelings of awe and exhilaration: "God is great and over all!"

After worshiping there, our small group descended the path again. Along the way we came upon a second natural chapel, a perfectly bowl-shaped hollow the size of a large room and perhaps twelve feet deep at center. The underbrush had been cleared and a few natural boulders left. We entered and sat on the ground, nestling into the curve of this natural bowl so like a great cupped hand. Trees growing all around the rim arched their branches above us in a canopy that completely enclosed us from the sky. The natural focal point of this rounded space was the center, down and in. The atmosphere was dusky, hushed, and quietly expectant. This place-in-the-depths called forth feelings of warmth and intensity: "God is intimate, deep, and underlying all!"

Both worship experiences were valuable, each shaped by its setting. In the same way, architectural design shapes our experiences of God within traditional houses of worship.

Even before entering most church buildings, worshipers encounter the unspoken message of a phallic spire pointing up, up, up toward the heavenly God who rules from on high. Inside, the congregation sits in rows of pews facing toward an elevated platform or chancel. A few special seats of honor on this raised area are for authorized church leaders and clergy. In harmony with the phallic imagery, whatever is most important is raised up, and higher is better. In Catholic churches usually the focal point is a large crucifix, in Protestant churches a cross—perhaps on the altar or communion table, perhaps suspended high above the congregation on the farthest wall of the chancel. The cross repeats the vertical emphasis, with its tall shape and relatively short horizontal member. Often ceilings are vaulted, windows tall and elongated, pulpit high and lifted up. All of these features resonate with the higher-is-better phallic value system.

In some houses of worship it is traditional for men to sit on one side, women on the other, enacting the differentiation and separation of opposites that is so valued in patriarchy. For similar reasons, priests, ministers, rabbis, and even gurus usually wear distinctive vestments setting them apart from those they lead.

All these structural givens predispose worship to follow phallic forms. Patterns that might otherwise flow authentically from the neglected strata of the tradition are blocked in such an environment. For example, nurturant affection of Christians for one another, such as described in gospel accounts of the early church, is not as readily expressed during formal worship services as it is in other settings.

Congregations who do "pass the peace of Christ" often must contend with a seating pattern that makes face-to-face encounter with one other difficult. It is awkward to reach across lines of pews for a handshake, much less a warm embrace.

As the female associate minister planning a special service for "Women's Sunday" in her church remarked, "It's as though we were to put up a sign WOMEN on the door of the men's room for one day—but still leave only urinals inside. There's only so much we can do to bring the feminine side of God into a sanctuary like ours."

Yet, even in such settings, words, actions, and music can open up nonphallic dimensions. For example, although the invocation from that Women's Sunday service was spoken by an ordained minister physically elevated above the people in a lofty pulpit, the words evoke the gestative and exertive womblike qualities of the Divine:

> Gracious, divine, and holy One, we come into your presence with a feeling of expectancy. Our deepest souls seem already to know that the time is ripe. All the moments of our lives to this point have been building toward this very hour. Secretly, as within the dark of the womb, you have been knitting together this piece and that, and now the time draws near when you will reveal a fresh glimpse of your New Creation.
>
> Those of us who have labored in advance to prepare the elements for this service—the music, the liturgy, the reading of the Word, the sermon, the Bread, the Cup—offer to you now all these elements, asking that you use them as vessels for holy joy and love overflowing. Having done our most and our best, we acknowledge that the real birthing labor is not ours, but yours. So bring forth this hour, we pray, authentic worship; and deliver each one of us forth into new life, the life offered to us through Jesus Christ.

Members of the congregation were not shocked by imagery of the Divine as womb, perhaps because as people of faith they recognized the ring of authenticity in these images. Although such imagery does not abound in Christian Scripture, it is there as an important harmonic, sounding a note that the soul recognizes and welcomes.

We can intentionally cultivate our soul's natural ability to discern the sometimes camouflaged presence of all four gender modes within the tradition. The four lists below give an indication of how elements from one's tradition can be correlated with the gender metaphors. These lists have been drawn together from the Bible, from words of hymns familiar to most Protestants, and from popular theology. Different sources would be appropriate for compiling lists from other traditions and paths. As you read through each list allow your deeper self to resonate with that cluster of images, noticing the differing tones of each set. Then see if you can create four similar profiles using phrases from your own belief system.

PHALLIC—Rising, Penetrating, Assertive Style

God is on high. King of kings, Lord of lords. Ruler of the Universe.

Almighty. Majestic. All-seeing. Powerful.

Mighty conqueror. Commander-in-chief.

Victorious over sin and death.

Sends his people forth to conquer new lands.

Wants us to win the race, fight the good fight, win victories for Christ.

"Onward, Christian Soldiers!"

"We are climbing Jacob's ladder, Soldiers of the cross."

We meet God in the mountaintop experience.

Vertical emphasis in church architecture and hierarchical polity.

We bow down before God, emphasizing our lowliness, His majesty.

GESTATIVE—Receiving, Nurturing, Serving Style

God as suffering servant.

Loving parent. Good shepherd.

The one "from whom all blessings flow."

"The Lord is my shepherd, I shall not want."

Promises a land flowing with milk and honey.

Bread of the world. Bread of life. Living water for all
who thirst.

"Let the little children come unto me..." "Jesus Loves Me"

"Come unto me...and I will give you rest."

Like a mother hen gathering her chicks under her wings.

Compassionate healer. "Comfort ye, comfort ye, my
people."

Shadow of a great rock. "Hide me, O thou Great Jehovah."

Holds us in the palm of his hand. "He's got the whole world
in his hands..."

"What a friend we have in Jesus..."

Manifested in the caring community of the church;
fellowship circles; community service.

TESTICULAR—Steadfast, Unchanging, Conserving Style

God is faithful, everlasting, steadfast.

The same yesterday, today, and forever.

Shows his nature in all we can count on.

The sure foundation. "Standing on the promises..."

"The church's one foundation..." The Rock of Ages.

"I will never forsake you." "Thou art with me, my rock and my
staff."

"O thou who changest not, abide with me."

Our duty is to trust in and depend on God.

This dimension is reflected in the longevity of Christian
tradition and the trustworthy sameness of the liturgy
each week.

EXERTIVE—Pushing, Birthing, Transforming Style

God as Destroyer and Recreator.

"It is a fearful thing to fall into the hands of the living God."

Whom he loves he chastens. Requires that we give up our
lives.

Dying with Christ.

Experienced in the "dark night of the soul." Being cast
into outer darkness. Being driven into the desert.

Surprises us. "Behold, I do a new thing. Do you
perceive it?"

Resurrection, always as a stunning surprise.

Good Friday through Easter morning.

In compiling these lists I have left male pronouns in place. It is
a revealing experience to reread the Gestative and Exertive lists
using the more appropriate female pronouns.

Making such lists is a good way to develop a conceptual
understanding of how one's Path correlates with all four gender
modes. Then drawing on the insights you have developed, during
sessions or services be aware and alert to the interplay of all four
modes. If you find it difficult to go directly from conceptual understanding to application within your faith community, you might find
it helpful to design four distinct imaginary services, each based on
only one of the four lists. If a few others in your community are
interested, actually worshiping together in accordance with those
designs would be an excellent way to become adept at recognizing
this or that gender mode subsequently within ordinary settings.
Samples of four such worship plans, developed from the above lists
and suitable for use with small groups, are found in *Appendix A*. As
with the lists themselves, these are meant as examples of what can
be done, to be modified as needed to fit your own situation.

In everyday usage, the most generic name for the Deity is "God."
Substituting the word "Goddess" to correlate with imagery related
to the two feminine body metaphors does provide a way of honoring
those hidden dimensions. At the same time, however, the use of
these terms side-by-side calls to mind the image of two deities,

rather than complementary facets of the One. Instead of Goddess, i use the name "God-Feminine," because it prompts us to begin naming the Lord and Heavenly Father as God-*Masculine* rather than simply God. This is important. It makes clear that "Lord" and "Father" are particular metaphors of the absolute Deity, whose full identity exceeds all particulars. It restores to the unadorned word *God* its authentic function as designator of the mysterious and unknowable One, with God-Masculine and God-Feminine each naming the single God from a different perspective.

Spiritual leaders who have themselves awakened to the presence of four gender modes within their faith will begin to notice resonances of all four as they study the Scriptures and engage in their own devotional practices. Being on intimate terms with the Divine in all four ways, they will quite naturally create prayers, litanies, homilies, teachings and rituals that draw on all four. I know ministers in traditional Protestant churches who have on occasion purposefully used expanded imagery, referring to the motherliness of God as well as the fatherliness, the well-like depths of the spirit as well as the mountaintop experience, the value of being at rest in God as well as aggressively working for the Kingdom.

The sacrament of Holy Communion is especially saturated with nonphallic meaning. The Cup/Chalice, by its very shape, invites comparison to the Divine Womb, which in its exertive mode uses destruction to bring forth new life. The body that bleeds but is not injured or diseased is like the Christ who bleeds and dies but is not, after all, destroyed. This facet of the feminine dimension of God is a deep mystery; it is explored somewhat in subsequent chapters. You can be in touch nonconceptually with that mystery by taking a moment before you drink to look down directly into the cup. Notice (or, if the light isn't just right, *imagine*) the reflection of your own eye gazing up at you. If you could look through the opening of the pupil into the depths of this cup, what would you glimpse?

Phallic imagery locates God in the upper direction. Most of us have been conditioned to project our energy only upward when seeking communion with the Divine. The cup invites us in and down. Both upward and depthward experiences of communion with the Divine are valid, each giving a different sort of connection. While meditating or praying, try orienting your energy first in one direction, then the other. See how your sense of communion with the Divine subtly shifts.

A friend told me she discovered by accident a visual cue that helps draw her energy down and in during pastoral prayers in the upward-oriented cathedral where she worships. One morning instead of folding her hands with interlaced fingers she brought her palms together with the fingers extended. During the prayer she became aware that her spiritual energy was being drawn toward the dark opening formed where her thumb joints left a gap. Suddenly she realized that the visual pattern made by her two hands resembled the female genitals, and that, figuratively speaking, her spiritual energy was being drawn to connect with God through that configuration (*Fig. 6*). This is the same sort of visual cue that the phallic spire provides to guide the attention upward.

Arriving a few minutes early and taking time for solitary preparation before the formal service begins helps me to worship with balanced attention to all four gender metaphors even when the service as designed is overwhelmingly keyed to the phallic metaphor. I may read through the Scripture lessons of the day, seeing what nuances sound when the gender is shifted by substituting female pronouns. Having personally interacted with the Scripture in this manner, I am able to listen with more breadth to the public reading of the lessons.

I regularly preview the words of the morning's hymns, noticing the assortment of imagery there. Despite consistent use of masculine pronouns, and the abundance of phallic imagery, many hymns also contain images correlating with the other three gender metaphors. As I read through the words I experiment with changing the pronouns and other gender words *to match the gender mode of each image.* If God is characterized as "high King of heaven"[2] (phallic image) or "thou who changest not"[3] (testicular), the masculine pronoun is congruent. "Shelters thee under his wings, yea, so gently sustaineth"[4] (gestative) calls for a change to feminine pronoun. I find this pluralistic approach more authentic than neutering the language.

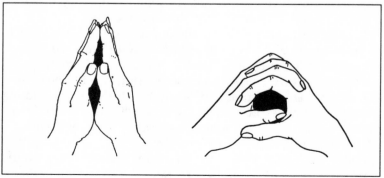

Figure 6

Having previewed the hymns in this way, I freely change the words when singing during the service. No one seems to mind, or even notice, that I am singing my own version. As I discovered how enlivening this practice is, I began bringing my own copy of the hymnal with me, to pencil in my changes so that while singing I can focus worshipfully rather than expending effort trying to remember which pronoun to use where. Here is one example from my modified hymnal:[5]

Praise, my soul, the King of heaven,   PHALLIC, HIERARCHICAL IMAGE
To God's feet thy tribute bring;
Ransomed, healed, restored, forgiven,
Who, like me, God's praise should sing?
Praise him! Praise him!
Praise him! Praise him!
Praise the everlasting King!

Praise God for her grace and favor   GESTATIVE AND EXERTIVE WOMB
To our forebears in distress;
Praise him, still the same forever,   TESTICULAR
Slow to chide, and swift to bless.
Praise God! Praise her!
Praise God! Praise him!
Glor-i-ous in faithfulness!   TESTICULAR

Mother-like, she tends and spares us;   GESTATIVE WOMB
Well our feeble frame she knows;
In her hands she gently bears us,
Rescues us from all our foes.
Praise her! Praise her!
Praise her! Praise her!
Widely as her mercy flows!

Angels, help us to adore God,
Ye behold God face to face;
Sun and Moon, bow down before God: BOTH MASCULINE AND
Dwellers all in time and space,   FEMININE IMAGERIES
Praise her! Praise him!
Praise him! Praise her!
Praise with us the God of grace![6]

In an analysis of the imagery in hymns actually used over a two-month period in Sunday services at churches representative of three denominations,[7] I found that 63 percent of the imagery was phallic, 17 percent gestative, 15 percent testicular, and 5 percent exertive. Despite the presence of *imagery* correlating with all four gender metaphors, unvarying use of the male pronoun gives the false impression that the tradition reveals nothing of the feminine idea of the Deity. Simply bringing the pronouns into congruence with the imagery of the tradition makes visible *as feminine* those elements that correlate with the gestative and exertive body metaphors. Because God is One, even in a tradition with a pronounced masculine bias we can expect to find hidden feminine features. Insofar as any tradition is inspired by glimpses of the One God, it will bear within it traces of the fullness of the divine nature, however partial and limited the conscious intentions of the founders might have been.

In addition to attuning our ears to traces of all four gender motifs in traditional hymns, we might even make up new words that unfold more fully those aspects least adequately honored in the tradition. For example, traditional hymns do not celebrate the correlation between the exertive-womb metaphor and the death and resurrection of Jesus Christ: at Easter the egg cracks open, the earth cracks open, the tomb cracks open, and new life comes forth. New verses making explicit this connection, as in my hymn on page 236, reveal a long neglected facet of the event most central to Christian faith. There is nothing contrived or heretical about such creativity, for it delivers forth meanings that have been implied from the beginning.

I yearn for the day when worshipers at Sunday service in my church sing together a new version of the Doxology[8] explicitly praising the honoring the multisided Divine One:

Four-Way Version

One God from whom
    blessings flow!
Praise him, all creatures
    here below.
Praise her above,
    ye heavenly host.
God-Goddess, Christ, and
    Holy Ghost

Traditional Version

Praise God from whom
    blessings flow!
Praise him, all creatures
    here below.
Praise him above,
    ye heavenly host
Praise Father, Son, and
    Holy Ghost.

Although that day is not likely to come soon, a fair number of individuals in various churches, as well as the staff of the Connecticut Conference of the United Church of Christ, the denomination's state-level body, have for several years been using a version that avoids the exclusively male terminology of the traditional version:

> Praise God from whom all blessings flow.
> Praise God all creatures here below.
> Praise God above, ye heavenly host.
> Creator, Christ, and Holy Ghost.[9]

This modification was not instituted as a denominational rule; it came into being within the actual worship practice of the women and men who work at the Conference office and worship together weekly. Subsequently, it has been appropriated by individuals and groups beyond that original circle. The point is that when *individuals* become excited about nonpatriarchal possibilities for liturgy, in addition to promoting their own immediate spiritual well-being, they may be helping to sensitize the larger community of faith to nonphallic resonances in the tradition. The effects of such revitalization may be long-lasting and may make a greater difference for the vitality of the faith over the long run than the individual could ever imagine. For although the Deity is eternal, religious forms are not. As the patriarchal story becomes less universal and humankind moves toward a new Age, spiritual truths still articulated solely in narrowly patriarchal terms will, in perhaps a few centuries, become but relics, as did matrical religious forms with the coming of the Patriarchal Age. Where those on the spiritual Path have midwived new authentic meanings forth from a tradition, that faith will continue to function into the Age to come.

Chapter Six

Genes, Embryos and the Turning of the Ages

An archetypal pattern pressing toward expression exerts great influence both within individual lives and in the functioning of communities, nations, and cultures. Human culture can be thought of as the aggregate expression of dominant archetypal patterns in the collective life of a people. The gradual transition from one cultural epoch to the next involves transformation of the collective (species) psyche, as well as changes in outwardly visible social patterns. So, for example, the outer social and cultural changes signaled by the Women's Movement are not simply ego-level initiatives, but evidences of deep, transforming processes occurring at the archetypal level.

I propose that each major cultural epoch or age correlates with the emergence of one of the four gender modes as the predominant archetypal keynote in the species psyche, and that looking at the history of human experience through this frame of reference can help us "place" our own lives not only within the Patriarchal Age, but also within the even larger context of what has come before culturally and what is to follow.

Of course, reconstructing the distant past and extrapolating to the unborn future are highly speculative endeavors. What results is not a literally accurate picture of either past or future. Nevertheless, through such picturing of alternatives to the Age in which we live, we become more deeply aware that the patriarchal pattern of life, so familiar and inevitable to us, need not be normative for humankind. If we can imagine other systems that reflect other gender modes as faithfully as the patriarchal system reflects the yang-phallic mode, our lives will no longer be determined automatically by patriarchal values. We and our children and grandchildren will no doubt live out our lives before the Age of the Patriarch has drawn to a close. Yet, having a larger view may make all the difference in the way we live our portion of the remainder of this Age, and in the significance of our lives as contributing to the turning of the Age. This is an effect somewhat on the order of the contribution each separate leaf makes to the continued growth of a tree. During the entire life of a great tree, what is one leaf among the many leaves of so many seasons? And yet each leaf does contribute to the growth of the tree—growth that consists not only of the adding of new branchlets each season, but includes a gradual reshaping and thickening of even the oldest, most original branches. In view of the fact that Jung described the archetypes as the deposit of humankind's typical reactions since primordial times, each with a long evolutionary history behind it,[1] it would be surprising if each subsequent deposit did not also have its effect on the totality.

A crucial factor in determining the degree of impact of a single life on a particular archetypal configuration lies in the degree to which the person is able to bring conscious awareness to the manifesting of that archetypal pattern within the actual life. Consciousness challenges the archetypes as they actualize, asking questions of them, discerning meanings, making counter demands, coming into a personal relationship with their personifications. If an archetype expresses without conscious awareness, its simply lives itself out. This is the usual case. If conscious awareness enters into active engagement with the archetypal pattern as it expresses itself, the resultant human experience will be different than the simple archetypal pattern. Although the conscious thoughts themselves do not get added to the archetype, the *changed human experience* resulting from interaction of archetype and ego becomes part of the psychic residue of the species.[2] This has a significant though minute effect, which, added to other minute effects from other conscious lives over long periods, in time can modify the archetype. For this reason, any widespread increase in conscious engagement with a particular archetypal pattern (such as is occurring within the Women's Movement, in terms not only of general consciousness raising, but also in the intense attention being paid by feminist scholars to women's unique experience as it pertains to such fields as psychology, anthropology, history, philosophy, spirituality, and religion) would accelerate the evolution of that branch of the archetypal tree.

Although the idea that the collective psyche is built up and evolved by the accretion of experiences of the species has been neither proved nor disproved, recent research by Rupert Sheldrake into what he calls "formative causation" supports this idea.[3] Bolen agrees with Sheldrake that when the gradual accumulation of experiences by members of the species reaches "critical mass," suddenly it crystalizes in the emergence of a new specieswide archetype, which is thenceforth part of the collective psyche, even for those who have not themselves had the prior experience. Such a "quantum leap is taking place now as a new archetype is in the midst of forming," Bolen writes.[4] I hypothesize that this new archetype will reorient both psyche and culture in a pattern metaphorically like the exertive, birthing womb.

The two great eons of human culture are the Matriarchal Age, named after the feminine parent, and the Patriarchal Age, named after the masculine parent. Both of these terms were coined by theorists for whom the contemporary patriarchal perspective is normative. *Within this perspective* it is self-evident that yin and feminine are synonymous; yang and masculine. Consistent with these patriarchal definitions, the Age that expresses the yin *half* of the feminine principle is named as though its features reflect the fullness of the species' female parent. And the Age that expresses the yang *half* of the masculine principle is named as though its features reflect the fullness of the species' male parent. Using the terminology developed in this book, however, we can specify that the Matriarchal/Matrical Age brings to cultural expression the qualities associated with the gestative half of femininity: yin-feminine nurturant containment. The Patriarchal Age brings to cultural expression the qualities associated with the phallic half of masculinity: yang-masculine goal-oriented objectivity, differentiation, and mastery. As we move out of the Patriarchal Age, there are signs that the next Age will bring to primary cultural expression the long-dormant yang half of the feminine principle, as seen in the exertive womb, with the cultural expression of the testicular mode waiting faithfully in the wings for another eon.

To say that each Age brings to cultural expression one of the four sexual modes does not mean the other three have no function within that Age. While key cultural features of each Age correspond to the characteristic qualities of one of the sexual spheres, within that frame of reference, each of the four then plays some role. The chart on the following page summarizes some of the features of the preceding, current, and emerging ages as I envision them. Reading down the chart within one column gives a unified description of one Age. Reading across the chart at any point provides a comparison of the three in regard to that feature.

COMPARISON OF AGES

	MATRICAL/ MATRIARCHAL	PATRIARCHAL	CONTEXTUAL- TRANSFORMATIONAL
Exemplary Reproductive Function	Containment, as of GESTATIVE WOMB YIN-FEMININE	Rises above and aims toward extrinsic goal, as does ERECTILE PENIS YANG-MASCULINE	Pushes from within context toward transformation as does EXERTIVE WOMB YANG-FEMININE
Parallel Chromosomal Patterns	AA . . . XX Matched pairs	X — Y Pair of Opposites	X^MX^P Egalitarian mosaic
Fundamental Human Unit	The CLAN or GROUP No true individuality— encompassment in a group, Nature, etc.	The INDIVIDUAL in distinction from a contrasting other	Contextually rooted SELF-TRANSCENDING independently centered Selves
Characteristic Socio-political Format	Participational containment Encompassment within a matrix	Opposites, polarities, asymetrical relation- ships; Hierarchies, rankings	Networking; Egalitarian; Interconnected self- transcendent integers
What constitutes a WHOLE	The Whole is collectively generated by the SUM of its PARTS	The Whole is an INDIVIDUAL UNIT differentiated out of chaos	MULTIPLE LEVELS of wholes; Perpetual birthing of new Wholes
Relationship of Ego and Unconscious	Ego carried by or encompassed by larger psyche; no clear differentiation	Oppositional, confrontational frontier between ego and unconscious psyche	Dialogical interconnec- tion. Each is context for the other, birther of the other.
Style of Consciousness	"Participation Mystique"	Objective; Discriminating; Linear	Contextual; Dialogical; Holistic
How Growth is Characterized and Promoted	Vegetative proliferation, natural growth; Nurturance; Cyclicity	Linear progress; Ascent; Competition and mastery-over; Begetting upon another	Transformations rooted in context; Multi- directional, fluid, unexpected, timely emergences
Style of Power and Source of Value	Power of participation and inclusion. Value lies in participating in collective.	Power over the other or the situation. Value lies in superiority.	Power of self- transcendence. Value as centered self in multiple contexts.
Geometric Analog	Borderless plane or "matrix" 	One center is determinator—the "bull's eye" toward which to aim 	Ellipse, with two equally ranked foci and perpetually changing radii

The matriarchal or matrical system consistently reflects the yin dimension of the feminine species parent or feminine principle. Containment and encompassment, characteristic of the gestative womb, shape the system at every level. Within that perspective, it would be self-evident that the fundamental human experience is of oneself-within-the-matrix. The basic human unit is not the individual person, but the tribe or clan, which encompasses all its participants. Identity is by virtue of containment within this matrix or "mother."

Theories of consciousness speculate that matriarchal consciousness is a participational awareness, or *participation mystique*, rather than the sort of objective consciousness that characterizes the patriarchal mindset. By patriarchal standards, that sort of consciousness seems "unconscious," for instead of a sharp discontinuity between ego and the rest of the psyche, matrical awareness is carried within or encompassed by the larger psyche. The type of consciousness characteristic of our Patriarchal Age depends on the ego differentiating itself clearly from the "underlying" matrix of the rest of the psyche, which is then called unconscious.[5] Within the current Age, it seems only natural that consciousness requires a solidly constellated ego with clear borders setting it off definitively from the murky mistiness of the larger psyche. Other possible relationships between the ego and the rest of the psyche are considered either immature, pathological, or "altered states." A less biased view would be that all the various states of consciousness (including the objective, nonparticipational, phallic sort) are alternatives, each with its sphere of validity.

Note that the format of the chart is itself an expression of patriarchally-toned consciousness, with its gift for differentiating and drawing distinctions. Because we perceive the world primarily through the patriarchal frame of reference, we are likely to assume a progression from a simpler or more primitive style toward a more advanced system. This is of course an expression of the longitudinally oriented, linear style of mentation, which parallels the phallic format. It takes an effort of imagination and will to suspend that assumption and envision the same factors as adjacent and unranked rather than as sequentially ordered and progressive.

The linear perspective is deeply ingrained in this Age, often seeming the inevitable and only way. For example, few people would dream of laying out a vegetable garden in any pattern other than long rows. In actual practice, however, the plants thrive at least as well when the rows are replaced by a honeycomb of four-foot *circles*, each of which is the equivalent of a twelve-foot row bent around to meet itself. My own garden has nineteen such circles in a hexagonal layout, separated by mulched walkways. Each circle is like a womb, the overall pattern nonlinear. In my experience, this system produces healthier plants and greater yield with less work.[6] The al-

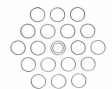

most universal preference for a linear layout has more to do with the expectations of a phallic-oriented mindset than with the actual needs and habits of the plants. For the same reason, it is assumed that a scholarly book will be written in linear style, beginning with foundational information and sequentially building a case step by step toward a final conclusion. This is the convention, regardless of whether or not it provides the best treatment of the material.

Starting with the next chapter, this book will depart from that pattern. Each subsequent chapter functions more as a spoke of a wheel than as a next rung in a ladder. Because all the spokes connect directly with the center, the chapters might even be read in random order. This nonlinearity may be disconcerting to some, exhilarating to others. Any sense of "getting somewhere" will depend not on progressing through a series of ordered steps toward a goal, but on being able to hold gently in awareness the whole field of unranked elements. In the fullness of time the central meaning binding all the spokes together may suddenly become evident to you. Each chapter touches directly on the process of releasing God-Feminine in us all, a quantum leap of consciousness to a new spirituality in a New Age.

The prevailing patriarchal system expresses the phallic or yang dimension of the masculine species parent or masculine principle. Like the erectile penis, its primary pattern entails rising up, standing out, advancing, overcoming, and penetrating. Individual identity is established by differentiating oneself from the matrix, and in contrast with an other. Opposites and opposition, polarity and polarization, competition and mastery are intrinsic to this system. Relationships are typically unequal, either competitive or with one party recognized by both as the superior, the other as subordinate. Hierarchical ranking seems natural. In this system power is thus the power to prevail over another person or a situation. In contrast, matrical power is the power of participation and inclusion.

Figure 13 is a graphic logo representing the participational nature of the matrical system. Both masculine (represented by the

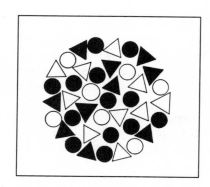

*Figure 13 - Graphic logo represent-
ing the participational nature of the
matrical system.*

triangles; dark for yin, light for yang) and feminine (circles) function
as integral parts of a whole that is "motherly" or "womblike" in the
sense of encompassing all. Each unit participates within a wholeness that is *collectively* generated. Each fragment is an unpolarized
component of the encompassing whole. Both feminine and masculine are immersed in this matrix.

Imagine yourself within the design as one of the many units.
Your identity is your place within the matrix. Your value and importance lie in participating in the collective pattern.Your sense of
belonging gives you a feeling of identity and value. Such participational
identity is analogous to the relationship of the bee to the hive. The
fundamental organism is not the bee but the hive, without which the
individual bee ceases to function, and cannot long survive.

In *Figure 14*, masculine and feminine elements are represented
as they function within the context of patriarchy. Here, instead of
inclusion in a common matrix, the primary feature is separation and
distinction. The two form a pair where each is other to its opposite.
The masculine is represented by the dominant figure, a large white

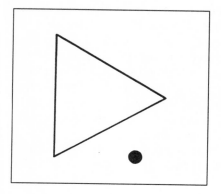

*Figure 14 - Graphic logo repre-
senting masculine and feminine
elements as they function within
the context of patriarchy.*

(yang) triangle that looms above the small dark (yin) circle representing the feminine. Although subordinate, the feminine is not encompassed by the triangle, for differentiated separateness of the two is the essential feature. Imagine yourself within this design as first one, then the other figure. As the larger masculine triangle towering above the little circle, you might feel either power or protectiveness. Whichever, your feeling is an expression of the contrast between yourself and the other. Your sense of identity depends not on immersion in a common matrix, but on differentiation between yourself and the other. Your value and significance consist of being the dominant figure in an unequal pair.

Now picture yourself as the small feminine circle. In your smallness you may feel childlike, dependent; either endangered or protected. Your significance lies in being the subordinate other against whom the dominant half of the pair takes its measure. In both instances your role and identity are based on the contrast between yourself and the counterpart. A simple reversal of shapes, with feminine as supreme ("matriarch") and the masculine as subordinate would still reflect the same type of structure.

The price paid for the possibility of succeeding in this system is that always there must be a counterbalancing "other" over whom to be superior. In the case of Western culture, both women and people of color (African-, Asian-, and Native-Americans, etc.) have provided this. When individual women (or Blacks or other "minorities" = those in the "minor" position) try to escape their lowly place by "climbing the ladder," they do nothing to transform the patriarchal system, since they continue to experience life through the hierarchical, competitive values, which require that they be in asymmetrical relationships—the only difference being that this time they are on top. No matter who is in the superior rank, the patriarchal model is maintained, not transcended. Likewise, simply changing the pronoun for God to the feminine, while maintaining the overlord image of the Deity's relationship to the world, does not really transcend the patriarchal model of the divine as a Supreme Being reigning on high.

Notice that if you have been able to experience these two diagrams by entering into them as suggested, your engagement has been somewhat like the participational awareness characteristic of yin-oriented consciousness. Such consciousness knows things not by objectifying them, but by becoming one with them. The fact that the verb *to know* refers both to cognition and to sexual intimacy (as in the phrase "carnal knowledge," or the Christmas scripture statement that Mary was pregnant although she had not yet "known any man") reflects this participational way of knowing, which once was the primary mode of human consciousness.

Figure 15 presents several ways of picturing the style likely to characterize the emerging Age. To make clear the meanings of these designs requires digressing into a detailed consideration of genetics and embryological origins of sex differences. Astonishing as it may seem, all four gender modes and their related cultural patterns are prefigured at the level of chromsomes, implying that the sequence of chromosomal evolution is later repeated in the development of human culture.

In humans and all other mammals, the fetus has an innate tendency to develop as a female, against which maleness must be actively imposed if the offspring is to be male. This parallels the pattern of cultural evolution, where the initial impulse was toward matrical culture, against which patriarchy was eventually actively imposed. The embryological factors predisposing toward femaleness or countermanding toward maleness reside in the genes. The nucleus of every cell in the normal human body has forty-six strands of genetic material called chromosomes, each carrying a patterned sequence of coded information or genes, arranged something like beads on a string (*Fig. 16*).[7] Imagine that you are to sort a box of forty-six necklaces and bracelets of strung, handmade beads into matching pairs, according to their length and distinctive color patterns.

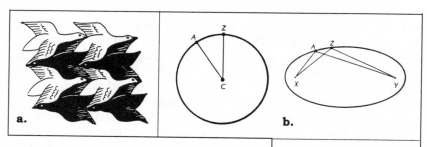

Figure 15 - Graphic logos for the emerging Age.

a. Mutual interpenetration of dark and light. (Patterned after Max Escher's many designs.)

b. While the circle has one center with all points on the circumference equidistant from it (AC = ZC), the ellipse has two "centers," or foci, and a compound radius (line XZY = line XAY).

c. Two magnets generate a forcefield.

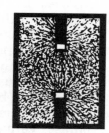

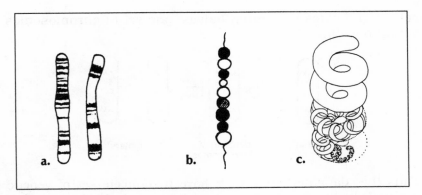

Figure 16
   a. Each chromosome has a distinctive pattern of bands. About one thousand bands are visible on human chromosomes (Therman, p. 43).

   b. Chromosomes are composed of sequences of genes, similar to strings of beads.

   c. A more accurate analogy is that the chromosome is formed of spirals of spirals of spirals of genetic protein. The smallest spirals are at the molecular level.

After pairing them, you notice that although of the same color and position on the two strands, matching beads are not quite identical, bearing as they do the marks of their individual origins. In similar fashion, each chromosome has a mate. The two are alike in size and in the way their "beads" are arranged, but with subtle differences between corresponding beads, or genes. We might label the paired chromosomes AA', BB', CC', and so on through twenty-three matched but not identical pairs.

The complex interactions of the matched but different genes orchestrate a person's particular inherited characteristics. Every cell in the body has a full complement of the person's genes. For example, the genes determining eye color are found not only in the cell of the eye, but in the cells of the big toe and the brain as well. And the cells of the eye contain the genes governing the development of the fingernails and the kidneys, even though they remain inoperative in this location. All genes are included in every cell, but function actively only in the circumstances for which they are specific.

To produce new body cells for growth and maintenance, the chromosomes in a cell pair up, then duplicate themselves. The cell then divides into equal halves, one set of chromosomes going to each:

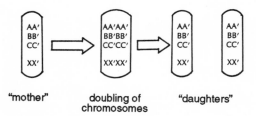

"mother" doubling of "daughters"
chromosomes

Thus the "daughter" cells each have a complete set of genetic material identical with the "mother" cell. In simpler life forms, before the development of dimorphic sexual reproduction (i.e., before the development of a masculine alternative), all offspring are produced by the simple duplication of the parent in this manner: generation after generation, all "mothers" and "daughters."[8] Culturally, this pattern repeats in the matrical system, where the male role in reproduction is not noticed and human lineage is pictured as coming through the womb, traceable ultimately to the divine Mother as Original Parent of us all.

In humans, this is the pattern of cell production everywhere in the body except the ovaries and testicles. There, a different process takes place in certain cells to produce egg or sperm. As before, the chromosomes align in matching pairs. However, instead of doubling before the cell divides, one member of the pair goes to each new cell:

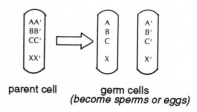

parent cell germ cells
(become sperms or eggs)

The resulting sperm or egg carries half the normal number of chromosomes. When sperm and egg fuse at fertilization, the full number of chromosomes is reconstituted in the new individual produced (*see box, next page*).

One particular pair of chromosomes, conventionally designated the twenty-third pair, governs inheritance of gender. In all the cells of a woman's body, these sex-determining chromosomes are a normal pair, with no more than the usual degree of variation

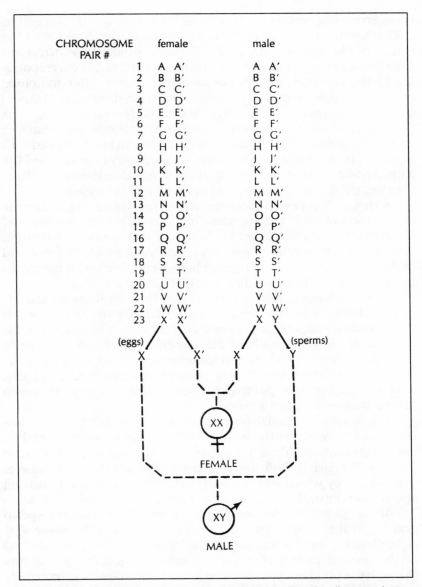

CHROMOSOME PAIR #	female		male	
1	A	A'	A	A'
2	B	B'	B	B'
3	C	C'	C	C'
4	D	D'	D	D'
5	E	E'	E	E'
6	F	F'	F	F'
7	G	G'	G	G'
8	H	H'	H	H'
9	J	J'	J	J'
10	K	K'	K	K'
11	L	L'	L	L'
12	M	M'	M	M'
13	N	N'	N	N'
14	O	O'	O	O'
15	P	P'	P	P'
16	Q	Q'	Q	Q'
17	R	R'	R	R'
18	S	S'	S	S'
19	T	T'	T	T'
20	U	U'	U	U'
21	V	V'	V	V'
22	W	W'	W	W'
23	X	X'	X	Y

(eggs)   X   X'   X   Y   (sperms)

XX
FEMALE

XY
MALE

Pairs of chromosomes are represented by letters. In the female, all twenty-three are matched pairs. In the male, the twenty-third is an unlike pair. Because only one of each pair of chromosomes goes into egg or sperm, all eggs have an X chromosome; half of the sperms have an X, half a Y chromosome. An X-sperm combines with an egg to produce an XX female. A Y-sperm combines with an egg to produce an XY male.

between corresponding genes. That is, the female sex chromosomes (XX) follow the matched-pair format, which is the norm for all the rest of the chromosomes (AA, BB, CC, etc.) *The male pattern deviates from this norm.* If you were to sort a box of strung beads corresponding to the chromosomes found in men's bodies, after matching twenty-two pairs you would be left with two dissimilar strands. Careful comparison would reveal that the larger one is just like the sex chromosomes found in women's cells; the other is much smaller and corresponds for only a small part of its length bead for bead with a portion of the larger chromosome. The ordinary type is called the X chromosome, whether found in males or females; the unusual one is called the Y chromosome, and is found only in males.

Although Y-type chromosomes made their debut long before the development of the human species, the basis of human sexuality (and of the patriarchal pattern) lies in "Adam's" Y chromosome. Without it, dimorphic human sexuality would not exist.[9] As in simple life forms and in the ordinary cells of the human body, reproduction of life plasm would follow the direct "mother-daughter" pattern.

The male's sex chromosomes (XY) are the only human chromosomes where the two constitute an unmatched pair. As outlined in the preceding chapters, a key psychological characteristic of phallic masculinity and the resultant male-oriented patriarchal system is the developing of a style of consciousness that emphasizes differentiation and discrimination of *pairs of opposites.* Even at this simple biological level, pairing of opposites (the X and the Y) is seen to be a masculine phenomenon.

The factor for sexual differentiation is consistently the contribution of the male, never the female.[10] All eggs are X-bearing, tending toward generation of daughters only. Half of the sperm produced are likewise X-bearing, half are Y-bearing. The gender of a baby is determined by which sort of sperm fertilizes the egg; if a Y-bearing sperm, the natural tendency toward femaleness is overridden.

Although genetic gender is determined at the moment sperm and egg unite, at first each tiny embryo develops the same way regardless of whether its genetic gender is XX or XY. Until the end of the second month of growth, nearly one-quarter of the way through the pregnancy, there is no discernible difference, internally or externally, in the development of male and female embryos.[11] The external genitals at first consist merely of a raised mound with a fold or cleft in it. Differentiation begins when the embryo is about 1.75 inches long.[12] Once again, the female direction of development is more basic, the male extraordinary. As can be seen from Figure 17, the androgynous embryo changes little to produce female organs, but greatly to produce male organs. Depending on your own bias, you might interpret this as portraying the female as the original, normal, standard, natural and thus more fundamentally human sex; with the male as aberration, oddity, deviant. Or you might see the male as an improvement, extraordinary, outstanding; and the female as primitive.

Regardless of whether XX or XY genetically, if the embryo is not dosed with male hormone at this stage it develops a female appearance.[13] Even if the developing embryo is deprived of both male and female hormones, the external genitals still develop the female form. Presence or absence of female hormones is irrelevant for the development of female-shaped genitals;[14] differentiation of masculine form requires a special hormonal stimulus. This hormonal kick originates in the gonads, located internally near the embryonic kidneys,[15] whose ducts connect to the outside of the body where eventually the external genitals will develop (*see Fig. 18*). Just before sexual differentiation begins, a second duct system forms in both sexes, parallel to the first.[16] One of the sets, called the wolffian ducts after their discoverer, is capable of developing into male organs. The other set, called mullerian ducts after their discoverer, can develop into female organs. In both sexes, the gonad is neutral to start with. From this initially neutral tissue the sexually differentiated ovary or testicle develops by emphasis of one set of its characteristics and deemphasis of the alternative.[17] The mechanism by which this first step toward a sexed body takes place is not yet well understood, but recent research ties it to a *single gene* on the Y chromosome.[18]

The presence of a Y chromosome in any cell causes it to produce a particular protein on its surface, which functions as a *histocompatibility antigen* (H-Y antigen)—a substance that rejects grafts of incompatible (that is, "non-Y," or female) tissue. The factor was first discovered in tissue transplant experiments with mice. It was later found that the same cell surface protein, H-Y antigen, is responsible for causing the neutral gonad to develop into a testicle. It is remarkable that "this single gene locus contributes to two of the most powerful *differentiating* attributes of individuals: male versus female and self versus other."[19] These are exactly the differentiations most basic to the patriarchal psychocultural pattern.

When the gland first begins to secrete hormones, the only difference between the male and female is that the XY gland makes a slightly greater amount of testosterone, whereas the XX gland produces a substance to convert its small amount of testosterone

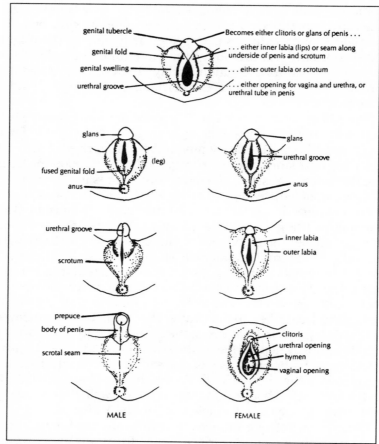

Figure 17 - Stages of differentiation of male and female external genitals.

into estradiol, a female hormone.[20] This small difference sets in motion a chain of events that results in the creation of a male or female body. The key factor is the effect of the male hormone, which percolates through the cells of the embryo, affecting those cells that are susceptible of becoming male genital organs.[21]

In summary, the XX or female sex is the neutral state on which maleness is superimposed by the hormonal secretions of the XY gonad.[22] Biological development of human maleness consistently involves imposing a pattern that is *contrary to the natural course of events.* The Y chromosome and the testosterone-producing male gonad function at the cellular and organ level in a style analogous to that of the proverbial patriarch at the sociocultural level: asserting themselves counter to the underlying world of nature; prevailing over the feminine; introducing and maintaining differentiation of unlike pairs, with all that goes along with such distinctions. In other words, the patriarchal pattern described in Chapter 1 may reflect the patterns literally programmed into the man's being at the level of his genes, gonads, and hormones. We might say the patriarchal system is uniquely *man's* contribution to the psychocultural evolution of the species. Through it, human culture enacts the primordial masculine impulse of the Y chromosome. Patriarchy's emphasis on differentiation, discriminating consciousness, objectivity, male dominance, subordination of the female, and development "contrary to nature" all aptly express at the cultural level the masculine contribution to biological evolution. Through this cultural incarnation of the masculine way, the entire species, both males and females, has been brought to a new degree of psychocultural development. It was a matter of course that men catalyzed it, out of the depths of their biological nature; but once the biologically founded pattern is brought into being at the level of psyche, culture, and spirit, conscious engagement by both men and women becomes possible.

To regret the development of patriarchy would make as much sense as to lament the advent of sexual differentiation on the

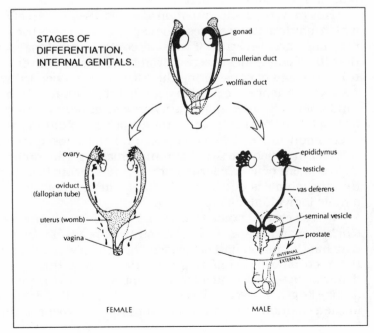

Figure 18

biological level. However, for the culture to remain oriented exclusively by the male-related pattern amounts to assuming that only those who develop according to the Y-masculine format are fully human, or that the X-feminine format offers nothing of value for cultural development.

The obvious question is, What pattern is programmed into the woman's being at the level of her genes, gonads, and hormones, and what gifts might cultural incarnation of this feminine way bring to humankind—to be catalyzed at first out of the depths of woman's biological nature, and thenceforth available for conscious engagement by women and men alike? One answer, which looks backward from the perspective of male-initiated differentiation and all it has brought with it, notes that the female way is simpler, less developed, more primitive, closer to nature, lacking in discriminating consciousness. The prepatriarchal Matrical Age of human development may be thought of as expressing in the psychological and social realm what the AA...XX pattern of mother-and-daughter replication typifies: identity by inclusion rather than by differentiation; self-evident lineage through the mother; primacy of mothers and daughters. Although the body cells of both men and women replicate in accordance with this design, it is a "feminine" pattern in that this matched-pair format encompasses the female (XX) but not the male (XY) chromosome pattern.

However, the XX formulation also has a second set of meanings, which may indicate features to be expected in the Age to come. These meanings are discerned if we shift context—recalling as we do so that the metaphorical exertive womb models attentiveness to contexts. Instead of considering the XX pair as embedded within the AA...XX sequence, we need to note that this pair functions in a way fundamentally *unlike any other chromosome pair*. This is discovered by looking to both the historical origin of X and Y chromosomes from a common antecedent eons ago, and the consequently unique manner in which the two X chromosomes together orchestrate the development of female form. For upon closer consideration we find that the female is not, after all, simply the residue left by default if a male individual fails to develop.

In less evolved species, male and female sex chromosomes are a single size and shape. To use the string-of-beads analogy, they have matching beads for most of their length, with only a minute segment of the Y chromosome differing from the X. It is this segment that determines sex differentiation and identifies this as the Y chromosome despite its general resemblance to the X. A recent theory proposes that in the evolution of mammals the ordinary segment of the Y chromosome broke off and linked itself to the X (*Fig. 19*). This would account for both the size differential between the X and the Y in mammals and many other factors too complicated and technical to detail here. If true, the process this theory describes is strikingly parallel to what I suggest has happened psychoculturally, with the projecting of the yin half of the masculine onto the feminine in order that discriminating, phallic consciousness might develop to the utmost. A portion of the originally large Y chromosome gets transferred to the X chromosome, resulting in more thorough differentiation. Interestingly, this also parallels the biblical story of the creation of the sexes: the female is created by borrowing a piece from the male.

Psychologically, at the right time the projection needs to be taken back. At the genetic level, of course, it is not feasible literally to restore the transposed section to the Y chromosome, as this modification occurred eons ago and is now built into the heredity of all mammals. However, an evolutional adjustment was made to neutralize the harmful effects of excess material, or chromatin, in the X chromosome. It is from this adjustment that we may perhaps gain a clue as patriarchal system passes its zenith and is succeeded by a yang-feminine modality.

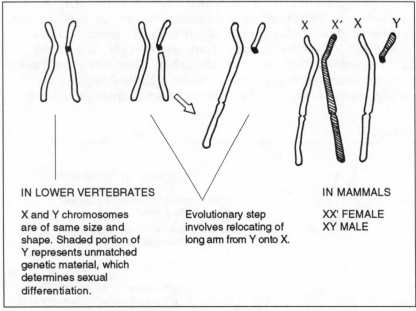

X   X'   X   Y

IN LOWER VERTEBRATES   IN MAMMALS

X and Y chromosomes   Evolutionary step   XX' FEMALE
are of same size and   involves relocating of   XY MALE
shape. Shaded portion of   long arm from Y onto X.
Y represents unmatched
genetic material, which
determines sexual
differentiation.

Figure 19 - Diagrammatic representation of evolution of Y chromosome from X.

Imagine the simultaneous conception of twins, one male, one female. The male receives a truncated Y chromosome from his father's sperm and an overloaded X chromosome from his mother's egg. The highly specialized Y chromosome is nearly empty of genes except for those governing the triggering of masculinization of the embryo. Even for its small size, it has few genes. Much of its length is genetically inert, as shown schematically in *Figure 20*.[23] Taken together, one "empty" Y plus one "overloaded" X constitute the full complement of sex chromatin needed for development. But what of the female twin, who receives overloaded X chromosomes from both father and mother? Taken together, two X chromosomes comprise an excess of genetic material, since each one already carries the equivalent of almost another whole chromosome, transferred from the ancestral Y earlier in the evolution of the species. To counteract the "overload," early in the development of the female embryo, in each cell one or the other of the X chromosomes actively "turns off" its genes, becoming inert.[24] In some of her cells, randomly, the X from her father (labeled henceforth as X^P for paternal) is the only functional sex chromosome; in the remaining cells, the X from the mother (X^M, for maternal) functions exclusively.

This has two effects. First, the overload is rectified, and each cell has the optimum amount of functional sex chromatin, about 5 percent of the total chromosomal material. Second, the ongoing development of about half the cells of her body is thenceforth orchestrated by X^M chromosomes from her mother, the other half orchestrated by X^P chromosomes from her father. Since this random division occurs early in the development of the embryo, each of those cells gives rise to many more, sometimes an entire organ developing

Figure 20

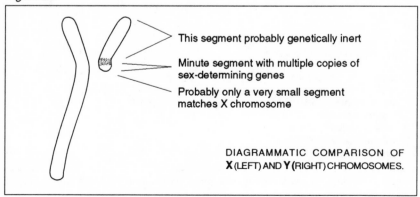

This segment probably genetically inert

Minute segment with multiple copies of sex-determining genes

Probably only a very small segment matches X chromosome

DIAGRAMMATIC COMPARISON OF
X (LEFT) AND **Y** (RIGHT) CHROMOSOMES.

in time from the one cell. The result is that a woman's body is a mosaic of X^M and X^P cells, in random masses. Instead of dominance of one over the other, both X^M and X^P are given expression. They retain their distinct identities in a mosaic of creative co-existence.

Herein lies the "message" encoded at the level of genes and chromosomes, which may in time manifest in a psychocultural system, in the same sense as the underlying pattern of masculine differentiation has found expression in the Patriarchal Age. In the Age to come, not only masculine and feminine, but any pair of opposites differentiated by patriarchal consciousness will be discovered to have equal value and stature. Of particular importance, as the $X^M X^P$ format so concretely illustrates, life and death will be recognized as coequal factors. This pattern teaches the feminine truth that, contrary to our usual evaluation, fulfillment and abeyance, advancement and regression, generation and entropy, development and atrophy, life and death—all are equally desirable as part of an intricate mosaic of meaning. Such an idea has profound cultural and spiritual implications, to be explored in later chapters.

To return now to the graphic logos in *Figure 15*, in a sociocultural system paralleling this pattern neither female nor male has dominance over the other. Such balanced interrelationship of "opposites" is pictured in many of Max Escher's enigmatic etchings. Black and white remain distinct, but in a state of mutual interpenetration in which neither predominates (*Fig. 15a*). The ellipse is a simple geometric figure that illustrates this type of interrelational pattern. It has two distinct foci of equal significance, which together generate the integrated whole of the figure (*Fig. 15b*).

By definition, an integer is anything complete in itself. In the coming Age, masculine and feminine will be integers in the sense that each has its own integrity and identity, knowing itself neither as an element in a matrix nor in contrast to an other, but simply in itself. The encounter of two such self-contained integers generates a third whole, of a new order—as illustrated by the ellipse generated through the relationship between two foci; the forcefield between two magnets (*Fig. 15e*); the pattern of intersection between two systems of diffraction rings (*Fig. 21a*). New Age consciousness will be attentive simultaneously to both levels of wholes, the integers and the integrated design their encounter generates.

The participational/gestative, the differentiating/phallic, and the interrelational/exertive systems each locate and derive "the whole" in differing manners (*see chart, page 93*). In the first, it is a summation of parts. The whole is greater than the sum of its parts

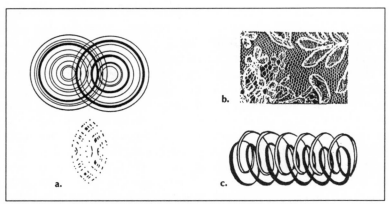

Figure 21 - Some graphic logos characterizing the emerging Age.
    a. Diffraction rings, generating a unique pattern of intersections.
    b. Lacelike network of interconnections.
    c. Double helix.

in the sense that it and it alone constitutes a true whole; any part extracted from it is not a "small whole," but simply an isolated component. In the phallic/differentiated model, what the prior model calls the whole is seen instead as chaotic mass, out of which various wholes may be separated. Here the whole is the individual unit, individuated from the mass and differentiated from every other whole. The mass is not a larger whole, but chaos. Finally, in the interrelational/exertive way of picturing reality, individual wholes interweave to produce a new order of wholeness. Thus there are two simultaneous orders of wholes: the integers themselves and the system generated by them. For example, in the second half of this book each chapter is a self-contained whole that might stand alone, as well as contributing to the larger whole of the book itself.

Not only pairs, but multiplicities of integers are to be seen in terms of the system of linkages between and among them. Like a piece of fine lace (*Fig. 21b*), such a network consists of non-uniform patterns of connection among constituents, giving rise to a many-textured design whose beauty and order results precisely from its nonhomogeneity. Individuals, clusters, cross-clusters, pairings—each with its own character—constitute the network. This is different from both the basically homogeneous gestative matrix and the hierarchical pattern typical of patriarchy.

In recent years a phenomenon known as "networking" has emerged simultaneously in many places. Top-down organizations are no longer the only respectable mode. Egalitarian shared-control and overlapping, rather than territorial, zones of influence are seen as viable possibilities, even in the corporate world. All of this departs from the patriarchal pattern and hints at the beginnings of a new Age based on exertive womb values.

Neither participational consciousness nor differentiating objectivity characterizes this third model. It encourages a "both-and" way of looking at things. Although uncommon in the Patriarchal Age, this sort of consciousness is sometimes experienced in mystical states or with the aid of psychedelic drugs. A pair of opposites that are mutually exclusive as seen by differentiating consciousness are no longer contradictory when comprehended by mentation that simultaneously holds awareness of various levels or orders of wholes. In other words, this is a style of consciousness that is attentive to varying contexts and can shift from one to another, or even hold several in awareness simultaneously.

Three Ways of Conceptualizing Wholeness

	WHOLE	PARTS	
PARTICIPATIONAL GESTATIVE SYSTEM			
	The whole is made up of parts. None of these parts is a "lesser whole" by itself.		
	CHAOS	**WHOLES**	
DIFFERENTIATING PHALLIC SYSTEM			
	Out of chaos, individual wholes are differentiated.		
		WHOLES	**NEW WHOLES**
INTERRELATIONAL EXERTIVE SYSTEM			
		Individual wholes interrelate to form new wholes.	

In such a system, we should expect to experience life as multivalent rather than focused, contextually transformative rather than goal oriented. Within the gestative system (*first column of chart, page 75*) movement was contained and cyclic. The metaphor for progress was natural, vegetative proliferation and succession of seasons. Phases succeeded one another in a repeating pattern, like a circle, or like the snake biting its tail. In the phallic system (second column), movement is goal oriented and linear, like an arrow. Progress is pictured as ascent, achieved through competition and mastery. In the exertive system (third column), movement is to be rooted in context and emerging out of it, like a spiral or helix. Each context is like a circle—but instead of closing on itself, the circle transcends itself. Each turn regresses back on itself, yet is a continuation of adjacent turns, each spiral transcending its own circularity in both directions. Another way of imaging this is the double helix (*Fig. 21c*), structural pattern of the basic molecules of all life. Interleaved ascending and descending coils suggest the contexting of "opposites" within a larger whole that retains their distinctions, yet transcends their opposition. In the coming Age we should expect to find experiences of transcendence commonplace, in the sense of shifting flexibly between smaller and larger contexts. Mystical truths formerly known only to exceptionally evolved individuals may become commonplace too, linked as they are to simultaneous awareness of multiple "planes of being," or contexts.

The contextual orientation and the capacity to consider multiple levels of context are already finding expression in the contemporary interest in holistic and ecological approaches. Although ecological values and holistic ideals can be imagined and are being articulated now, actual implementation is uncommon because such values are at odds with the prevailing patriarchal pattern. Ownership of natural resources by this or that individual, corporation, or state, and exploitation of the natural world are automatic corollaries of the patriarchal world view, which is still the norm for us. In an Age expressing the exertive womb rather than the phallus, property ownership and exploitation would simply cease to be meaningful concepts, based as they are on phallic principles of separating-out and power-over.

It is as yet beyond imagination to picture concretely a world based on exertive-womb principles of egalitarian networks, contextual transformation, and holistic transcendence. To appreciate how alien exertive-womb principles still are, try to imagine what sort of pattern would replace "ownership" of animal pets by "masters" in an Age in which hierarchical patterns no longer pertain.

To recapitulate, in an Age incarnating culturally the $X^M X^P$ pattern and the exertive womb metaphor, these are the watchwords: context; egalitarian; transformation; multiple wholes; self-transcendence; non-uniform multiplicity; "both-and" simultaneity without loss of distinctions; network.

During the Matrical Age, patterned on the qualities of the gestative womb, yin-feminine attributes would have been most valued and promoted. For example, both women and men would have tended to develop the participational style of consciousness. Because they embody the physical organ upon which that Age is patterned, and can readily catalyze the parallel psychological style, females would have been the primary carriers of culture in that system. In the current Age, where the phallic mode predominates, the yang-masculine qualities are most valued and promoted. Thus both men and women tend to develop the objective, differentiating style of consciousness that corresponds to the phallic nature. Because they bear the physical organ upon which the Age is patterned, and display parallel psychological proclivities, males are seen as the primary carriers of culture in this Age. It follows from this that within the Patriarchal Age there is a tendency to equate "patriarchy" with masculine, male, and men. Therefore as the patriarchy comes under criticism, some may feel that saying no to the continued hold of patriarchal patterns requires rejecting of men and masculinity. *It is crucial to grasp that both men and women, and all four of the sexual modes, play a part in each Age.* What needs to be discarded is not men, but outmoded, extreme cultural expressions of phallic values. Furthermore, in turning away from patriarchy let it be with a sense of its value, as a stage of human growth.

The impression that patriarchy must be rejected outright in order to move into a new Age is itself an expression of the patriarchal tendency toward *either-or* choices and ranking of alternatives as good or bad, rather than as simply different. From the phallic perspective, transcending this *either-or* duality requires building bridges between opposites. Such configurations as truces and treaties, even the gesture of shaking hands, express the motif of bridging between alien opposites. In patriarchal terms, the route to the next Age is a bridge connecting the old world view to the new one. From the perspective of the exertive womb, what is needed is not a bridge, but a more comprehensive context, transcending and embracing both.

As humankind develops facility in discerning multiple contexts, it will become more and more commonplace for people to unite across ethnic and other lines while retaining a sense of individual identity. This differs both from the ideal of the "melting pot" (where immigrants from varied ethnic origins quickly merge into a single culture) and from the pathology of mob psychology (where the individual loses separate identity, merging into the collective matrix). The 1985 recording "We Are the World," created to raise funds to send aid to those starving in Ethiopia, offers a prototype of such multiple contexting. First, the enterprise was undertaken with a sense of the larger context linking all humankind: the famine in Ethiopia is comprehended not as something happening to "them," but as afflicting the broader "us" of humankind, we who are the World. Secondly, singing stars of widely differing styles came together to produce a single recording in which each retains his or her distinctive style, yet all are united in the context of a single song. It is not the hodgepodge that might have been expected; it holds together as a whole. Third, the recording stars function as a nonprofit benevolent organization, collecting and redistrbuting funds, both maintaining and transcending their identity as musicians. Fourth, many radio stations in many countries worldwide participated in synchronized playing of the song, with numerous gatherings of people "singing along" to generate a worldwide network for those few moments.[25] The unprecedented public response also cut across many group identities. People who would not normally listen to, much less purchase or sing along with, recordings by these stars, did so. "We Are the World" has been movingly sung in churches, at commencement ceremonies, and even funerals, equally authentic in such diverse contexts.

Similarly, the peace marches of 1983-86, the women's marches of 1978 and 1986, and marches on behalf of the poor and homeless in the early nineties mobilized people across a broad spectrum of identities, not solely to benefit this or that small group but also on behalf of all humanity. Such movements grasp the grass roots imagination and hint at Contextual Womb patterns.

This book is based on the premise that biological facts suggest meanings that inform our understandings in the psychological, cultural, and spiritual spheres. At the same time, the biological "facts" at our disposal are themselves in part the products of psychocultural attitudes. Thus in ancient times the role of biological paternity was overlooked not because the means of discerning it were not at hand, but because the matrical mindset predisposed a focus on the maternal half of the procreative process. Until recently the clitoris was deemed nonfunctional, not because the means did not exist for discerning and analyzing its function, but because the patriarchal mindset was predisposed to overlook in the female "other" the homologue of the organ symbolic par excellence of masculinity as defined within the patriarchal system. Perhaps in subtle ways the egalitarian ideals promoted by the Women's Movement and New Age prophets predisposed geneticist Mary Lyon to look for the balanced alternation of maternal or paternal expression characteristic of the $X^M X^P$ chromosomal pattern she discovered. Such biological "facts" are not merely objective, but are discovered and formulated in accordance with the mindset of the Age.

Little or no genetic research has yet been done to determine the role of the male's X chromosome. In looking at the genetic basis of maleness, all attention has been on the Y chromosome, which correlates symbolically with phallic psychological traits and patriarchal culture. It is sometimes erroneously said that the male's X chromosome is "female." When paired with a Y, the X is a component of male genetic makeup. The tendency to imagine that the male's X chromosome is "feminine" correlates with our tendency to label testicular psychological traits as "feminine." It is also the consequence of underdeveloped attentiveness to the fact that the context in which the X is found in part determines its nature. Within the context of the male, the X in the X-Y combination carries that portion of the ancestral protomale chromosome that split off in producing the original Y. In other words, it is the conservator—a quality that harmonizes with the testicular attributes already described. I venture to predict that as the long-belittled testicular masculine qualities gain their rightful stature, genetic researchers will begin to take notice of the unexplored question of the special role of the X in the male.

It appears that the Patriarchal Age has already passed its zenith. Its gifts to human cultural development become detriments when carried too far. The threat of nuclear war is the ultimate expression of the danger of overemphasizing such phallic values as territoriality, competitive power styles, superior-subordinate relational structures, technological exploitation of nature. The superpowers have developed huge arsenals of penislike missiles that carry nuclear warheads. The purpose of such penis power is to be able to say "fuck you" to any who challenge their spheres of dominance. Ironically, it has become evident that to carry out this threat would be to rape the entire planet, destroying not only the human species, but all life on earth. Even the sort of "surgical," non-nuclear military operation seen in the Gulf War had dire ecological consequences, with longterm effects not yet fully assessed.

Thus it becomes less and less possible to operate on the "fuck you" principle. Phallic power becomes so exaggerated it is impotent. There is no way out except the relinquishing of the patriarchal world view. The old order will pass away, either through nuclear/ecological annihilation or through transformation to a new Age—based, I predict, on exertive-womb values. If indeed only "death" of phallic dominance and the "birth" of the Contextual Womb Age can save the world, then peace efforts that reflect exertive-womb values will be most effective.

Whether we look ahead to the coming Age or back to the prepatriarchal Age, there is a tendency to imagine it as a Golden Age. This is a matter of projection. Both the unknown past and the unknown future function as blank screens upon which to project the cultural manifestations of human characteristics that have been neglected during the Patriarchal Age. Whether we look to the past or the future, we are likely to see our missing selves: what we most need for new life and vitality as the current Age wears itself out.

Chapter Seven

Counting Serpent Skins

The lost parts of ourselves are lost parts of our image of the Divine. As we come to know ourselves more fully our ways of worshiping will take into account the gestative, testicular, and exertive body metaphors as well as the phallic. Even our names of God and our most personal ways of relating to the Deity will likely change. The God beyond all our notions about God may be the same yesterday, today, and forever, but human concepts of God change as surely as the butterfly sheds its chrysalis or the serpent sheds its skin.

All our words about the Divine (including such names as "God-Masculine" and "God-Feminine") are metaphorical rather than literal statements. They function well as *pointers* aiming us toward the God beyond the words, or as *vessels* welcoming us to encounter God between the lines. Even the most hallowed formulation becomes idolatrous if we mistake the name for the Reality toward whom the names leads. Unfamiliar names for God are heretical only if old names have become idolatrous. All of our images of the Deity are both true and false: true, insofar as they function as authentic metaphors, pointing to or embracing the mystery of the Deity; false, insofar as we mistake the metaphor for the Deity Itself/Herself/Himself.

Although ultimately God is One, no one image or title is adequate. Even within a single tradition, multiple images, often contradictory if taken literally, coexist. For example, God is both intimate father to his chosen children and awesome lord of the universe; both a jealous, devouring fire whose vengeful touch is to be feared and a still small voice in the silence after the tempest. Further, within the integrity of each religious tradition lie *as yet unborn* images of the divine. The fourfold framework developed in this book provides a way of calling forth from the tradition of a faith community new names of God correlating with each of the four body metaphors.

99

Willingness to address God in new ways goes hand in hand with intimate relationship with the divine. It is akin to the proliferation of terms of endearment that we spontaneously invent when we are in a love relationship with another human being. Parents seldom call their infant children solely by the formal name given on the birth certificate. Punkin, Button, Bruiser, Champ, Bunny, Kitten, Big Boy, Sugarbun—such names are a sign of lively parent-child bonding. Similarly, lovers may call each other Sweetheart, Lovey Dove, Honey, Baby, Sugar. Just as it would be absurd to take such names literally, imagining that the parent thinks this baby is a pumpkin, button, or animal, or that the lovers really consider each other to be hearts, babies, or doves, so it is a mistake to imagine that in naming God as Father, or Rock of Ages, or King, or Mother, for example, we literally identify the Deity as any of those. All our various names for God originate as forms of endearment springing to the lips of those who are on intimate terms with the Deity. Thus Jesus calls God "Abba" (Poppa); the Song of Solomon and many Christian mystics address God as the soul's beloved; and the Psalmist sings,

> As a doe longs
>   for running streams,
> so longs my soul
>   for you, my God.
> My soul thirsts for God. (Ps. 42:1-2, JB)

The converse is also true. If names that were intended as terms of endearment become abstracted from a living relationship between human and divine, they become frozen as orthodoxy. Then gradually they lose their power to catalyze human-divine intimacy and devotion. Being willing to entertain new names for God has the unexpected bonus of bringing to life again the traditional ones. If religious communities and people of faith remain unable to express the truths of their faith in any except narrowly patriarchal terms, then as the human species outgrows the Patriarchal Age the old formulations will lose their power to connect people to God.

Historically, each successive style of spirituality has been shaped in part by reaction against the outgrown formulations of its predecessor, in part by the emergence of a new guiding metaphor. The Jewish religion emerged early in the Patriarchal Age, when the old matrical patterns were still influential. In the matrical system, holiness is a participation or immersion in the divine matrix by such means as sexual intercourse in temple or fruitful field, faithful observation of natural cycles and processes, living in the presence of manifold images of the Deity, and drinking or bathing in the blood of an animal representing the Deity. In contrast, for the People of Israel holiness means being *set apart*. God's chosen people are to cultivate a sense of separateness from all others. The Deity, no longer experienced as immanent in Nature, is likewise set apart as transcendent Other. Visual representation of God and even speaking the Holy Name is forbidden. The consequently immense gulf separating human and divine is a progressive counteraction to the matrical tendency for merging. God and Satan become a pair of opposites engaged in a cosmic power struggle. In the new religion of Israel, obeying the matrical circularity of the snake (*Figs. 22 and 23*) has become evil; salvation comes from being chosen as a people apart and given "unnatural" laws to keep. These include dietary laws that prescribe ritual enactment of strict separation of one kind of food from another, reiterating in daily life the overall separational motif. Rejecting the uroboros (symbol of gestative containment) in favor of phallocentric values results in a curse upon both the exertive and testicular gender modes: the exertive womb must labor painfully to give birth; tending the seed, symbolic of the testis, is no longer natural, but laborious and toilsome.

The importance of breaking free from the containing matrix is enacted by the founding patriarchs. Abraham is required by Yahweh to leave behind the old country, where life was circumscribed by agricultural cycles, and embark instead on a linear path toward a distant goal; cyclicity is replaced by sequential history and a linear sense of time; earthy agricultural rites are replaced by manna from above; natural wonders as revealers of the Deity are replaced by the supernatural bush that burns but is not consumed.

Moses leads the people not only out of Egypt, but out of matrical bondage and into a forty-year exile in the wilderness during which their identity as the *Lord's* people is tested and shaped. Backsliding to the old ways takes the form of yearning for the nurturing stewpots of mother Egypt and worshiping a golden idol in the shape of a cow, both symbolic of the old Mother religion. Moses raises up an image of the serpent, its uroboric power (circular, self-fertile, self-spawning, self-devouring, matrical; *Fig. 22*) broken upon a phallic rod (*Fig. 24*). In a mountaintop experience Moses is given the holy Law: morality requires obedience to the Lord. Sacrifice is less a rite of immersion in the Deity, more a matter of making amends with the transcendent God for having broken divine Law.

All of these changes mark a species-beneficial counterbalancing of the outworn matrical system. However, once sufficiently ac-

Figure 22

a. Is this snake devouring itself? Mating with itself? Giving birth to itself? If it were an animated cartoon, what would the next few frames show? The snake curled upon itself mouth to tail (called the uroboros, meaning "tail eater") represents participational immersion characteristic of the matrical system, with merging and overlapping rather than the sort of clear separation typical of patriarchal consciousness and spirituality.

b. In patriarchy, matrical circularity is considered evil. The uroboric snake becomes the serpent in the Garden of Eden (Gen. 3). *From a carving in Andlau Church, Alsace, ca. 1100.*

Figure 23

When the male God-image became dominant, the snake came to seem evil. In earlier times goddesses were frequently represented as accompanied by the snake or serpent as a positive symbol of wisdom, transformation, subtlety, and flexible power.

a. Ceres-Demeter.
Terra-cotta relief, Hellenic.

b. Dea Syria.
Bronze figure, Roman.

c. Hathor-Ashoreth- Astarte.
Egyptian, 1250 B.C.E.

d. Athena.
Greek, 5000 B.C.E.

complished, the very separateness that was the means of salvation begins to be a problem. Earlier, the need of the soul was to separate from the matrix. Later what the soul needs most is "at-one-ment." Separation is experienced not as salvation, but as alienation. Jesus comes as Emanuel, meaning "God *with* us," to effect at-one-ment (atonement), reuniting humankind with the transcendent God whose distance has become the central problem of the alienated soul. He himself becomes the one "lifted up" as Moses lifted up the serpent (*Fig. 25*). On the cross he enacts the painful bridging between opposites (*see Fig. 26*). In this event, linear time is inrupted by *kairos*, the fullness of time, the turning point of history. Holiness by obedience becomes holiness by rebirth through grace or gift, "purchased" by the blood of the sacrificed Christ. The Law is condensed to the commandment to love: to connect again with what has been separated, "that they might all be one" (John 17:11-23).

These brief characterizations suggest how each religion follows a guiding gender metaphor and is both related to its predecessor and departs from it. Of special interest is the departure of the Christian configuration from the phallic mode. Although the historical expression of Christianity has been predominantly phallic in tone, *key motifs actually resonate with exertive womb imageries.* If humankind is nearing the threshold of a new Age where the exertive womb is to be the guiding metaphor, it may be that these resonances will take on great importance. Perhaps the newly emerging spiritual focus of the Women's Movement will bring these to more explicit expression in this century or the next.

To summarize the main themes of this progression:

Matrical Mother Religions

- Holiness is by participation in the divine flux of cyclic natural life, represented by the circular snake swallowing its own tail. (GESTATIVE CONTAINMENT)
- Time is cyclic.
- Morality is natural behavior.
- God is all over, roundabout. (GESTATIVE CONTAINMENT)

Early Patriarchal Age: Jewish Religion

- Sin is obeying the matrical circularity of the snake. (REJECTION OF GESTATIVE CONTAINMENT)
- Cyclic time is replaced by linear, historical time. (PHALLIC ORIENTATION TOWARD GOALS AND EXPLORATION OF VIRGIN TERRITORY)

Figure 24

Bronze serpent that Moses lifted up in the wilderness to save and heal the people (Num. 21:9), as represented in an eighteenth-century manuscript.

- Natural law has been superseded by the Law from above. *(PHALLIC EMPHASIS ON HIGHER AS HOLIER AND SEPARATION OF MAN FROM NATURE)*
- Morality is obedience to divine Law. *(PHALLIC PATTERN OF MASTER AND SUBORDINATE)*
- God is over all *(SUPREMELY HIGH PHALLIC "MASTER")*, rather than all over *(CONTAINING GESTATIVE MATRIX)*.
- God acts to separate out a holy nation. Holiness is by separation— of Israel from all others; of God from Satan. *(PHALLIC SEPARATION AND POLARIZATION OF OPPOSITES)*

Late Patriarchal Age: Christianity

- Sin is alienation, separation from God. *(CORRECTION OF EXAGGERATED PHALLIC DIFFERENTIATION)*
- Linear, historical time is inrupted by *kairos*, the fulfilled moment. *(EXERTIVE-WOMB TIMING)*
- God acts to effect at-one-ment. *(A COMING TOGETHER IN A NEW WHOLE, AS BY EXERTIVE WOMB.)*
- A new law of the heart replaces the Law from above; inner attitude is as important as overt obedience. *(CONTEXTUAL WISDOM, AS OF EXERTIVE WOMB)*
- Morality is reconnecting with (loving) both God and others.
- Holiness is by grace/gift/rebirth rather than obedience. *(TRANS-FORMATION, BIRTHING FROM EXERTIVE WOMB)*

Such an evolutionary overview may seem to suggest that there is no "true religion" on which to stake one's life and in which to center one's soul. If earlier religions are "corrected" by later

Figure 25

LEFT: The two sides of a medieval coin show Christ crucified and the serpent crucified. "As Moses lifted up the serpent in the wilderness, so must the Son of man be lifted up" (John 3:14).

RIGHT: Contemporary Lenten motif of cross draped with burial shroud is derived from early Christian images of the serpent crucified, as shown here from a drawing ca. 1500.

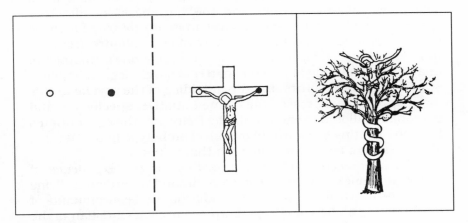

Figure 26

LEFT: The patriarchal system polarizes opposites, including human-divine, good-evil, God-Satan, self-other. On the cross, these opposites are reconnected.

RIGHT: Design from a medieval Italian fresco shows Christ crucified on the Tree of the Knowledge of Good and Evil (the opposites), around which the uroboric serpent still entwines. Christ and the serpent each represent an alternative to patriarchal separation of opposites. The serpent merges them, dissolving their distinctions. The crucified Christ is a figurative bridge between opposites that retain their distinctions.

understandings, doesn't that make them "false"? Or, if all are somehow "true," then are we free to pick and choose this or that piece from each one?

The answer to these questions that I find most satisfying is based on the Jungian understanding of the psyche as an extremely complex totality, with many components held together around an ordering center. The most central archetype of a person's psyche, the one functioning as the most comprehensive center providing the maximum coherence and integration of these manifold elements, constitutes that person's experiential image of the living Deity. If the most central archetype corresponds to the Christ as incarnated in Jesus, then for the person centered on that archetype it is literally true that no one comes to the Father except through him, and there is no other salvation from alienation. If the most central archetype ordering one's psyche corresponds to the Law of the Holy People set apart, then membership in that nation and keeping the Law is the only salvation possible. Whichever archetype functions as the ordering center of the psyche determines the "truth" of the symbol system correlating with it, and the "falseness" of all other systems. The Christian symbol system is utterly true for those grasped by it, false for those whose psyches configure around a different center. This is not to suggest that one's manner of imaging and relating to God is a matter of psychological happenstance. Rather, I picture that the unfolding of the psyche in this manner or that expresses the divine initiative, specifically and personally tailored to each soul. The Deity, not the ego, initiates the constellating of a particular central archetype in the psyche. The ego's task is to cooperate with that initiation.

The phenomenon of conversion, then, is the experience of discovering one's psyche to configure around a particular divine archetype—with all the subjective and behavioral concomitants of that ordering archetype. To be "born again" as a Christian is the subjective experience of the Christ as constituting center of the psyche. To make a commitment with heart, mind, soul, and strength to keep the holy Law of Israel is an expression of having one's psyche configure around the Yahweh-Israel revelation.

Conscious commitment to the central archetype corresponding to a particular faith may entail an actual shift from a different centering archetype (radical conversion), or may instead involve explicitly recognizing and naming the archetype that had already been ordering the psyche, unnamed (confirmation, bar mitzvah). In any case, religion (whether institutional or individual) is a matter of the *interaction* between the psyche and the Deity per se; what we experience is that interface, rather than God alone.

Each institutional religion is a distillation of spiritual wisdom relating to human experience as configured around a particular central archetype. Each reflects the collective experience of many whose souls have related to divinity in the manner imaged by that archetype. The theology and practice of an institutional religion thus provides a strong vessel for ordering and containing the raw energy of spiritual libido, which otherwise could easily overwhelm the individual ego. This is a major reason for maintaining ties to one's traditional faith. Although the "tried and true" ordering symbols and practices of a faith tradition might sometimes deaden the experiences of the faithful by limiting expectations, those same symbols can also carry into new territories. This is because *their meanings may evolve*—as has the significance of the serpent, for example.

God images that live within the soul and are mapped by collective religions are not frozen solid. When they are in danger of rigidifying, they "shed their skins" and show forth new facets of the Divine One, who is ever beyond full comprehension. For those whose psyches no longer perfectly cohere around a central archetype defined in terms of the Holy Law of a people set apart, nor of the atoning Son of God as traditionally preached, there is no choice but to participate in a creative process to make visible the unnamed center in new terms: to dare to speak new names of God.

In each faith tradition resonances of all four body metaphors are detectable, and part of our challenge is to discover and consciously name these as they function within our own traditions. Moreover, each institutional religion centers on one gender mode as its keynote. For those who are called to it, the present-day task is to *name the Deity who emerges when the exertive womb becomes the keynote* and the other modes take new places in resonance with that central motif.

Chapter Eight

Conversion to the
Divine Womb

Zeus, Mars, Pluto, Apollo, Neptune—we have heard their names in stories read in childhood. No modern person would rank these old Greek and Roman gods on a par with the Lord God Yahweh or the Christian trinity of Father, Son, and Holy Spirit. Although at one time they perhaps corresponded to the central archetype around which the entire psyche cohered, no longer do they fulfill that function the way Yahweh and the Christian God still do for many in this era.

Vesta, Hera, Diana, Venus, Athena—we have heard their names, too, and perhaps have read about their continuing role in the psyche as "goddesses in everywoman."[1] Although it is worthwhile to know how these goddesses still function as subsidiary organizing nodes of the personality, what engages us today is the possibility of experiencing a feminine personification of the self-center: a feminine experiential image of the Deity on a par with Yahweh and the Christian trinity; a Deity who correlates with the exertive womb as the Lord correlates with the phallus.

Every personality is held together by a central ordering principle, regardless of whether or not the person is affiliated with a particular community of faith. As this center-of-self has tended to personify itself specieswide in phallic terms for many centuries, so now a specieswide shift is underway toward yang-feminine personification of the self-center. It is unlikely that any of the old goddesses *per se* can function as central ordering archetypes for modern women and men. The value of recalling imagery from an era when the central archetype did have feminine form is that doing so may help us to perceive and name in feminine terms the divine center as it configures anew. In particular, the *yang* feminine elements in the old stories provide points of connection between the ancient feminine trinity and newly emerging feminine manifestations of the Deity.

The resurgence of interest in tales of the triple Goddess, not as curious relics of long-dead religions, but as dramas that have the power to stir the soul today, indicates the readiness of the human psyche to enter into the next phase of divine-human encounter. As a Christian, I am keenly concerned with discovering how the revelation in Jesus Christ correlates with this tendency for conversion from the phallic Lord to the exertive Womb. Exploration of conversion from the phallic emphasis of other faiths can be undertaken authentically only by devotees of each faith.

Although adherents of the three great patriarchal religions (Judaism, Islam, and Christianity) disagree on many points, all know the Divine One as God, never Goddess. "Behold, Israel, the Lord your God, the Lord is One." "Allah is the One God; Muhammad is His Prophet." "In the name of the Father, and of the Son, and of the Holy Spirit." "Jesus saves." If that One begins now to enter human experience and awareness again in female form, It is still the same One, presenting new facets of Its mystery to humankind.

So imagine. . . Once, long ago, there was no winter. Sprouts, buds, flowers, fruit, and seed followed one another in uninterrupted succession. This was the Original Age as pictured by women and men of old who knew the divine power as the Great Goddess, eternal source of both life and death. She was known in three aspects, which likewise follow one another in uninterrupted succession, much as the phases of the moon turn perpetually from one to another. As each of the phases of the moon is distinct, yet still a single moon, so each of her phases is distinct, yet still One Goddess. Her names may be familiar from patriarchal Greek mythology. However the following story about her predates the phallic Age.[2]

The Story

In ancient times, mortals knew that Demeter and her daughter Cora, called Persephone, together watched over the perpetual process of sprouting, flowering, fruiting, harvesting, and seeding. It was said that Demeter herself had taught mortals to grow and cultivate crops instead of foraging in the wild for food.

Together Demeter and Cora inspirited all growing things. The maiden especially delighted in the tender new shoots, lovingly coaxing them to grow. The mature plants were in Demeter's care, and at that season Cora-Persephone was free to wander the countryside gathering bunches and garlands of narcissus, hyacinth, myrtle, and red poppies. Often Mother and Maiden would dance together in the fields, bedecked with the flowers Persephone had gathered. So full of life force were they that shoots of grain would spring up behind them wherever their feet touched the ground.

One day, Mother and Daughter sat together on a high hill, serenely surveying the fields of grain. The younger woman stretched out and laid her head in her mother's lap. As Demeter absently stroked her hair, Persephone mused about the spirits of the dead, whom she had encountered on her wanderings. She described them to her mother, how they milled about in bewilderment, not understanding their new state or knowing where to go. "Is there no one," she asked, "to receive the newly dead into the underworld?"

Demeter sighed and answered, "I myself have responsibility for the underworld, for it is from under the earth that I draw forth all vegetation. When the seeds are underground my boundless energizing spirit from below fills them, readying them to burst forth in new life. So the realm of the dead is my domain; but my most important work is here, to feed the living."

"Yes, Mother, I can see that you are needed here. Yet, the dead have need of us too." Persephone reflected awhile. Then she decided, "I will go to them."

Demeter shuddered with dread. She called Persephone's attention to the joy they shared in this beautiful world—the warmth of the sun, the fragrance of the flowers, their times of dancing and of reverie together. She told Persephone that the underworld was a place of perpetual gloom and darkness and begged her to reconsider.

Persephone sat up and hugged her mother. They rocked each other, weeping quietly for a long while. Finally, each knowing in her heart that Persephone's decision was true, together they walked silently and slowly down the hill toward the fields. They paused in the midst of Demeter's fine grain and looked tenderly at each other one last time, realizing and accepting the cost of what Persephone would do. Then with a tender smile Demeter gave her blessing to her daughter's venture. "It is right that you go. Yet, you are my daughter, whom I love, and for as long as you remain in the underworld, so long will I mourn your absence." Persephone in turn blessed Demeter's wholehearted acceptance of the mournful half of the undertaking.

Persephone gathered three blood-red poppies and three sheaves of ripe wheat. Demeter herself led Persephone to a deep chasm, portal to the underworld, and gave her a torch to light her way into the darkness. Then she watched her daughter go down into the deep cleft in the earth.

In the crook of one arm Persephone held her mother's grain close to her breast. With the other arm she held the torch aloft. She shivered from the sudden chill as she descended. Deeper and deeper into the silent dark realm she ventured, slowly making her way along the rocky path. After many hours she became aware of a droning sound that grew louder as she descended. Finally she entered an enormous cavern. There thousands of spirits of the dead milled about, moaning with bewilderment and despair.

Persephone made her way through this throng to a large, flat rock. She climbed upon it and found there a stand for her torch, a vase for Demeter's grain and poppies, and a large bowl piled full of rubylike pomegranate kernels, the food of the dead. As she looked out upon the throng her aura grew brighter and warmer.

"I am Persephone," she announced. "I have come to be your Guide. You have left your earthly bodies and now reside here in the realm of the dead. Come to me now, and I will initiate each of you into your new world."

She beckoned to those nearest the rock to step up onto it, into her aura. As each one came, Persephone embraced the form, then stepped back and looked full into the eyes. She reached for a few pomegranate seeds and squeezed them between her fingers. She marked the forehead with a swath of the red juice, saying, "You have waxed into fullness and waned into darkness. Enter now into the mystery of the eternal womb that bleeds but is not wounded. Be renewed!"

For months Persephone unceasingly received, blessed, and initiated the dead into their new condition. Above, on the earth, Demeter yearned for her return. She wandered disconsolately from one secret cleft to another, hoping to find her daughter emerging at last from the underworld. So profound was her sorrow that she withdrew her power from the fields and woodlands, the crops and trees and wild-flowers. They withered and died. Unable to bear reminders of her daughter's delight in young, sprouting things, she forbade new vegetation to grow. The mortals planted their seed as usual, but the fields remained barren. Eventually her grief became so great that she ceased her searching and sat still as a stone on a bare hillside, gazing out at the drab fields with blank and sunken eyes, waiting. Waiting.

One morning green shoots of crocus pushed through the bare earth, encircling her where she sat. Demeter was too lost in sorrow to object to this defiance of her order that no new vegetation was to grow. Then, as the purple buds swelled and opened Demeter heard them whispering together. She leaned closer and heard them murmuring excitedly, "Persephone returns! Persephone returns!"

With a gasp of surprise and joy, Demeter leapt to her feet. She clapped her hands, she shouted and laughed, she ran and skipped, waving her arms and crying, "Persephone returns!" As Demeter ran down the hill, through the fields, through the forests, her renewed energy surged into the dormant plants and seeds, stirring them to fresh growth. In response to her jubilation the birds, the insects, all life took up the message, crying out joyfully, "Persephone returns! Persephone returns!"

When Persephone emerged from the underworld, Demeter was there to meet her with a robe woven of white crocus. They ran into each other's arms, embracing, laughing, dancing together, renewing the whole earth with springtime energy.

Ever after, Demeter and Cora-Persephone willingly repeat this drama each year with the turning of the seasons.

❖ ❖ ❖

Time after time, I have witnessed how this ancient story still has the power to move listeners to tears. If it can so stir the depths, then it must be more than just an anthropomorphic attempt to explain the succession of the seasons. We who understand the scientific reasons for the changing weather patterns have no need of fanciful explanations. I believe we find this story exciting and satisfying because, dating as it does from an Age when subjective experiences of the divine regularly came in feminine form, it reawakens in us a latent capacity to experience the divine mystery in its feminine guise. Goddess stories such as this one about Persephone's venture and Demeter's sacrifice were not simply made up, but reflect the experiences of spiritually attuned women and men in that Age—who encountered the triple Goddess as authentically as today's born-again Christians have encountered Christ.

"Ah," you say, "but Demeter and Persephone are just characters in a story, whereas Jesus was a real person." The implication is that we can trust the Father-Son-Holy Spirit triune image of the divine nature because one of its members is an actual person, whereas the Maiden-Mother-Crone triune image of the divine nature is simply a figment of the collective imagination, with no basis in reality. To me it seems equally astounding that the Divine One reveals Itself through an historical configuration or through visionary images of the collective imagination of an Age. I believe both make a significant impact on the spiritual evolution of the human species, and that the effect of personal encounter with either can be life changing.

Although the historicity of Jesus is an important factor to be reckoned with in Christian theology, simply hearing an account of the historical events does not bring about faith in Christ. Something other than a listing of historical facts is responsible for conversion experiences. People do encounter the living Christ, do undergo radical transformations, being "reborn in Christ." It is such a subjective experience of the Divine One encountered in the guise of Jesus that convinces the convert of the authenticity of the Christian faith. "I know that my Redeemer liveth"—not because it is a comforting, logical, or historically sound idea, but because I have had a personal experience of the Christ, touching and transforming me. In other words, I have recognized in Jesus Christ the central archetype organizing my psyche as a whole, ordering chaos into cosmos. It is at this deep subjective level that the Cora-Demeter-Persephone story may also stir us, unfolding theological insights pertinent today.

The triune Goddess typically comprises maiden, mother, and old woman expressions. Although this version has only two characters, the three names—Cora, Demeter, Persephone—relate to the three functions. Demeter's name contains the word *meter*, meaning "mother." The prefix *de-* or *da-* may mean either "grain" or "earth,"[3] or might be connected to the Greek letter delta, sometimes said to be the "letter of the vulva" because its triangular shape resembles the female genital.[4] The corresponding letters in Sanskrit (dwr), Celtic (duir), and Hebrew (daleth) mean "door." As the divine genital, Demeter is the sacred doorway of both birth and death, *and all other major changes or transformations*. The letter delta (Δ) as used today in mathematical notation likewise signifies changes or differences.

The triangular shape also represents the trinitarian nature of the Goddess. Demeter, "Δ–mother," is one Goddess with three phases. On the one hand, she is the Mother phase. At the same time, she is the *triune* Goddess, expressing herself now as Maiden, now as Mother, now as Mistress of Death. In this triple sense, all the characters in the story are phases of Demeter, rather than sharply distinct persons.

As Divine Mother she presides over the growing and harvesting of vegetation, bringing forth plenty from the earth. In this aspect she is Demeter Ploutos, meaning "riches." From the same root come our words plus, plural, and plenteous. Her Roman name, Ceres, is said to derive from Cora, meaning literally "maiden" (Greek *kore, korasion*).[5] Our words *cereal, corn, kernel, core,* and *cardiac* are related. Cora is the kernel, the heart, the germinal center hidden in the buried seed, which initiates new life. Thus Demeter's divine power permeates the dark realm, where transformation is wrought. The daughter who ventures into the underworld and the mother who grieves above, are the same One. Both bear the cost of blessing and initiating the dead.

The third phase of the triple Goddess is directly concerned with wisdom and death. Her titles include Destroyer, Black One, Subterranean One, Queen of the Blessed Dead, and Avenger. Usually she is pictured as a very old woman or crone, from word roots meaning "old, dry, withered." The word is related also to *carcass, carrion* and *hag.* [6] Although the old death hag is wise and holy as well as ugly, sifted through patriarchal sieves what usually remains is a caricature of repulsive ugliness: the Halloween witch. In this story Persephone retains the youthful appearance of daughter-Cora, maturing into the hag's qualities of wisdom and holiness without becoming ugly, old, and withered. The withering shows instead in the shriveling of vegetation during Persephone's sojourn in the underworld. Because Persephone is a young woman in both the aboveground and underworld scenes, we are perhaps able to look at what she represents without immediate distaste. Nevertheless, she is not simply lovely maiden, but death-crone as well.

To our linear minds, virginal maiden and old crone would seem to be at opposite ends of life. We picture the maiden coming first, followed by the matron, and finally the old woman. If the Demeter trio simply represented successive life stages, or the succession of the generations, the *kore* phase should begin as a little girl, who grows into a matron and finally an old woman. But in stories of the triple Goddess, the Kore consistently is pictured as a full-grown young woman, rather than a prepubescent girl. The fact that there is no child, and that the youngest woman sometimes is designated simply "maiden" rather than "daughter," alerts us that the three have some other significance than to show generational succession or sequential life stages. The three nodes are simultaneous, rather than successive, components of a true trinity.

If we arrange the three phases of Demeter at the points of a triangle (*Fig. 27*), Persephone's mixture of maidenly and deathly qualities may seem less surprising. Instead of being at opposite ends of a line, Maiden and Death Goddess are adjacent and thus easily interchanged. So in the story it is consistent for Cora and Persephone to be alternative names for Demeter's maidenly daughter whose destiny is to fulfill the duties of Death Goddess, initiating the dead into their new condition. It is at this point of *initiation* that Death Goddess and Kore are interchangeable. Significantly, this is also the

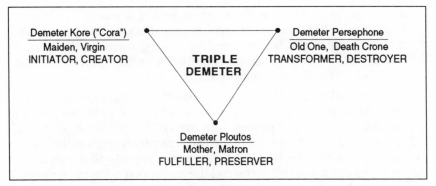

Figure 27 - This trinity rests upon Demeter Ploutos, the bounteous mother. From the matriarchal perspective, the matronly aspect is naturally foundational.

locus of assertive feminine energy, which I postulate as the point of connection between the ancient trinity and new feminine archetypes of the deity.

Both are initiators. The Kore is an initiator in the sense of taking initiative: self-starting energy to make a new beginning. In the story, she corresponds to the bursting forth of fresh, new growth. The Death Goddess is an initiator in the sense of orchestrating rites of initiation. An initiation process typically entails the undergoing of ordeals and the learning of secret knowledge, in order to enter into the new group, estate, or office. Thus, literally, Death Goddess (initiation) and Kore (initiative) are interchangeable.

In ordinary life, typically it is a young woman who gives birth, thereby becoming a mother. In contrast, psychologically and spiritually the old woman representing death is the birther. The following dream by a middle-aged woman at the "change of life"[7] illustrates this truth:

I see a very, very old woman dying in the street. I kneel by her side to give aid. She is a frail skeleton, with fragile, birdlike bones, almost like a fossil in the pavement. I place my hand on her lips and heart—no breath or pulse. I rest my left hand on her head as for baptism, to speak the Rite of Passage for the Dead. I am weeping. Her skeletal form is still on the ground, but her Being materializes briefly, standing nearby. I turn and converse with her, tears running down my cheeks. She and I affirm together that her death came at the fullness of time, when she had completed putting all her things in order. There is a rightness about it, for she leaves a wholesome heritage to her descendents. I turn back to the corpse. No longer a frail skeleton, but a very pregnant young woman! Her belly a huge, round ball. Suddenly I realize that though she is dead, her unborn baby might be delivered by cutting open her belly and lifting out the baby. Just then her belly splits open like a ripe pod, delivering forth a healthy infant.

The paradox that the old crone and the young maiden are One is the central feminine mystery. Contrary to the phallic view, life and death are not warring opposites, with resurrection as the final triumph of life over death. The mystery of their secret unity repeats in the phases of the moon. Whereas the phallic perspective expects all things new or good to be bright and shiny, instead the *new* moon is the *dark* moon. It corresponds to the point of initiation (*Fig. 28*), where the Death Crone extinguishes the old cycle and gives birth to the new; where the virginal new life springs forth at the initiative of the Maiden.

Like the paradoxical new moon, the Cora-Persephone composite hides within itself the turning point from oldest to newest, from waning to waxing, from death to life, from destruction to creation. This dark moon directly counterbalances the bright full moon of the plenteous, sustaining mother with her full breasts and perfect nurturance. Whereas the full moon is fully yin, fully open to receive light and passively reflect it back again, the darkness of the new moon veils secret *yang* activity.

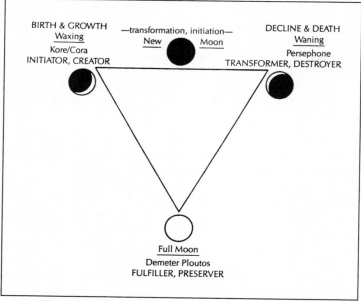

Figure 28 - Moon-phase correlation in Demeter trinity.

This is a reversal of the usual identification of light with yang, dark with yin as seen in the Taoist landscape analogy cited in Chapter 2. Within the limits of that analogy, sunlight and shadow aptly represent yang and yin. In an unrelated analogy central to patriarchal symbology, sunlight and shadow *also* signify good and evil, respectively.[8] The bright light of the sun as symbol of the divine nature and of humankind's finest impulses casts a dark shadow as symbol of evil. This analogy is helpful in its own way and is the basis of Jung's important work on the archetype of the Shadow. However, prevalent mixing of these distinct analogies results in false conclusions:

> If yang is light,
> and good also is light,
>> then yang must be good.
>
> If yin is dark,
> and evil is also dark,
>> then yin must be evil.

Yet a third traditional symbol is that sun is masculine, moon feminine. Putting these together, patriarchal symbolism equates light and brightness with yang, good, sun, and mascuine; and sees dark, shadow, yin, evil, moon, and feminine as an opposite cluster. These configurations must be broken open if we are to appreciate the meaning of the new moon as dark without being evil, as yang without being bright, and as feminine without being yin.

This entails shifting out of solar symbology into a lunar frame of reference. So long as the sun is our reference point, the moon in its *full* phase will seem most desirable, for it receives and reflects light from the sun most fully. From this solar perspective, the dark new moon is a nonentity, for it reflects sunlight not at all.[9] *From a lunar perspective,* however, *bright and dark phases of the moon have equal significance.* The dark of the moon is not a negation, as is the dark Shadow in solar symbology. Nor is it a complementary opposite of the bright solar yang-masculine, as is the dark yin of the Taoist analogy or the yin anima of Jungian psychology. Once we shift from solar to lunar orientation, the bright and dark phases of the moon symbolize balanced aspects of femininity: as the bright full moon is perfectly yin-feminine, the dark new moon is utterly yang-feminine. Lunar darkness is not evil, not to be approached as Shadow in the Jungian sense. Neither is it receptive in either positive (nurturant) or negative (devouring) ways. Its fiery darkness is the exertive, active, transforming power of the womb. Because this phase is a nonentity in a solar-oriented symbol system, what it might show us about the Divine One has been mostly invisible in patriarchal religions.

Although not explicitly named, this yang-feminine aspect of the divine is in fact at the heart of the Christian mystery of incarnation, death, and resurrection. Despite contrary patriarchal overlayers, the Christian revelation, like the ancient Goddess trinity, shows God not conquering death, but using death as the doorway to new life. The three days in the tomb are finally revealed as an incubation in the Divine Womb, which, though it bleeds, is neither diseased nor wounded. Both the womb and the Divine One bleed, suffer, die, and renew. Illuminating Jesus Christ with the lunar light of the triple Goddess rather than the solar light of patriarchy emphasizes his connection with the Divine Womb and supports the possibility that the Christian religion carries within itself the seeds of conversion from a phallic to a birth-oriented central archetype.

The Maiden as she connects with the Mother (*Fig. 29*) correlates with the moon *waxing toward the yin side* of femininity. It is not surprising that the figures of Virgin and Mother, and particularly Virgin-Mother, fare well when the patriarchy takes over, with its vision of femininity as all yin. In contrast, the Maiden as she connects with the Crone is assertive, yang initiator—exactly the opposite of the patriarchal ideal of femininity. Thus in patriarchal piety the Virgin has been venerated exclusively in terms of her connection to the Mother dimension, ignoring her connection with the Crone and the dark moon. In devotional art the Virgin Mary has often been pictured with the waxing crescent moon at her feet, symbolizing her yin identity. She is idealized as pristine Virgin who is the Mother in a sanitized way that ignores her womb, her vagina, and the bloodiness of giving birth. The fiery, dark, assertive powers associated with the Maiden's connection to the Crone and the dark of the moon play no part in Mariology. Likewise, goddesses who correspond to the dark moon, such as Persephone, Hecate, Lilith, and Kali, fell quickly into ill repute with the coming of the Patriarchal Age.

As the patriarchal system displaced the matriarchal, the story of Demeter and Persephone underwent major revision to bring it into harmony with the new patriarchal standards and values. A comparison of the two versions of this story alerts us to the sorts of patriarchal emphasis we may also expect to find in accounts of Jesus' life, for though Jesus was an actual person rather than a character in a myth, the way in which the historical events of his life are understood and represented has been similarly shaped by the values of patriarchy.

Here then, is the classical Greek form of the story, known more widely by far than the more ancient version:

The Modified Story

One day while Demeter was busy tending the grain, her daughter Persephone was in the fields gathering wildflowers. With her were Artemis, Athena, Aphrodite, and some nymphs—virginal maidens all. Seeking ever more beautiful blossoms and attracted by the lovely Narcissus (some say the scarlet poppy), Persephone wandered away from the others. As she reached to pluck the most beautiful flower, suddenly the earth was rent open at its roots. A great a chasm formed, and out of this cleft rose Hades, ruler of the underworld, driving a fine chariot drawn by black horses. He seized Persephone and carried her off into the underworld to be his consort. The other maidens heard her cries, but none could tell Demeter just what had befallen her.

In a frenzy of grief, Demeter left her work and began to search for her daughter. She wandered the earth, seeking her everywhere. She even asked dark Hecate if she knew what had become of Persephone. Finally Helios, the sun, who sees all things from on high, told her of the abduction and rape by Hades, and that Persephone now resided in the underworld.

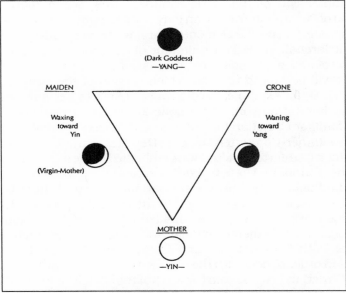

Figure 29 - Waxing toward yin; waning toward yang.

Demeter appealed to Zeus, greatest of the gods, to intercede, only to find that Zeus himself had approved Hades' plan. In anger and grief, Demeter withdrew her power from earth's vegetation. Her purpose was to bring pressure on Zeus, for if mortals had no crops they could make no offerings to Olympus. Finally Zeus relented and sent Hermes to the underworld to fetch Persephone home. But Hades had forced upon the maiden a few pomegranate seeds, and having eaten these she was forever bound to him. A compromise was struck. Persephone would return to her mother for part of the year, during which the earth would experience summer with full access to Demeter's power. For several months each year she must return to Hades in the underworld. During those months, Demeter sulks and grieves, and the earth falls barren for winter.

❧ ❧ ❧

By comparing this later version to the pre-patriarchal one, we can chart the sorts of changes introduced by patriarchal values. This same patriarchal orientation likewise has shaped accounts of the life of Jesus, accentuating those elements that fit, systematically de-emphasizing others. Precisely those yang-feminine characteristics that are central to the original goddess story and voided out in the patriarchal revision provide clues to the repressed yang-feminine dimension of the Christ drama. Thus, the prepatriarchal version of Persephone's mission may point the way for noticing in the Jesus material specific elements that have been mostly invisible in the patriarchally-toned formulations of traditional theology.

For clarity in the following discussion, references to the Goddesses will be tagged to show which version of the story is being cited. Thus, for example, Persephone-1 refers to her nature in the pre-patriarchal version; Persephone-2, the patriarchal version.

A familiar Christian formulation is that God is Creator, Savior, and Sustainer-Comforter. In the Demeter trinity, Creator and Sustainer-Comforter functions are embodied in the initiating Maiden and the abundant Mother—both of whom are retained (although with diminished roles) in the patriarchal system. Where the two trinities most diverge is in regard to the remaining Person. Instead of Jesus Christ the Savior, in this trinity we find Persephone the Destroyer. Despite their dissimilar titles, the two bear much resemblance. Both Persephone-1 and Christ willingly leave the Divine Parent in order to deal with the problem of human death. One of the great Christian insights into the ways of the Divine One is that in the sacrifice of God the Son, God the Father likewise suffers. The same truth is portrayed by Persephone and the Mother. In both instances the Divine Parent bears great suffering, participating fully in loss and diminishment of divine wholeness and bliss.

Both Persephone-1 and Christ deal with death not only as the end of physical life, but also as an ongoing phenomenon of spiritual growth throughout one's lifetime. Thus the Christian is to willingly participate in "dying daily" (1 Cor. 15:31). Persephone's initiates are to attune to the cyclic succession of waxing, waning, waxing; not only as tied to the moon, but as the rhythm of the life process at all levels. Waning and withering are to be valued, not avoided.

In the original goddess story, yang energy is centered in the exertive womb rather than the phallus. Half of this assertive energy is devoted to actively destroying the old, half to pushing to birth the new. It is the destructive half that is most feared and misunderstood within the prevailing patriarchal milieu. Persephone's main title is "the Destroyer." Although no certain derivation is known, her name resonates with various Greek roots that evoke a sense of her stark destructiveness. *Peras* means "uttermost." *Sepo* is "corruption." *Phoneuo* is "kill, slay, murder." During the destructive phase, the entire trinity participates in the transforming work of the Crone. The withering of all vegetation is not an after-the-fact or incidental expression of Demeter's grief, nor a manipulative spoilsport reaction. It is integral to the work of the Crone, the "withered one." Withering, waning, destruction are her gifts. When this mode comes to the fore the virginal Kore no longer is manifested in the spontaneous blossoming forth of the life force. Instead she is experienced as initiator into death as transformation. Because the three are One, Mother Demeter participates in the Crone's energy; everything withers.

Both Persephone-1 and Christ relativize the seeming finality of death. The Persephone-1 resolution is to reveal acceptance of death as inevitable for initiation into new life. The Christ resolution is that death as an ending is unexpectedly followed by resurrection and new life. They differ in that whereas death is seen by patriarchy as the final enemy to be overcome once and for all by the victorious, phallic Christ, it is for Persephone-1 the creative instrumentality for her perennial work of initiation. Despite the predominance of triumphal imagery at Easter, there are indications that Christ's relationship to death more closely resembles Persephone-1 than at first appears to be the case. Contrary to phallic theology, he taught the value of death: "Unless a grain of wheat falls into the earth and dies, it remains alone; but if it dies, it bears much fruit" (John 12:24);

and "If any man would come after me let him deny himself and take up his cross and follow me. For whoever would save his life will lose it, and whoever loses his life for my sake will save it" (Matt. 16:24).

This runs counter to the prevailing patriarchal mind-set, which predisposes us to view the bright moon of fulfillment and the dark moon of destruction as a pair of opposites, and to rank them so that one is called good, the other bad. Withering, waning, destruction, and death are seen as negatives, often as the work of the Devil rather than as part of the divine nature. At best, patriarchy counts them as necessary evils, to be accepted and passed through as quickly as possible so that we can emerge again into the light side. The original goddess story suggests a different valuation, and one that exists in the Christ material alongside the image of Christ crowned as victor over death.

In the original goddess story, the underworld forces of death, initiation, and transformation were willingly engaged by Persephone. In the later version, she has lost her natural connection to the exertive womb, which spontaneously pushes to birth in the right time and place. Instead Hades' abduction, inharmoniously imposed from outside, is required to force change upon her. Persephone-2 has been turned into a wholly passive object whose fate is determined completely by others: Hades, her mother, Zeus, and Hermes. Gone is every trace of her former yang initiative. Now the only way she can participate in creative or transforming experience is to be "carried away" by an intrusive, coercive phallic figure.[10]

Jesus, too, is portrayed as the victim of intrusive phallic coercion. As Persephone-2 was abducted and raped, so Jesus was roughly arrested, violated, and pierced by nails and sword. Even though his death might best be described in terms of the divine yang-womb, because assertive femininity is not recognized as a divine force by patriarchy, the death of Jesus must be attributed not to the purposeful timing of God's womb, but to an evil adversary: the hands of evil men or the cosmic power of sin and death as personified in Hades or the Devil. So long as the human psyche is oriented by a *phallic* central archetype, the orderliness of the cosmos is inevitably experienced as pairs of opposites. Within that cosmos, God and Satan *are* adversaries and it would be dangerous to take either one lightly.

As the central archetype ordering both psyche and cosmos moves away from the phallic toward the womb metaphor, the adversarial model loses centrality. In repeatedly affirming that he was entering into death by choice rather than through defeat by the Adversary, Jesus invites such a change of guiding metaphor, for like

Persephone-1, Jesus actively embraced his mission into death. He announced in advance the means by which he would die, spoke of the importance of the divine timing ("my time is not yet come")[11] and asserted, "I lay down my life. ...No one takes it from me, but I lay it down of my own accord" (John 10:17-18). In this he resembles Persephone-1's personification of the dark yang womb. Seen as the labor of the divine womb, this death and resurrection mark the *kairos*, the divine fullness of time, the perfectly timed push that brings forth new life from blood, pain, destruction, death.

The patriarchal values of hierarchical dominance and assertion of power over one another, absent in the earlier story, significantly shape the later Greek version. Once imagined to be an expression of sexual passion, rape is now recognized by psychologists and sociologists as a crime of phallic aggression. In kidnapping and raping Persephone-2, Hades asserts his dominance and power over her, much as the patriarchy itself came to dominate the earlier matriarchal pattern. Moreover, before carrying out his plan, Hades had it approved by his superior, Zeus. The chain of hierarchical authority ranks Zeus above Hades, and Hades above Persephone-2 and Demeter-2. As Persephone-2's abduction was approved and engineered by the hierarchy, so was Jesus Christ's death sanctioned and accomplished by the machinery of the religious and political hierarchy. He was killed not by a wild hoodlum or lone madman, but through the coordinated efforts of the hierarchical chain of command.[12]

Within that hierarchical system he was the lowest of the low, despised and rejected. He taught repeatedly that high rank was not important. This revolutionary idea is contrary to the very essence of patriarchy. Although his supporters called him Lord, and his enemies parodied him as a mock king, Jesus identified himself not with power and high rank, but with the subordinate half of humanity. He showed that the way out of a hierarchical system is through the bottom: any one who would be great without buying into the hierarchical pattern must become like a servant. Thus he knelt and washed the feet of those who called him Lord and King and ended his life executed as a no-account criminal. It is ironic that his resurrection was nevertheless hailed in hierarchical terms as proving that he is Lord, King, and Victor after all—thus confirming rather than modifying patriarchal ideals.

Demeter-2 was already at the bottom of the heirarchy, without power to effect the rescue of her abducted daughter. She appealed to the highest authority in the hierarchy for help. When Zeus refused her request, she resorted to the only remaining way to opt out of the system. She withheld the yin nurturance that was her assigned contribution to the hierarchy. Such passive resistance, much the sort practiced by Gandhi, is an apt weapon for those deprived of direct power within a system. Zeus finally agreed to her demand, only to find that Hades had outmaneuvered them both. By forcing his seed upon Persephone-2 he bound her to him forever. Ownership rights of the male over the female, or of master over slave, is another patriarchal motif. Jesus, by willingly submitting to the ultimate subjugation, identified fully with such ritually subjugated "others" of the patriarchy. From the phallic-solar orientation the "powers of death" are envisioned as holding Jesus against his will until on the third day he finally triumphed and broke free of bondage. As seen from the yang-lunar-womb orientation, however, the three days are not an imposed bondage but the fulfilling of a mission; the underworld is an aspect of the Divine Womb rather than the kingdom of evil Hades.

An alternative form of Hades is Pluto, the masculinized hypostasis of Demeter's epithet, "Ploutos,"[13] That Pluto-Hades has usurped qualities that formerly resided in Demeter Ploutos is substantiated by the fact that he was considered to be not only the god of death, but also the giver of fertility to the crops. It was said the seed corn could sprout only after exposure to his fertilizing power, having lain beneath the dark earth. This power was formerly an attribute of Demeter's Divine Womb, in her role as Ploutos.[14]

Pluto-Hades at first enjoyed a place as a respected god in the hierarchical chain of command. However, eventually the patriarchal tendency for polarizing opposites resulted in underworld Hades coming to be regarded as the enemy of God the heavenly Father. As the divine Father is the highest of the high, Hades is the lowest of the low. So, paradoxically, both Hades and Jesus are aptly characterized by the same phrase: Hades is the lowest of the low as God's evil adversary in the patriarchal system of opposites and hierarchies; Jesus is the lowest of the low by virtue of voluntarily identifying with the bottom of the hierarchical pyramid as the way out of that system—and as such is God's beloved, in whom he is well pleased. I fantasize that part of the ultimate at-one-ment accomplished by Christ will be the reunion of Hades-Pluto with the central Deity.

Such an idea departs radically from traditional theology, where Hades as the Devil is Jesus' adversary, embodying death, darkness, and evil. In the old theology, based on phallic values, death is the enemy of both God and humanity, to be avoided or vanquished. In yang-womb theology, death is the means to life, to be entered into with awareness of the Divine Womb that bleeds nonpathologically. Death-bringer and Life-giver are one Womb.

The ancient lunar trinity rested on the Full Moon and worship was characterized by participational immersion in the plenteous Mother. The shift to a solar orientation entailed separating from the immanent divine Mother and discovering God in a new way, as the transcendent divine Lord. The upward, sunward displacement of divine power in the revised goddess story is shown in that no one but Helios, the sun on high, can tell Demeter-2 what has happened to her daughter. In the old dispensation, surely Hecate with her dark-of-the-moon wisdom would have known. In the patriarchal cosmos the bright light of solar-phallic consciousness is to be relied on exclusively. Contrary to this, Jesus connected wisdom not solely with light, but with the serpent: "Be wise as serpents" (Matt.10:16). That ambiguous symbol originally associated with the feminine Deity (recall *Fig. 23*) and later equated with the Devil may become again an important symbol of the wisdom and holiness of yang-femininity. Jesus' spiritual insight (Matt.21:42) that the stone the (phallic) builders rejected is the very one destined to become the cornerstone in the coming Age, may be seen to apply not only to himself, but to to other rejects, including the serpent of wisdom and the (originally feminine) divine qualities that Hades-Pluto represents.

The church has for the most part continued to see Jesus as a solar King of Light, not yet appreciating that he points toward a new divine archetype, a revelation of the divine nature in nonphallic, nonsolar terms. Psychologically, to attune to this revelation means that the psyche arranges itself around a central organizing principle patterned after the exertive womb and the dark new moon rather than the phallus and bright light of the sun. From this lunar perspective Jesus Christ is a paradigm for disidentifying with patriarchy and living out of womb values.

For men who have assimilated standard phallic values, the need is to disidentify with the overlord, relinquishing their position of "godgiven" superiority and identifying instead with their subordinate counterpart—the slave, the woman, the oppressed. No longer is greatness to be measured by high position, but by willingness to relinquish not only this or that hierarchical privilege, but also the centrality of the phallic archetype itself as organizing principle for both psyche and cosmos. This means relinquishing the world view that polarizes humankind into superior and subordinate halves and that predisposes the man to experience mankind as the human

standard and himself (and the phallic gender metaphor he carries
in his body) as more directly in the image of God than is the woman,
who bears in her physical being the womb metaphor. Jesus models
this willingness to let go the phallic orientation and enter the womb-
tomb daily to die with Christ.

For women, the task is to disidentify with being the subordinate
"other" and to find their own feminine identity,[15] which in its essence
is contextual and egalitarian rather than hierarchical. They find
true release from their subordinate "place" at the bottom of the
hierarchy not by making their way to the top, but by beginning to
know their own value and dignity in the image of God-the-birthing-
womb.[16] For both men and women it means recognizing that
womanliness, with its equal emphasis on both birth and death, is
as much a divine attribute as is manliness.

This implies recognizing, as I propose in the final chapters of this
book, that Christ (meaning God in human life and form) is not
exclusively masculine. Even if we prefer to limit our experience of
Christ to the life of the man Jesus, we can perceive his divine
femininity once we set aside exclusively solar understandings.
Despite the predominantly solar orientation of the age, Jesus
sometimes characterized himself in terms that resonate with the
qualities of the womb. He said he had come to seek and save the lost,
inviting them to "come unto me," and offering to gather Jerusalem
to his breast as a mother hen gathers her chicks. This correlates with
yin-womb enfoldment and nurturance. His own involvement with
death and the tomb, and his message that we too must be willing to
die with him, is another way of saying, "You must be born again,"
and correlates with yang-womb powers of death and transformation.

> "Can we enter a second time
> The womb of God the Mother?"
> "If ye would be born again,"
> Answers Christ our brother.
>
> Birthing power of God brings forth
> What is least expected.
> Tomb of death is Womb of birth,
> Christ is resurrected![17]

Not surprisingly, his female contemporaries seemed to recognize more readily than did men the womb metaphor underlying
Jesus' life, death, and resurrection. Particularly, meanings relating
to the dark, deathing-birthing side of the divine seemed beyond the

understanding of even his closest male followers. Peter was the first man to recognize Jesus as the Christ, yet immediately after showed that he had no understanding of the role of the womb-tomb in this identity. When Jesus spoke of his imminent death, Peter replied emphatically, "God forbid, Lord! This shall never happen to you" (Matt. 16:16-25). Jesus sharply corrected him, affirming that all who would enter into the Christian way must willingly enter into death, or as we would say, into the transformative labor of the divine womb.

When we remember how male-dominated the culture was at the time, it is impressive that the four gospels recount so many instances of women witnessing to the yang-womb affiliation of Jesus. Repeatedly, they seem to home in on the dark birthing meanings that the cultural bias made invisible to most men. His mother, Mary, was the very first person to know of his coming birth. Her kinswoman Elizabeth was next to know: her womb leapt up in greeting when Mary came to her in the early stages of pregnancy. When the shepherds came to see her newborn son, telling of the angel's message that this baby was Christ the savior, everyone wondered—but Mary "kept all these things pondering them in her heart" (Luke 2:19). And again, when the boy was twelve years old and disappeared for three days, only to be found at last in the temple, "his mother kept all these things in her heart" (Luke 2:51). This heart of Mary is like a gestating womb. It was his mother who, out of the wisdom of this womb, prompted Jesus to begin his public ministry at the marriage at Cana, despite his protest, "Leave me alone, woman. My time has not yet come" (John 2:1-6). Such timing is a function of the exertive womb, and Mary evidently was in touch with its rhythms, for despite his reluctance, Jesus did transform the water into wine at this wedding—his first public display of divine power.[18] In contrast, on other occasions when he told various men "my time has not yet come" he did not then go ahead and fulfill their expectations. Their requests evidently were not in harmony with the divine womb-timing, as was Mary's.

A woman came to Jesus midway through his ministry and while he was at table knelt to wash his feet with her tears and dry them with her long hair (Luke 7:37-48). She provided the model according to which Jesus later washed and dried the feet of the disciples as they were at table, thereby taking upon himself the subordinate place at the bottom of the heirarchy.

Just prior to his arrest, a woman[19] came up to him as he was eating with friends and poured precious perfumed oil on his head. When the men there protested at her wastefulness, Jesus praised her for preparing his body in advance for its time in the tomb.[20] She alone was in tune with the rhythm of the time, which was leading Jesus toward fulfillment of his mission in the tomb-womb.

After he was arrested and tried by the religious council according to Jewish law, he was taken to the Roman authorities to be tried in accordance with the law of the civil hierarchy. Neither Herod nor Pilate, the two Roman governors to question him, seemed to know what to make of him. It was Pilate's *wife* who recognized that Jesus was not to be trifled with. She sent Pilate an urgent message saying she had had a nightmare about this man and advising her husband to have nothing to do with him (Matt.27:9).

As the divine timing came to fullness and Jesus went to his death, for the most part his male followers deserted him. It was the women who were able to stay present through the terrible enactment of the divine womb's deathly transformative power. At the cross, many women stood watch through the hour of Jesus' death.[21] The women were at the tomb when he was laid there, and only the women returned to the tomb first thing in the morning to complete the death rites of anointing his body. These women were the first witnesses of the resurrection, commissioned to go and tell the men, who at first thought they were talking nonsense (Luke 24:11). When the men did come to believe, they immediately construed his resurrection in solar terms, proclaiming him victorious over death. From the phallic perspective, this is an appropriate interpretation. From the perspective of the dark New Moon, the resurrection is not a victory over, but a birth out of death. Death is not an evil enemy, but the divine destroying-creating Womb, who transforms and brings forth.

This birthing of the nonsolar Christ is still in process. It involves more than a conversion of the individual soul: a conversion of the collective psyche. As we begin individually and as a culture tentatively to relate to the divine yang womb, new personalities and a new cosmos will be shaped around that central image. Such a conversion entails a nonadversarial attitude toward darkness, destruction, death, and the devil as attributes of the uncensored Divine Womb.

Chapter Nine

The Body that Bleeds but Is Not Wounded

Appreciation of the divine as feminine goes hand in hand with positive attitudes toward the full female sexual cycle. Each supports and furthers its counterpart. If a woman (or a man who cares about her) yearns to know the divine as feminine, then nothing less than full respect for both "light" and "dark" phases of her sexuality will suffice; if she (or he) hopes to accept and fully cherish her biological nature, nothing less will do than knowing it as an image of the divine nature.

The exertive-birthing and the gestative functions of the womb are but two nodes in the complex cyclicity of feminine physiology. They have been especially emphasized in developing the basic body metaphors because they aptly represent the yang and yin expressions of femininity. To develop the fullest possible body metaphor for the Divine Womb it is next valuable to consider all that is known about the bodily womb and its cycles, including hormonal, physical, and emotional components of menarche, menstruation, ovulation, pregnancy, and menopause. The menses and menopause merit particular attention, since both are connected with the yang side of the Divine Womb—and therefore have been maligned as curses.

The physiology of feminine cyclicity has not yet been adequately studied by scientists. Investigations have been slowed and flawed when researchers have proceeded from unexamined phallic biases that devalue some phases of the natural cycle and focus on symptoms, syndromes, pathology, and disease at the expense of charting normal female experience.[1] Nevertheless, within the last two decades a great many papers have been published concerning various aspects of feminine cyclicity. This research has modified the available body of facts about menstruation, menopause, and female sexuality in ways that support and strengthen the notion that femininity has both yin and yang expressions.

129

Two feminine cycles (circles) will be traced. The first is the *monthly cycle* marked by ovulation and menstruation. Generally ovulation has been considered the end and purpose of the process, and menstruation as the disintegrative aftermath of a lost opportunity for pregnancy. These attitudes resemble the patriarchal valuation of the full moon as "better" than the dark moon, which is considered to be absent or depleted. To fully appreciate the monthly cycle means valuing its menstrual aspect.

The second is a lifelong *developmental cycle* whose segments are menarche, pregnancy, parturition, and menopause. Within patriarchy, menarche and pregnancy have been considered the positive, definitive signs of femininity; birthing and menopause have been defined as difficult, painful, dangerous, damaging, undesirable. It may be hard to imagine that these, too, are worthy aspects of the divine image.

Body facts about the menstrual cycle include both hormonal and organic patterns of change, the most noticeable of which is the flow of blood from the vagina about once a month. (*Menses* actually means "month.") Multiple studies have confirmed that although the normal periodicity of individual women varies between twenty and forty-four days, the average menstrual cycle (as determined for both statistical mean and median) is twenty-nine and a half days—exactly the length of the moon's cycle.[2] Reflections about symbolic connections between moon phases and female cyclicity are thus not mere speculation, but rooted in physical facts. A composite moon-menses symbolism provides a basis for imaging and relating to God-Feminine, just as a composite sun-phallus symbolism underlies ideas and experiences of God-Masculine.

Within the body this periodicity is timed by a delicate hormonal feedback system. A variety of hormones (primarily FSH, estrogen, LH, and progesterone) from three locations (hypothalamus, anterior pituitary, ovaries) directly orchestrate the system. We shall look first at the biological facts, then at their metaphorical meanings.

The hypothalamus is a node of specialized brain cells equilibriating such states as hunger-satiety, sexual appetite and response, increase-decrease of body temperature, sleeping-waking balance, and simple emotional states such as pleasure and rage. In response to certain stimuli, the hypothalamus sends a chemical message to the anterior pituitary, a gland located near the base of the brain. The pituitary responds by secreting FSH (follicle stimulating hormone) into the bloodstream. When FSH reaches the ovaries, it stimulates several cocoonlike capsules called follicles, each containing an immature egg. Thus stimulated, the follicles begin to manufacture estrogen, secreting it into the bloodstream. When estrogen in the blood reaches a certain level, it blocks further FSH production in the pituitary, which begins instead to manufacture LH (leutinizing hormone, meaning "yellowing"). At the ovary, LH changes the pattern of follicle stimulation so that only one follicle and egg continue to grow. As this follicle enlarges, its wall thins at an outer point, eventually breaking open to release the ripened egg. The empty follicle fills with a yellow fluid and begins to function in a new way as corpus luteum, literally "the yellow body." The corpus luteum continues to manufacture estrogen, as did the follicle, and in addition produces another hormone, progesterone. When the level of progesterone in the blood reaches a certain point, it triggers the pituitary to cease manufacturing LH. Without continued LH, the corpus luteum begins to disintegrate—thus halting the production of both progesterone and estrogen. When progesterone and estrogen reach their lowest points, menstruation begins. About two days into the flow the hypothalamus responds to the absence of estrogen in the bloodstream by signaling the pituitary to start production of FSH again, beginning a new cycle.

Throughout the cycle, both highs and lows of hormone level are equally important as signals moving the cycle along. *Periodic absence of a hormone is as significant as its abundance.*

The time between the manufacture of FSH and its cutoff in response to the production of estrogen by the ovarian follicles is called the *follicular phase* of the cycle (*see chart, page 132*). The length of this phase varies from month to month and from person to person, within a normal range of six to thirty days. The *luteal phase* begins when LH production stimulates ovulation with consequent formation of the corpus luteum. This phase is consistently fourteen days, ending with the onset of menstruation.

The rise and fall of these various hormones in the bloodstream affects the uterus, or womb. Increasing levels of estrogen produced by the follicle prompt the uterine lining to proliferate. During the luteal phase, the combined effects of estrogen and progesterone stimulate even greater growth, producing a deep, spongy, blood-rich lining. When the corpus luteum disintegrates, progesterone and estrogen levels drop abruptly, prompting tiny vessels in the lining to contract for several hours, cutting off blood supply to the surface layer of spongy tissue, which in turn begins to shrink and disintegrate. After some hours, the vessels again expand, bringing blood to the tissues. As vessels near the surface of the lining burst under the suddenly renewed pressure, patches of blood-soaked tissue sepa-

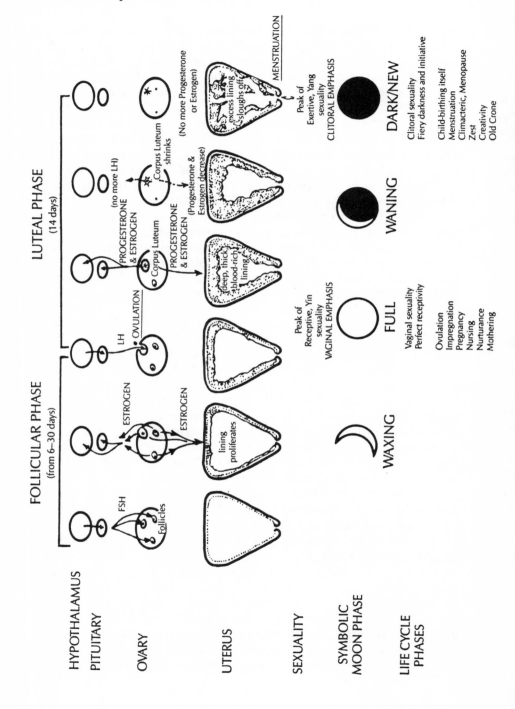

rate off from a thin lining of cells that remains intact—from which another thick and spongy proliferation will arise when the estrogen and progesterone levels again increase.

We have been conditioned to assume that the focal point of this cycle is ovulation and that impregnation is the only purpose of female sexual activity. Although procreation is one valuable end, for the woman herself (and by implication, for God-Feminine) all phases of the cycle have meaning. To honor only the ovulatory function is a bit like saying that the only purpose of the moon is to be full, and that the other three phases are passed through solely to produce a full moon again. From the lunar perspective, the bright full moon is no more valuable than waxing, waning, and dark phases. The feminine way is intrinsically egalitarian. If it builds up, it also destroys; if the abundance of a hormone is important to the cycle, equally of value is its absence; if one X chromosome functions actively, the other functions correctly by turning itself off; if it promotes life, it also brings forth death. To insist on honoring only the proliferative, life-increasing mode is to deform femininity, precluding the constellating of a fully feminine God-image in the psyche.

Stages in the menstrual cycle correlate well with the symbolic meanings of the moon's phases, as shown in the chart:

• The waxing crescent corresponds to the increase of hormonal levels in the follicular phase. Like the enlarging moon, the follicles wax or grow fat; the lining of the uterus begins to thicken.

• Ovulation and the formation of the corpus luteum correspond to the full moon. As the full moon is maximally receptive to the light of the sun, at this point both egg and uterus are most receptive to possible fertilization and implantation. Hormone production from the corpus luteum is at its highest, stimulating the production of a deep, thick, receptive lining in the uterus, a physiological paradigm of receptive and nurturant yin-femininity.

• The ongoing luteal phase corresponds to the waning moon. Just as the moon grows smaller and smaller, so the corpus luteum shrinks and hormone levels fall.

• Menstruation itself correlates with the dark new moon. What has been built up, breaks down; expulsion replaces receptivity. In an apt metaphor of yang-femininity, life-blood pours forth rather than being reabsorbed within the body in a process of simple involution.

This yin-yang cyclicity is observable in women's dream patterns as well. Periovulatory dreams are more passive, relaxed, contented (yin-ish); perimenstrual dreams more active and energetic in content (yang-ish.)[3]

Conventional wisdom has it that women are most "feminine" and "sexual" at the time of ovulation. This would make sense in the interest of procreation, since only around the time of ovulation can intercourse result in pregnancy. Accordingly, the sexuality of most primates follows an *estrus* cycle, having a rather short breeding period, just at ovulation, marked by a bloody discharge from the vagina. In species having an estrus cycle, the female is sexually active only during this specific period. However, humans, Old World monkeys, and apes have departed from this estrus pattern. In these few species female sexuality is organized around the *menstrual cycle*, in which bleeding no longer coincides with ovulation but with the opposite side of the circle, and females are capable of enjoying intercourse and other kinds of sexual activity throughout the cycle. In fact, for human females arousal response to erotic stimuli has been found to be *weaker* in the periovulatory phase than at some other times in the cycle.[4] Nonovulatory sex has no direct procreative value, since impregnation is impossible except at ovulation. That it has developed as a natural phenomenon in several species suggests that it expresses another aspect of the feminine principle, alerting us to appreciate nonprocreative values.

Recent studies have found that many women actually feel more sexual around the time of mensruation than around the time of ovulation.[5] Kinsey found that women are more likely to masturbate just before menstruation than at any other point in the cycle. Masters and Johnson fround that just prior to menstruation women are most orgasmic.[6] Some studies have shown that women seem to have two distinct types of sexual urge.[7] Around ovulation their sexuality expresses itself in a desire to surrender, to be receptive and responsive to overtures by the man, and to enjoy vaginal penetation. In other words, it has a yin nature, corresponding to the Full Moon and to patriarchy's image of ideal femininity. Menstrual sexuality typically is more assertive. Whether in relationship to a partner or alone, women are likely to take initiative for sexual experience during the time just before, during, or just after menstruation, when the locus of sexual intensity is the clitoris rather than the vagina. Enjoyment of clitoral sexuality predates menarche and the onset of fertility; during the fertile years it is more intense when the woman is *not* ovulating; and it continues past menopause, when the woman is no longer fertile.[8] So clitoral sexuality evidently serves purposes other than promoting procreation. Anthropologists puzzle over what could be the survival value for the species to have developed nonprocreative, clitoral sexuality; they have yet to agree on a satisfactory rationale.[9] As women themselves can attest, a strong clitoral orgasm is a powerful experience of womankind's intrinsic yang nature.

Thus ovulatory, vaginally-oriented sexuality expresses femininity as yin: receptive, responsive, enfolding, leading to gestation. Perimenstrual, clitoris-oriented sexuality expresses the yang side of femininity: assertive, "fiery," eager, initiating, nongestative.

Even after two distinct peaks of female sexual interest had been mapped, some researchers asserted that only the yin-style sexuality (near ovulation) was truly feminine. The yang-style peak was dismissed as "pseudomasculine," because characterized by initiative and assertiveness, qualities assigned *a priori* to masculinity.[10]

Hormones generally are given names that describe the function first identified by investigators. For example, progesterone means "promoting gestation or pregnancy" in consideration of its role in stimulating the lining of the uterus prior to ovulation and maintaining the placenta during pregnancy. Despite its name, which identifies it as a female hormone, progesterone is found naturally in *men's* bodies as well as women's.[11] If the same hormone is produced naturally in bodies of both sexes, it seems a methodological error to attach gender-specific labels in this way. However, since gender oriented names have been coined by scientists, in exploring metaphorical meanings it is important to remember that so-called female (or male) hormones regularly and naturally appear in the physiology of the opposite sex. Neither sex has exclusive ownership of any hormone.[12] In the male body so-called female hormones are normal; in the female body, so-called masculine hormones are normal; and in fact, the "male" hormones or androgens are regularly changed into the "female" hormones or estrogens, and vice versa, in the normally functioning body. The designations "male" and "female," and the root meanings of their names, are thus misleading.

The hormone that stimulates sexual interest and behavior in both women and men has been named as though it were a "male" hormone—even though it occurs naturally in women and is in fact associated with peak orgasmic sensitivity in the woman's cycle.[13] An apt neutral name for this hormone would be prolibidone, "libido-promoting hormone," rather than testosterone, "hormone made in the testicle."[14] In women it is found in greatest concentrations around the time of menstruation, correlating directly with the surge of assertive sexuality that many women experience then. It also increases as a woman nears menopause, the phase of the life cycle that correlates symbolically with the yang-femininity of the Crone.

If this hormone were to be named in accordance solely with its role in *female* physiology, it might be called yangynone or YSH, "yang-femininity stimulating hormone."

In general, the naming of sex hormones by the scientific community reflects unexamined phallic-patriarchal biases natural for our culture. For example, if the so-called male hormones are named androgens, from *andro-*, "male," and *-gen,* "producing," the parallel female form should be a word combining the root for "female," *gyno,* with the same suffix: *gynogens.* Instead, the generic term for all female hormones is *estrogen,* from *estrus,* implying that the ovulatory-receptive yin phase is the exclusive norm for femininity. This is an example of the subtle ways yang-feminity is made invisible, literally anomalous in a phallic-dominant culture.

If a woman goes along with the culture's disapproval of her natural yang-femininity, the rejected gift can only be experienced as "the curse." This is not to suggest that perimenstrual or menopausal symptoms are "all in the woman's head," and that if only she had a more positive attitude such discomforts as cramps, hot flashes, and irritability would disappear. It is as much an error to imagine that menstruation and menopause should have no effect on a woman as it is to consider them pathological conditions. The ideal is not to paint the Dark Goddess white, nor to eliminate the dark New Moon in favor of a perpetually Full Moon; rather, it is to appreciate the dark phase of femininity on its own terms and to discover how these bodily experiences are metaphors not only of personal assertive femininity, but of divine attributes as well.

In the first century, the natural historian Pliny compiled a catalog of the ill effects a menstruating woman has on her surroundings. It was said her presence would turn wine sour, damage fruit on trees, tarnish mirrors, dull knives, kill hives of bees, and more. Such ideas continue in force to the present day. A hairdresser once told me that many women will not come for a perm while menstruating, explaining matter-of-factly, "It wouldn't 'take' at that time of the month." My mother remembers her grandmother scolding her for going near the young cucumber vines in the vegetable garden while menstruating, and that indeed those vines she had stepped near *were* stunted thereafter. So far as I know, no scientific study has been undertaken to determine whether verifiable effects of these sorts actually occur. Perhaps our readiness to dismiss these ideas as empty supersitition, without bothering to test them, has more to do with eagerness to dismiss yang femininity once and for all than with having outgrown the superstitious attitude of mind.

Regardless of whether or not objectively founded, these stories symbolically express important truths about the dark, yang side of femininity. They represent it as a potent force that can bring about radical transformation, usually of an "undoing" or disintegrative sort, reminiscent of the withering that accompanies the descent to the underworld in the Demeter-Persephone myth.

In the movie version of Alice Walker's novel *The Color Purple*,[15] when Celie finally decides to leave her oppressive husband she stretches forth her arm, sighting along it to fix him with intense eyes, telling him firmly that until he does right by her and her long-lost children and sister, things will go ill with him. It is a simple statement accompanying a simple gesture, but infused with such power and authority that it has the force of a curse. After Celie leaves, his life does indeed disintegrate progressively until at last he secretly helps Celie's sister and the children, now grown, to return from Africa. This secret altruism not only fulfills the terms of the curse, but has a saving effect on his character as well.

We need many more models of how the zap of yang-femininity can initiate a process of salutary disintegration. Because of strongly pejorative associations, the evil witch is an inadequate model—even though, as a number of Jungian scholars have observed, without the witch there would be no unfolding of the story at all.[16]

Both perimenstrual and menopausal women often are characterized as "witchy." It may even be that actual witch persecutions in the seventeenth century particularly targeted menstruating and menopausal women, for besides whatever overtly peculiar behaviors may have been at issue, during those times in their feminine cycle their very bodies expressed the fiery, dark, assertive nature of forbidden yang-femininity. Even the mode of executing the estimated 8 million women burned at the stake for witchcraft resonates with the fiery nature of the yang-femininity which was their fundamental crime. Jungian analyst Jean Shinoda Bolen, in a 1991 interview for *Sounds True*, points out that women carry archetypal memories of this holocaust, experienced unconsciously as generalized anxiety as menopause approaches.

Women tend to be as frightened of their own yang-femininity as little Red Ridinghood was of her Grandmother's fierce teeth. Let your imagination play with that story a bit. Imagine that it really *is* Grandmother in that bed, ferocious teeth and all. What an arresting image of the Crone that is! All these years, we've thought we were afraid of "wolves," when actually what terrorizes us most is the *rejected* Crone. If all our unclaimed yang energy gets projected on men, their exaggerated phallicism casts them either as our "saviors" (in this tale, the huntsman who rescues the helpless girl) or as dangerous "wolves."

It is time our culture retells this story. As our daughters approach menarche (the first yang-feminine outflow from the womb, figuratively portrayed by the girl's flowing red garment) our cultural values program them to focus on *yin*-feminine qualities, represented by Red Ridinghood's basket, a womb-like receptacle filled with nurturant goodies. Identifying solely with yin femininity at a time when her body is about to initiate her into yang energies insures that she must enounter her unacknowledged yang-femininity as separate from herself. In the tale this appears as the wolf she meets on the way.

Let's imagine this personification of yang-feminine energies as a *she*-wolf. Picture the daughter recognizing She-wolf as her sister; imagine them frolicking freely together. In fairy tales, animals can talk and teach humans. So picture little Red asking She-wolf to teach her all she needs to know about the yang energies soon to express through her first menstruation.

In the traditional story, alas, instead of recognizing She-wolf, little Red remains true to her culture's prescription for femininity. She continues on her way, still demurely carrying her exclusively yin-style basket of goodies. Her intention is to have milk and cookies with her sweet Granny. Instead she is heading, as are all females, for an encounter with the fierce energy of the Crone.

Played here by the Grandmother, the Crone is actually her own eventual destiny as a woman. Without the teachings of She-wolf, Red Ridinghood is ill-prepared for this rendezvous with her mature yang-oriented self. The traditional solution is for the phallic hero to come to her rescue. In the New Story, little Red, Granny, and She-wolf will learn to party together.

Menstrual and menopausal changes in the female body demonstrate the principle of radical transformation, represented in witch stories as the ability to "cast spells" changing things from one form to another. As her exertive womb expels its contents a woman experiences in her body a physical metaphor for psychological and spiritual femininity in the yang mode. Whereas the birthing womb emphasizes timely labor yielding forth new life, the bleeding womb makes known the timeliness of darkness, disintegration, and death in the transformational process.

Menstrual blood flows not as the result of either wounding or pathology, but in the natural course of events. Such bleeding is not the blood of sacrifice, where something of value is surrendered for

Figure 30

• ***Medusa and Athena*** *are aspects of the same Goddess. Both are associated with wisdom, Medusa as destroyer-Crone, Athena as eternal Maiden. (Metis is the Mother aspect.) The serpents radiating from Medusa's head and those springing from her blood represent feminine wisdom. The blood may originally have been menstrual rather than from a wound, for both Medusa's face and the eye of a menstruous woman were said to turn men to stone. Eventually patriarchal values named Athena as benevolent, Medusa as evil, and cast them as opponents. The Medusa aspect was beheaded by the solar hero Perseus, with the help of Athena, whose original feminine wisdom had by then been modified into an expression of the head of Zeus. Thereafter Athena wore the head of Medusa on her breastplate, a continuing token of their underlying identity.*

• ***The twin serpents of wisdom,*** *Life and Death, twining about the winged staff, are reminiscent of the serpent twined around the Tree of Knowledge of Good and Evil in Eden, of the serpent lifted up by Moses for the healing of the people, of the serpent crucified as an alter-image of Christ (see Figs. 24-26) and of the double helix of the DNA molecule. This sign marked ancient temples of healing (Asclepius, Hygeia, Panacea) and is today the emblem of the medical profession.*

the sake of something more valuable, or where a higher power makes demands on those subject to it. Those patterns make sense within a hierarchically ordered system. Menstruation belongs to a cyclically ordered system. This blood mystery hints at a cosmos where life and death are as intertwined as are the fibers in spun yarn or the two snakes on the Caduceus. According to ancient legend, these serpents reflect the power of female blood for both life and death. One snake is said to be poisonous, having sprung from blood flowing from the left side of slain Medusa's severed head. Its bite brings death. The other is said to have materialized of blood dripping from the right side, and its bite brings renewal of life. They intertwine as partners, not adversaries. Wisdom lies in discerning the timeliness of life or death, rather than choosing always to prolong life.

Once she atunes to it, a woman's cycle is something she can count on even when the rest of the world is unstable. The deity can be experienced as trustworthy in the same sense as the menstrual cycle. For a deity who menstruates, this blood is sacred not as an extraordinary sacrifice of life, but as a sign of participation in trustworthy cyclicity encompassing both life and death.

To gaze deeply into the Christian communion cup may bring to awareness the menstrual blood mystery. To "drink this cup," as Jesus spoke of it, was to undergo initiation into death.[17] Numerous symbolists have noticed the parallel between grail and womb, each a vessel flowing with blood of death and of new life.[18]

Blood rites have always been a powerful means of making sacred connections. To intermix token portions of blood from two people signifies the establishing of a sacred bond. To partake of (or be sprinkled with) a token portion of ritually sacrificed blood effects a bond between the person and God. To carry in one's own body the blood that flows without wounding could be a powerful experience of connection to the deity in female form.

A girl's first period, then, would be a time of profound religious ceremony celebrating the yang-femininity she shares with God. More often it is ignored, treated as a somewhat shameful secret, or at best valued as an indicator that the girl is beginning to ovulate.[19] Ovulation is highly valued by patriarchy, since it signifies receptivity to impregnation, the essence of yin-femininity. For most women, ovulation itself is silent and undetectable, although a few do experience a twinge of abdominal pain as the bursting follicle releases the egg. The most dramatic evidence of cycling is menstruation. This is why the first menstrual period may be celebrated, even though subsequent periods are characterized as a curse. The first period is taken as signaling the onset of ovulation; subsequent ones as signs of failure to conceive, failure to perfectly exemplify yin-femininity.

Pregnancy epitomizes yin-femininity: welcoming, embracing, and nurturing another even to the point of being parasitized.[20] Suckling the infant at the breast continues this nurturant mode. The gestative womb and the bounty of the breast convey an impression of the unearned, unconditional love of God—if not as God the Mother, then as God the motherly Father. The actual labor of giving birth is likely to be considered an unfortunate and dangerous interruption between the twin blessings of gestation and suckling, for the forceful expulsion of the fetus demonstrates *assertive* femininity—and who thinks of God as a pushy woman?

As menarche marks the beginning of a woman's fertile years, so cessation of menstruation, or menopause, marks their end. Medically, the term "menopause" refers explicitly to the final menstrual period, as though this mere point in time were the significant event. Most women wisely "misuse" the term to designate the years-long process of transition, which they also call "going through the Change." This lengthy transitional stage surrounding the final menstrual period technically is called the climacteric. Unfortunately, this word suggests that life after menopause can only be anticlimactic. Actually, the climacteric is more of an initiation than a finale. Women today reaching menopause around age fifty can expect to live twenty-five to forty more years—one third or more of their lives. These years, corresponding to the mythological figure of the Crone, are marked by the emergence of yang femininity physiologically, emotionally, sexually, behaviorally.

Conceptualizing menopause as a point of cessation rather than as a phase of development reflects the natural patriarchal bias against honoring the Crone. Having contracted the stage of the Crone to a single point, the scientific community then largely ignored that point as a subject of inquiry until the mid-1970s, and a comprehensive study of menopause as a natural stage of life has yet to be made. In April 1991, the National Institutes of Health announced the government's first major study of *female* health problems. This is a milestone because prior studies have used male subjects to establish generic norms, even though women's bodies differ from men's in many subtle ways. From early reports, however, it appears that the emphasis of this study will still be on pathology, illness, and causes of death, rather than on gathering data about the spectrum of healthy female functioning. Recently, a number of research projects have been undertaken to chart the non-pathology of the menopause process. First initiatives in this regard have come from the nursing profession. For example, Ann M. Voda, R.N., Ph.D., Professor of Nursing at the University of Utah, in collaboration with Phyllis Kernoff Mansfield, Ph.D., of Pensylvania State University, has developed a "Midlife Women's Health Survey" (May 1990) designed to collect data about the physical and emotional changes experienced by healthy women as menopause approaches.[21]

Without the Crone dimension neither woman nor God-Feminine is complete. The "change of life" is a universal and normal process for all women, not an aberration or disease. Yet the predominant medical attitude is that the bodily changes accompanying the perimenopausal period define a pathological condition requiring treatment as a hormone-deficiency disease. The treatment of choice is "estrogen replacement therapy," (ERT), sometimes called "hormone replacement therapy" (HRT) when a combination of estrogen and other hormones is prescribed. The goal is to artificially elevate estrogen levels to premenopausal levels, thereby preventing the bodily and behavioral changes that naturally-reduced estrogen levels would bring about.[22]

During the reproductive years estrogen rises and falls cyclically, peaking at each ovulation and lowest at the onset of each menstruation. At about age forty, hormones from the hypothalamus and pituitary begn to lose their triggering effect on the ovaries. During the ten-to-fifteen-year climacteric period, ovulation becomes occasional and estrogen levels begin to even out. These biochemical changes result in various bodily and affective patterns that are new to the woman, may be unpleasant, but are the predictable and normal accompaniments of this transition into the final third of life.

Nearly 90 percent of women experience hot flashes. Their cause is still unkown, but seems linked to a brief pulse of LH. The hot flash is a sudden perception of heat located within and/or on the body. The heat has an origin and a spread and may be accompanied by sweating and flushing of the skin.[23] Some women are awakened by night sweats, a variant of the hot flash. Most women find flashes and sweats annoying. Many are embarrassed and try to conceal the fact that they are having a flash, for to be known as "menopausal" within a culture that rejects the Crone is to invite ridicule, distaste, and put-downs. Yet, women who become comfortable with the qualities represented by the Crone, perhaps within a therapy group, sometimes even report finding hot flashes pleasurable.[24] A woman whose sense of God-Feminine is developing may spontaneously think to herself as she feels a flash starting, "The Goddess is touching me."

During the years of "the Change," many women experience unaccountable "blue" feelings, irritability, anxiety. The severity of emotional distress may be influenced by nonphysical factors as well as by hormonal variations. Some studies suggest that women who have invested themselves very intensely in mothering have the greatest difficulty adjusting when their bodies bring them to the point of initiation into the final third of life, where nonmaternal modes of fulfillment are to take precedence. Having no resource of shared knowledge and stories can leave women feeling isolated and abnormal. Anthologies such as *Women of the 14th Moon,*[25] a new genre of book containing women's own stories about menopause, can help fill this gap, as can mid-life conferences such as the one sponsored at Cabrillo College by the Santa Cruz Women's Health Center in 1991. "Celebrating Changes: Midlife, Menopause & Beyond" drew nearly 150 women, even though it was the first event of its kind in the area. There is clearly a need for such celebrative gatherings for sharing experiences and honoring this phase of life.

The face of the young Maiden represents ideal femininity; the face of the Crone is considered ugly, evil, disgusting. As lines and wrinkles inevitably appear, and perhaps moles, liver spots, warts, and facial hair as well, women may feel shame grief, anger, disgust with themselves. At the same time, new resources of yang energy are becoming available. Anthropologist Margaret Mead is reported to have said that the greatest creative force in the world is a zesty menopausal woman. If environmental circumstances or the woman's own habitual attitudes block the flowing forth of this zestful creativity, the thwarted potential goes sour within. The consequences may range from irritability to mental breakdown.

A serious physical difficulty for some postmenopausal women is progressive depletion of calcium from bone tissue. The origins of this problem, called osteoporosis, are laid down many years before menopause by a diet deficient in calcium. Lower concentrations of estrogen after menopause accelerate loss of calcium, resulting in bones that are porous and brittle. Compression fractures of cervical vertebrae are common as the bones become unable to support erect posture, resulting in the "dowager's hump." A woman may gradually lose several inches of height, her body literally charicaturing the diminutive, "spineless," fragile image of ideal femininity she has accepted as her role.

Prevention begins with adequate intake of dietary calcium while the woman is still in her twenties and supplemental calcium tablets during later years. Some loss of bone calcium is an inevitable part of aging for both men and women, but lower estrogen levels at the menopausal transition seem to exaggerate the process for some women.

Estrogen is manufactured in fat cells throughout the body, as well as in the ovaries.[26] After menopause, when the ovaries no longer produce periodic surges of estrogen, this hormone stabilizes at a decreased level. With decreased estrogen the lining of the uterus no longer proliferates and the tissues lining the vagina undergo changes as well. The vaginal walls become less robust, secretions from glandular tissue decrease. Some women find intercourse uncomfortable without use of a lubricant. Cocoa butter, unsaturated oils, and *non-estrogen* creams and jellies are effective remedies.[27] Because at this time libido is becoming centered in the clitoris rather than the vagina, expressions of sexuality other than intercourse may spontaneously take precedence even when vaginal discomfort has been alleviated.

As the clitoral (yang) style of sexuality takes precedence over the vaginal (yin) mode, the woman may experience a parallel shift in other areas of her life. She may find herself generally less nurturant and more assertive in both her relationships with others and her style of creativity. Ideally, she discovers how to be a pushy woman in the positive sense as she grows into the Crone dimension of her feminine identity.

While a case could be made for considering certain aspects of menopause a deficiency disease, some statements in the medical literature reveal that an underlying bias against the full spectrum of femininity also motivates such a view. Menopause is said to bring about a "deterioration of feminine attributes"[28] and menopausal women have been described as "castrates," "sexless," and without value or purpose once past the childbearing years.[29]

A full-page 1990 ad for physicians by CIBA pharmaceutical company reads, MENOPAUSE MYTH NO. 1: "NO MAN IN HIS RIGHT MIND WOULD BE INTERESTED IN A MENOPAUSAL WOMAN." While control of osteoporosis *could* be a motive for prescribing the advertised product, this ad mentions only the unattractiveness of estrogen-poor women. CIBA's solution: the estrogen patch for continuous, longterm replacement therapy. Never mind that the appended prescribing information for physicians warns that in three independent studies "estrogens have been reported to increase the risk of endometrial carcinoma [*uterine cancer*]", and that longterm continuous use "may increase the frequency of carcinomas of the breast, cervix, vagina, and liver" as well. These risks are presumably deemed worth taking in view of the alternative, namely, that postmenopausal women typically develop characterisics that are considered unattractive and "masculine"— coarser hair on the face, slightly deeper voice, assertiveness.[30]

Women as a class typically mature into these qualities. How absurd it is to consider such *universally female* features as "masculinization." It would make as much sense to characterize males as prematurely resembling old women. To define either one in terms of the other does justice to neither.

Estrogen replacement therapy is promoted as a way of "staying feminine forever." Many physicians would routinely begin every woman on E/HRT at the first sign of the Change. During a routine check-up around my fiftieth birthday, without first inquiring whether I was having any menopause-related "symptoms," my physician recommended, "You're at the age now where we like to begin Estrogen therapy." From interviews with other women, I find this is a common experience, and seldom are the serious side-effects mentioned. Such casual prescribing is all the more disturbing, according to Voda,[31] since E/HRT *affects the genes of the cells*. From the start, that fact should have been reason enough for great caution, even before serious side effects had actually been noted.

Taking supplemental estrogen, whether orally, via vaginal creams and suppositories, or through a dermal patch like the one in the advertisement, maintains the appearance of continued fertile femininity, but does nothing to extend actual fertility. Ovulation ceases at the time specified genetically, regardless. E/HRT postpones but does not eliminate such objectionable effects as hot flashes and growth of facial hair. As soon as E/HRT is discontinued the woman begins a period of adjustment characterized by all the features typical of menopause at its natural time. Therefore, proponents of E/HRT recommend that women continue estrogen treatment for the rest of their lives. Aside from philosophical objections to such systematic elimination of the Crone, long-term E/HRT is of questionable value because it poses such serious physical dangers. The risks have long been known. Following private research reported as early as 1975, the Federal Drug Administration issued a warning in 1977 that E/HRT increases the risk of uterine cancer, and the National Institute of Health independently reached the same conclusion in 1979.[32] One theory is that post-menopausal use of estrogen stimulates uterine cells that have been preprogrammed genetically to shut down, and that these cells turn malignant under continued stimulation. The very treatment intended to hold at bay the Death Crone instead opens wide the door for her in a different guise.

In the United States, 35 million women—one third of the female population—are now post-menopausal. A larger portion of the population than ever before in history now are Crones. This shift is due to repeated increases in average life span.[33] While in ancient times few women lived much beyond menopause at age fifty, now the average life expectancy is some twenty-five years longer. Thus most women can expect to experience "being the Crone" physically and emotionally—with concomitant opportunity to explore and integrate the spiritual meanings of that aspect of God-Feminine. As Crones abound more and more, the *spiritual values* of yang-femininity may gradually become commonplace as well.

Tribal cultures traditionally have recognized their few post-menopausal members as wise women, holy women, healers. In this regard, these so-called "primitive" peoples model for us an attitude alternative to our culture's denigration of "old ladies."

There may also be a connection between the phenomenon of hot flashes and the heat-like experiences associated with the process of spiritual transformation called in Eastern philosophy *kundalini*. Ancient yogic records[34] teach that significant spiritual transformations typically are accompanied by sensations of intense heat moving through the body. In Eastern spirituality, numerous practices have been defined for the purpose of stimulating and controlling the movement of "vital energy"(*prana*). As a practitioner of Kripalu Yoga, I learned the rudiments of such breathing patterns (*pranyama*) and body postures (*asana*) shortly before I began having menopausal hot flashes. I have noticed that some of these practices produce "on-demand" *pranic* rushes that are astonishingly similar to the spontaneous hot flashes of menopause: experiences of sudden heat, beginning at a point, and expanding or running through the body, sometimes with breath-taking speed.

The mind-body connection now being documented through scientific medical experiments, as well as anecdotal accounts, focuses on how mental attitudes and thoughts can bring about physical ill health or healing. Both ancient writings and modern *kundalini* research[35] suggest that radical spiritual transformation may permanently alter the physiology of the body. Moreover, yogic practices imply that modifying physiology (through *pranayama* and *asana*) can induce spiritual change. Given this foundation, it is not such a leap to imagine that the physiological changes of menopause might go hand-in-glove with major spiritual effects. Those "symptoms" we tend to dispose of with pejorative and pathological labels are strikingly similar to prized signs of increasing spiritual maturity!

All this supports a new view of menopausal experiences. Women reaching this stage of life may be feeling the effects of a *transformational clock*, built into the human organism. It might be that the symptoms we so dread and dislike are actually signs of an incipient spiritual breakthrough, affecting not only each woman individually but, with so many women now involved, collectively pushing the entire species toward its next evolutionary step.

The Monroe Institute in Faber, Virginia, is world-renowned for its research into the nature of human consciousness. During lab sessions, subjects are linked via electrodes to a 24-channel high-resolution topographic brain-mapping computer system.[36] Technicians were surprised to find that when a subject reports having a menopausal hot flash, skin temperature remains steady. However, concomitant with the flash, monitors note a rapid, complete reversal of the body's electrical polarity. The sensation of heat is evidently due not to changes in physical temperature, but to shifts in the electrical field surrounding and permeating the body.[37] This tallies with women's descriptions of the speed with which flashes sometimes proceed. Gross temperature changes or the purely physical dispersal of a hormone surge through the body are both slower processes. To picture the relative speeds of the three modes imagine first a venetian blind with slats that are blue on one side, red on the other. Simply changing the angle of the slats (their "polarity") instanteneously reverses the color. A gross temperature change would be akin to changing the color by adding paint. And the dispersal of hormone surges through the body would be analogous to unrolling an alternative window shade. Only the polarity shift affects the entire system instantaneously.

Research at The Monroe Institute has shown that when such a reversal of polarity is purposefully induced (through the use of precise audio signals) the subject typically reports psychic-spiritual experiences, such as visions, profound insights, and altered states of consciousness. Whether occuring naturally (menopause), or induced in the lab (using patented audio signals), or self-induced by the yogi (through *pranayama, asana,* etc.) the subjective experience of heat may be a *bio-psycho-spiritual event.*

Such phenomena have been most thoroughly observed and studied within Eastern philosophical and religious systems, where the transformative principle is called *kundalini.*[38] The symbolic imagery associated with *kundalini* fits strikingly with motifs of yang-feminine spirituality. *Kundalini* is envisioned both as Goddess and as snake. She is pictured (and experienced) as a sleeping serpent, coiled three and a half times around herself, at the very base of the spine. In that condition, she provides the foundational energy of life and form, infusing our every ordinary movement and thought. Either spontaneously or as a result of stimulating spiritual practices (i.e. *pranayama, asana, shaktipat,* etc.) She may awaken. This corresponds to the spiritual awakening of the person, initiating a period of growth and change. Upon awakening, *kundalini* (also known as the Goddess Shakti) uncoils herself and begins to move upward through a subtle energy channel approximately parallel to the spinal cord. In this mode, She epitomizes the yang nature of God-Feminine: exertive, fiery, transformational. The movement of energy through this channel may produce sensations of heat, tingling, pressure. Enroute upward, this energy may encounter obstructions in the channel causing physical, mental, or emotional distress. Ancient writings warn that awakening *kundalini* through forceful practice can be dangerous. Modern studies show that mental-emotional conditions (mis)diagnosed as schizophrenia or other mental illness may result from a poorly integrated kundalini process[39] Even in an ideal scenario, the spiritual seeker must expect to undergo "death of the ego" enroute to the hoped-for outcome.

Kundalini/Shakti is experienced as both Goddess and Serpent.

Once the obstructions are cleared—"burned away"—*kundalini/* Shakti proceeds upward toward rendezvous with her counterpart, pictured as God-masculine (Shiva), who waits at the uppermost limit of the energy channel, at a location corresponding to the pituitary gland. There, the two energy modes, or poles, ultimately unite. This is pictured as a sexual embrace, bringing bliss, super-human psychic abilities, and permanently modified physiology.[40]

While it may not be valid to impose this Eastern symbology in total on the menopausal configuration, there are sufficient points of similarity to support the intuitive impression that menopause may be spiritual transformation in disguise: experiences of heat moving through the body; risk of mental illness; the imagery of spiritual energy as serpent bringing both wholeness/bliss and disruption/disintegration.

Menopause is an invitation to confront disintegration and death while there is still time to live. It is a true initiation, a doorway through death to a new phase of life. Fear of natural menopause, fear of the Crone, translates into dread of death. Through bodily experiences of yang-femininity, in both menstruation and menopause, women (and men who relate sensitively to them) have opportunities to encounter the dark death side of the Divine.

Chapter Ten

Gift of the Thirteenth God-Mother

The number thirteen has long been associated with dark, mysterious forces, with evil, chaos, destruction, and death. Like the Dark Goddess, unlucky thirteen was held sacred in ancient times but came to be viewed with distrust and fear in the Patriarchal Age. In Goddess symology, thirteen is the number of completeness and transformation. There are thirteen new moons in the year; thirteen is the symbolic age of initiation into womanhood (menarche); and, traditionally, thirteen sanctified women meeting together constituted a holy covenant group, or coven. In Judaeo-Christian and patriarchal symology, however the number of completeness is twelve: the twelve tribes of Israel; the twelve disciples of Jesus; twelve jurors in a court of law; twelve hours on the clock face; twelve months in the solar calendar. The loss of the thirteenth corresponds to the banishment of Lilith, the demonization of Demeter Ploutos as Pluto-Devil, the repression of the yang-feminine qualities represented by the exertive womb, the naming of menstruation as curse, the rejection of the dark moon and the old Crone.

The interplay of twelve and thirteen as divine numbers is evident at the Last Supper of Jesus. The thirteen gathered at table were twelve plus one. They can be thought of as twelve disciples plus Jesus, who was set apart on the one hand as divine, and on the other as "despised and rejected," soon to be killed; or as twelve good men plus Judas, the traitorous son of the evil one. Either way, its association with numinous power, evil, and death sets the thirteenth apart from the in-group of twelve. After the departure of both Jesus and Judas, the remaining eleven quickly chose a replacement to bring their number to the magical twelve again (Acts 1:21-26). Our task today is to restore the missing thirteenth. This requires a radical change in collective attitudes toward death.

In a familiar fairy tale,[1] the patriarchal ruler of the kingdom had only twelve golden plates, and so did not invite the thirteenth fairy God-Mother to the party celebrating his daughter's birth. This powerful and holy God-Mother came regardless, bringing a gift that was experienced as a curse, eventually resulting in the entire kingdom falling into a deep sleep on the princess' thirteenth (many versions say fifteenth) birthday. Thus, when the daughter reached the age for initiation into adult womanhood, instead of awakening to mature awareness of her feminine identity as the image of the triune Goddess, she entered a state of suspended animation, remaining a child-woman.

Fairy tales are products of the collective psyche. No single mind produces them; they emerge within a community or culture and grow into inevitable forms that satisfyingly reflect some part of the story of the evolution of the species' psyche. This natural congruence is the secret of the fascination they perennially hold for us. Many tales tell of the phallic hero who slays dragons and performs great feats: that is, the story of the effortful separation of the human ego from its original matrix. The story of the thirteenth fairy God-Mother alludes in the same sort of way to humankind's as yet unrealized potential for developing collective values harmonious with the exertive-womb metaphor and identifies our fear of death as the main obstacle.

Death was the gift offered by the thirteenth God-Mother. The others blessed the princess with all the traditional attributes of the ideal Maiden: beauty, modesty, sweetness of nature, and so on. The thirteenth promised that at the time of menarche the princess would cut her finger on a spindle and die.

Although a spindle normally tapers to a point no sharper than a knitting needle, not sharp enough to pose a physical hazard, it represents the point at which the thread of life is to be either spun out or cut off. In many stories the triune Goddess appears as spinner of fate.[2] Death comes when, as Crone, she cuts the thread.

In some commentaries on this tale, it seems that the spindle is confused with the distaff, a staff upon which *unspun* fibers are wrapped and held ready for spinning.[3] This error probably reflects our cultural bias toward seeing femininity always as yin. The stationary distaff giving forth the material for spinning is suggestive of nurturant yin qualities. The energetic activity of the spindle, actively transforming one substance into another, correlates with the yang side of femininity and is in fact the essence of the gift. What the thirteenth God-Mother offers is yang-femininity, as symbolized in the spindle, transformational turning point between life and death. The God-Mother's intended gift to humankind was not simply death, but death as part of the deathing, birthing, transforming power of assertive femininity, as known through the womb metaphor. In the tale this promised death was to coincide with the age of menarche, the first flow of menstrual blood marking the turning point from childhood to maidenhood. At a strictly animal-biological level, such changes occur without psychic trauma, indeed without conscious awareness at all, purely as phenomena of the world of nature. With human consciousness comes a capacity for awareness of the spiritual cognates of this natural process. It is just such an awakening to the symbolic meaning of the womb that bleeds (in distinction from the womb that contains), which the thirteenth fairy God-Mother offered the princess, and which humankind has yet to fully develop.

Although the God-Mother's gift is not simply death, but the entire repertoire of human behavior and experience modeled by the exertive womb, to receive it requires welcoming death as part of the package. In accordance with phallic values, which define death as the ultimate enemy to be defeated, the human response typically is aversion and avoidance, whether it be of death as the end of physical life, or death as the destroyer of old patterns of living. And so the King found a way of turning this threatening gift aside. When the spindle of fate drew blood from the Maiden's hand at the turning point of her birthday, instead of dying (i.e., transforming, growing up, appropriating the spiritual energy signified by the bleeding/birthing womb), she and the entire kingdom fell into a deep sleep, lasting an eon. The bursting forth of new psychological and cultural developments, perhaps even a new sort of consciousness patterned after the exertive womb, was deferred. Human consciousness remained in the model of participation mystique, embedded in the yin-nurturant womb of "mother nature," represented in the tale by a ring of heavy, vegetative growth that sprang up to enclose the kingdom.

The patriarchal solution for the freeing of humankind from this matrix has been the development of masculine phallic consciousness, carried by the Prince, who successfully penetrates the vegetative barrier of briars surrounding the sleeping kingdom. His kiss awakening the sleeping Princess, and with her the entire kingdom, represents the wonderful and timely emergence of the objectifying ego in the evolution of human consciousness. The Maiden awakened not to a new sort of feminine consciousness, as prefigured and proposed by the thirteenth God-Mother, but to her role as carrier of the yin dimension within a new world determined by yang-masculine advances in consciousness. Not until the fulfillment and passing of the Patriarchal Age will the eventual acceptance of the

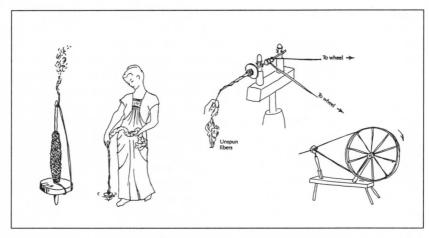

Figure 31 - From left: "'What sort of thing is that, twirling round so merrily?' said the girl, and took the spindle and wanted to spin too." As this quote from the tale shows, the old woman in "Sleeping Beauty" was using a simple drop spindle rather than a spinning wheel. A drop spindle is a tapered rod attached to a flywheel, which is spun 'round and 'round to twist loose wool, cotton, or flax fibers around themselves, forming yarn. The resultant yarn is wound on the base of the spindle as it is produced. The fluffy, unspun fibers are fed out through the spinner's fingertips just fast enough to be twisted firmly together by the rotation of the spindle.

The drop spindle is twirled and let drop toward the floor as it pulls the fibers out and twists them into yarn. It looks much like a spinning top. When the new yarn reaches such length that the spindle dances on the floor the spinner retrieves the spindle and winds the yarn upon its shaft, securing it around a notch; then twirls the spindle again to begin twisting the next span of fibers.

A spinning wheel orients the spindle horizontally and attaches the fly-wheel via a belt to a large drive wheel. When the large wheel is turned, either by hand or treadle, the belt drives the spindle around at high speed, to twist the yarn in the same manner as a drop spindle.

thirteenth fairy God-Mother's gift result in the emergence of a yang-*feminine* mode of consciousness and spirituality, and an accompanying cultural style.

The objective, egoic mode of consciousness brings forth benefits and problems to humankind, as outlined in previous chapters. Its hallmark is the separating of subject and object, and thence the fostering of a sense of self as separate from nature, distinct from all others, separated from Deity. In the process of human spiritual evolution, to separate from the participational matrix (represented by the yin-womb of the ancient Great Mother) the emerging ego had to slay the many dragons that would have swallowed it back into the gestating womb. This was a truly heroic species accomplishment, repeated again by each individual who achieves egoic consciousness today. The consolidated ego correctly guards against the regressive pull of the yin-womb of unconscious Nature, because to fall back into that mode would be to lose egoic consciousness, to die as a self-conscious subject. However, in bracing against the regressive pull of the matrix out of which it has arisen, phallic (egoic) consciousness takes a stance that defends also against the transforming power of the Divine Womb. All forms of death equally are feared and rejected by egoic consciousness. The insight that death is a divine force remains alien to Western consciousness.

"What a shame," we murmur when we hear that someone has died. Literally, death often seems an almost shameful secret, as carefully closeted and disguised as were sexual impulses during the Victorian era. The lifeless body is immediately covered to hide it from view and quickly removed to a funeral home where preservative is pumped into its tissues to counteract the withering, disintegrative process. Heavy cosmetics are applied to simulate the bloom of youth. At the cemetery the bare earth around the grave, reminder of Demeter's isolation and the Crone's withering touch, is concealed beneath a carpet of artificial grass.

At the same time, death holds a paradoxical fascination for us. The thrill of a carnival ride is that it flirts with destruction. Movies and television shows featuring violence and death are popular. The death-defying feats of an aerial acrobat, a free-fall parachutist, or a professional stuntman spellbind us. We are avidly attentive to detailed news specials about natural disasters, plane crashes, terrorist acts, and other events entailing sudden death. We are drawn to death in spite of ourselves.

This mixture of abhorrence and fascination is indicative of a problematic relationship between egoic values and the larger perspective of the Divine, whether conceived as God, Goddess, or transcendent Self. Mystics of all the great religions have recognized that the so-called death wish is at root the yearning to transcend the limits of the separate-self sense characteristic of egoic consciousness.[4] Both individually and as a species the human pattern of development is one of progressive differentiation from the original Matrix or Source, accompanied by a yearning for reunion with the divine Ground of Being. Separation from our Source is at once the great accomplishment and the sin of humankind. As accomplishment, separation of the individual self marks a crucial stage in human development, though not its end point. As sin, separation from the Ground of Being requires healing through atonement or "at-one-ment." Either way, the separated state of egoic consciousness bears within itself the urge to transcend its own limits—thus to "die" as a separate self. At the same time, it resists and abhors the possibility of losing its hard-won identity. The separated self faces three possibilities for resolving this dilemma: by repressing, by regressing, or by transcending.

Most often the death urge is denied and repressed as we identify exclusively with the egoic task of defining who we are in distinction from all we are not. Any revision of our carefully developed sense of identity is experienced by the ego as loss or death. Major changes in our self-sense are typically painful, often having the character of crisis. The old identity dies and a new perspective emerges. When we deny the urge toward transformative death it can only manifest covertly through unconscious projection. Then instead of accepting our own necessary transformation, we channel that death-urge energy toward others, releasing it into efforts to make the world conform to our solidified vision of how things should be, resorting if necessary to aggressive behavior, murder, or war to coerce conformity.

As the time drew near for my older child to leave home, she and I became entangled in such efforts. We found fault with each other, hurt each other, angered each other. The abundance of destructive energy unleashed between us was the deflected and repressed death urge, whose purpose was to transform our relationship. Accustomed to experiencing myself in the Demeter Ploutos mode as motherly provider and care giver, I was unable to shift into a wholesome acceptance of the *mourning half* of Demeter's example. To send my daughter into the next stage of her life with my blessing required that I willingly engage in the pain and grief of losing both my daughter and my established and valuable mothering identity.

The situation called for honest weeping in the face of loss and death. I repressed that grief and instead mounted an angry offensive against my daughter, disapproving of her because she refused to conform to my expectations and demands. She and I both became witchlike reflectors of the Dark Goddess, destroying by force and unconsciously what we could not relinquish willingly. The tears that her witchlike nastiness finally provoked in me were in lieu of the tears I legitimately should have shed had I been able to accept directly the Demeter task of giving her my blessing and honestly mourning the passing of a way of life. Had I entered with some awareness into this real-life Demeter-Persephone drama, I would have experienced simultaneously Demeter's willing tears and Persephone's calling toward death, destruction, and transformation.

I was unable to accept gracefully the gift of death and transformation that the thirteenth God-Mother was offering. Willingly or not, I did undergo the death of transformation. It has been more than ten years since my daughter left home. My old connection with my daughter has passed away and we now enjoy a satisfying relationship as two adults who, most of the time, savor knowing each other. Having truly given my blessing now to her departure does not relieve me of the sorrow of missing her daughterly presence again and again. On the contrary, it guarantees that I will never grow immune to mourning her absence each time my arms remember the feel of her infant body cradled against me; each time memory recalls some past moment of perfect mother-daughter togetherness; each time she "comes home" for a visit and leaves again. Such tears are legitimate expressions of the eternal Demeter presence within life, and only if I can willingly shed them can I continue to give my blessing both to my daughter's continuing maturation and to my own continuing transformation. I am perpetually tempted to repress this ongoing process of death-in-the-service-of-transformation. In other words, I am tempted to deny the value of womb power with its timely push toward death.

An alternative response of egoic consciousness to the death urge is to regress to a predifferentiated mode. The ego recants what it has accomplished and loses its identity and sense of separate self. A psychosis entails just such a disintegration of the ego. The vernacular term "nervous breakdown" accurately describes the process. Although it can in some instances lead to a breakthrough, in its initial stages a nervous breakdown is a regressive and disintegrative expression of the urge to transform old ego definitions through at-one-ment with the perspective of the larger Self. Often suicidal wishes, thoughts, plans, and actions are a concretizing of an unconscious death urge, which secretly yearns toward at-one-ment at any cost.

Because of the appeal of experiences of at-one-ment, mind-altering drugs that blur the boundaries of the self-sense are attractive. If the ego is well developed, strong, and resilient, such drugs can be an aid to authentic spiritual growth through transcendence of the ego state. The problem is that more often the ego regresses and simply merges into the mists of pre-egoic potentiality.

Such regressive merger with the matrix negates rather than transcends egoic consciousness. It entails breakdown rather than breakthrough, deformation rather than transformation. What is needed is for the former limits and boundaries of the individual self to be *transcended*, not voided. This cannot be accomplished by ego alone. It requires a divine push—the push of the divine yang womb, of the fairy (literally, "fate-dealing") God-Mother, of the death Crone who destroys in the service of new life. Left to itself, the ego would entrench itself more and more firmly in its definitions of itself and its world. The divine death force undermines the ego enough to allow a transcending of its otherwise tightly drawn limits. Mind-altering drugs used sacramentally and ritually within a religious framework can enhance the devotee's relationship to the transformative Divine One, even though the same substances may endanger the ego when taken casually.

Imagine yourself standing on a beach near the waterline. You gaze out over the ocean, delighting in the ever-changing colors and textures of its sun-lit surface. The wet sand is so solid and firm beneath you that your feet leave only the faintest of imprints when you take a step forward to stand just within reach of the leading edge of the waves. Imagine doing that now. As each wave curls around your ankles and then rushes away again, notice that it sucks the sand out from under your feet, unsettling you. You are forced to take a new stance, again and again. This is something like the relationship between the ego and the larger, divine perspective that both attracts and undermines. Whatever "stand" the ego takes it struggles to maintain, while the death urge nibbles at undermining it. The power of death is our ever-present companion, perpetually undermining the ego—sometimes sufficiently to allow a true transcending of its limits. Whenever that happens we are in the presence of the Divine One as slayer-birther.

In prosaic ways we have opportunities every day to recognize consciously the operation of this slaying-birthing principle in our lives. As separate body-selves we must repeatedly kill other life in order to sustain ourselves. Through metabolic processes the flesh of another (whether animal or plant life) is transformed into our own substance. The starkness of such death in the service of life is camouflaged when we either avoid eating meat or buy it precut and uniformly wrapped in plastic. We prefer not to associate the rare roast beef on our plates with the bloody death of a living, breathing animal. I propose that just such awareness could be an aid to learning to know the Deity as slayer-birther. Our need is to experience a sense of the Divine as worker of death in the service of transformation, beginning at the level of biological growth, and then psychologically and spiritually as well.

In naming the death side of the universe *Goddess*, we affirm it as an ontological and transpersonal reality. Our own dying, and death itself, are to be seen in light of what the new moon and the birthing womb reveal about this transpersonal process: death does not come through either fault or default, but as an active principle of transformation.

Like birth, death is an active, yang-feminine initiation into a new condition. This same pattern is found in the functioning of the female chromosome pair, where both the chromosome that continues to function and the chromosome that turns itself off *actively contribute* to the correct functioning of the female organism. Whether at the level of chromosomes, or of physical sustenance, or psychological development, or spiritual values, *death is one-half of the function of the feminine-divine energy.*

If instead of valuing the two halves equally, we choose against death, siding with unchanging "life," we reject the yang-birthing womb. If the feminine-yang energy is refused, masculine-yang energy must try to take its place. This exaggeration of the phallic role results in an experience of death as a coercive and intrusive power. Death as intrinsic process with its own timing (that is, as a function of the exertive womb) is replaced by death understood as the result of untimely aggressive encroachment by disease or injury (expressive of the invasive exaggerated phallus). Thus Persephone's timely mission to the realm of death in the more ancient myth is replaced in the phallicized version by externally imposed abduction and rape. The mocking and crucifixion of Jesus Christ likewise have the intrusive quality of rape. Within a firmly patriarchal system, death can be experienced in no other way, because awareness of the yang-womb has been repressed.

In the patriarchal world view, all that assertive womb power represents is mistrusted, the physical birthing function no less than physical death. Significantly, the birthing labor of the womb has been construed as a dangerous, even pathological process. Intervention by the medical profession is deemed necessary to protect mother, baby, and society from the direct expression of exertive womb power.[5] In an uncanny parallel to the fairy tale, the birthing woman is literally "put to sleep" by the anaesthesiologist. The current grass-roots movement toward natural childbirth, midwifery, home births, and nonmedical birthing rooms may be a sign of our readiness, collectively, to begin valuing the assertive feminine qualities symbolized by the birth-pushing womb.

Continued mistrust and even horror of everything the exertive, out-pushing womb stands for may be one of the underlying reasons for the extremely strong feelings of those who passionately abhor abortion. In the process of aborting, the womb's exertive function is displayed in isolation from the (patriarchally more acceptable) yin-nurturing-breast phase, which follows quickly upon the birth of a full-term baby. In abortion, the *yang* symbolism of the womb stands alone. Through patriarchally conditioned eyes, its labor, like the work of the Dark Goddess, is perceived as evil, death dealing, and utterly destructive. That there could be meaning and value to death, including the death of abortion, is a possibility alien to patriarchal values.

Yet the leading edge of human spiritual development may lie precisely in the freedom sometimes to *choose* physical death, rather than automatically striving to preserve biological life; in other words, to love and respect the Crone as much as the Maiden or the bountiful Mother. The prototypical "pro-life" orientation is that of egoic consciousness defending its own identity against the death urge, resisting the regressive pull toward submergence in the divine matrix. At the same time, however, the death urge also nudges egoic consciousness to *transcend* its self-defined limits. To be "pro-choice" in this most fundamental sense, then, is to align with the tendency toward self-transcendence.

So at base the pro-life versus pro-choice opposition is between self-preservation and self-transcendence. The pro-life position makes an across-the-board assumption that in all circumstances the continuance of biological life is the highest value. The pro-choice position forces a consideration of context, leading to contextually appropriate decision and action—as is characteristic of the exertive womb—and in the process may catalyze the transcending of former limits of self-identity and ethical awareness. The woman or man who struggles contextually with whether or not to abort a particular fetus, or whether or not to undergo experimental chemotherapy for advanced cancer, or whether or not to authorize life-prolonging technology for an aged parent, is pushed to grow in consciousness and ethical maturity.

The emergence of pro-choice as an attitude counter to an exclusively pro-life position signals a shift toward yang-feminine values as the Patriarchal Age begins to wane. While the specific context is abortion legislation, the issues are broader. The passionate rebuttal by pro-lifers, even to the point of violence against abortion clinics, demonstrates the continuing rejection of yang-womb values, across the board, by many.

This is a conflict between value systems resting on differing patterns deep in the collective psyche, one founded upon the phallic metaphor, the other upon the exertive-womb metaphor. In the final decade of the century, the two perspectives vie for eminence politically. Legislation by individual states challenge the Supreme Court's 1973 prochoice Roe vs. Wade decision, thus requiring repeated re-examination of the basic issue. In the spring of 1992, more than 500,000 pro-choice marchers converged on Washington, D.C., in the largest demonstration in the capital's history. At stake is whether or not the gift of the thirteenth God-Mother can at last be received, not only by this or that individual, but as a new stage in the ongoing development of the species' psyche.

A pro-choice attitude goes hand in hand with greater willingness to have optional dealings with death, including spending time studying it as a phenomenon. Kubler-Ross' examination of death and dying and Moody's study of near-death experiences surprised everyone by becoming best-sellers in the seventies. The success of such books intimates that a collective shift toward exertive-womb values is already under way.

The pro-life/pro-choice dichotomy applies not only to attitudes about abortion, but to every situation in which death is an issue. In the face of aging or illness, the traditional medical ethic has been pro-life. Heroic efforts are routinely ordered to preserve biological life as long as possible. During the last few decades a strong pro-choice movement has emerged, affirming the right of the individual to *choose to die* without submitting to extreme efforts to prolong biological survival. Many states now recognize as binding on family and physicians "living wills," such as the one found in Appendix B. These are legal documents stating the person's choices regarding medical treatment in various circumstances.

Even in cases where the patient is unable to make his or her own choice, the premise that heroic medical efforts should always be undertaken to maintain life as a matter of course no longer prevails universally. Consider, for example, the "Baby Jane Doe" case of 1984-85. The courts upheld the right of parents and physicians to decide together to forego surgical intervention to repair her severe spina bifida, disclaiming the right of governmental agencies to require that all available technology be applied to preserve the child's life. And in 1986, the American Medical Association's Council on Ethical and Judicial Affairs decided that it is ethical for doctors to discontinue all life support for patients who are in irreversible comas, even if death is not imminent. The list of treatments that may be withheld includes not only elaborate technologies and medications, but even ordinary nutrients and fluids given intravenously.

All such choices involve mere withholding of treatment, never active assistance to end a life. In 1993, ballot initiatives in both California and Washington state proposed legalizing physician-assisted suicide for the terminally ill, as long as the patient provided a signed and legally witnessed directive. At least one medical doctor, Jack Kevorkian, believes individuals suffering severely from chronic but not terminal illnesses should have the right to choose to end their own suffering. Kevorkian invented the so-called suicide-machine, intended to permit a person in such circumstances the dignity of choosing a quick, comfortable death. After a series of grievously suffering women used his death technology, Kevorkian was indicted on murder charges in 1992. The amount of attention to this case, and the fact that a member of the medical profession is siding with the "left-hand" serpent on the medical caduceus (*recall Fig. 30*) is indicative of the degree to which traditional attitudes about death are being re-examined.

Not many physicians would go as far as Kevorkian, but many these days are willing to consider redefining the doctor's identity to include roles other than aggressive efforts aimed at curing. The international hospice movement, which draws together physicians, nurses, mental health workers, clergy, and others to create terminal care teams, shifts health-care emphasis from preserving life to supporting the patient and her or his family once efforts to cure the illness have been discontinued. To engage the hospice support team is tantamount to choosing the work *with* the dying process, rather than against it. The hospice approach holds forth the possibility of actively choosing death, not as a defeatist, regressive merger with the matrix, but with dignity in keeping with the timely rhythm moving the dying person toward transformation through death.

Chapter Eleven

Delivered by the Crone

The tale of the thirteenth fairy God-Mother, usually titled "Sleeping Beauty," makes an entertaining and satisfying Disney movie. It appealingly portrays the emergence of phallic consciousness and patriarchal culture, and their saving effect for humankind as a whole. A great many movies, stories, and fairy tales share with this one the plot of the young woman awaiting rescue by the hero. For the human race as a whole, such a rescue has, in principle at least, taken place. With the turning of the past Age, the penetration of phallic-style consciousness has freed the soul from its former immersion in the containing matrix, represented by such plights as falling unnaturally asleep, being threatened by a monster, or held fast by a captor. Both the heroic ego and the languishing soul have awakened to a cosmos no longer contained within the mythical Mother, but created afresh by patriarchy's great gift of objective consciousness. This awakening is often portrayed as a heroic battle against the forces of evil, the reward of success usually represented by the life and love of a beautiful young woman. This story line, retold in such varied guises as *Star Wars, King Kong,* and the adventures of Agent 007, James Bond, will continue to fascinate and satisfy so long as individual men and women find reflected in it the continuing story of their own soul's progressive awakening to phallic spirituality.

The damsel in distress shows the predicament of humankind prior to the triumph of the phallic principle, when to be human was still to be a Daughter of the Mother. Her distress arises when the evolution of the human spirit needs a shift in central metaphor from matrical to patriarchal. Then the Mother is no longer experienced as benevolent containment, but as captor; no longer as all-inclusive matrix, but as the Evil Other against which the Good Father can be contrasted, and over whom to triumph. The hero of this story is always a man,[1] representative of the new humankind of the Patriarchal Age, bringing to cultural and spiritual expression patterns prefigured in the Y chromosome and the phallus. The damsel, once rescued, takes her place as the phallic

161

hero's mate in the new kingdom of patriarchy, complementing his assertive yang-masculinity with her quietive yin nature, being the subordinate "other" in contrast to whom he knows himself.

The opening moments of the 1986 hit movie *Aliens*[2] show a scene familiar to us from such tales as "Sleeping Beauty," "Snow White," and "The Glass Coffin."[3] A beautiful woman lies sweetly sleeping in a glass-encased bed. Are we about to witness her rescue by the hero? Using laserlike beams of light, three workmen from a "deep salvage team" (i.e., savers or saviors) cut an opening in the spaceship within which the casket rests. They enter, look upon the woman, then scan the glass with some instrument. One announces, "Looks like she's alive. Well, there goes our salvage operation." From that moment, instead of a variation on the old story, a new kind of story unfolds, with a new kind of hero(ine) who is both assertive (yang) and feminine. Her name is Ripley, bringing to mind both the astonishment of Ripley's "Believe It or Not!" and the long sleep and waking of Rip van Winkle. Ripley has been in a state of "hypersleep," floating in deep space for fifty-seven years. Thus she is actually an eighty- to ninety-year-old Crone, even though her appearance, like Persephone's, is that of a young woman. Also like Persephone, she leaves the beloved, familiar world to journey to an alien place on behalf of the dead or doomed.

As with a fairy tale, this story is engaging and satisfying just as it is. As we watch the movie, we are simply entertained, without need for understanding why. Yet, as with fairy tales and myths, "we interpret for the same reason as that for which such stories are told: because it has a vivifying effect on us and gives a satisfactory reaction."[4] In short, it is fun. And there is the possibility that the initial impact of the movie will, through this process, become understood in terms that help us savor its meanings for a long time to come—and perhaps even play our own parts better in "The Story" as told in our actual lives. For all the stories we tell ourselves about the nature of God and life and the world are variations of a single story, the story of humankind making real its identity in the image of God. We ourselves are the players—within whatever version of the story catches our most profound attention. Fairy tales, movies, religious mysteries that move us do so because they are variations of our own version of the Story. From this perspective it makes no difference whether the author-director intended this movie to mean what I experience it to mean. Both the uninterpreted movie and my analysis of it are valuable insofar as each casts its particular light on the mystery of our evolving human identity in the image of the Divine One. I believe this movie has captivated a huge audience because it hints at the next chapter in humankind's collective story. It tells symbolically of the process through which qualities long personified as ugly old Crone or evil Witch can be reclaimed as positive forces in human nature, culture, and spiritual life. Taken together, the fairy tale "Sleeping Beauty" and this movie indicate the evolution of the species' psyche from matrical culture through patriarchal and toward the promise of a new Age centered on an archetypal pattern that is simultaneously yang and feminine.

Ripley, a spaceship flight officer, entered hypersleep for the return journey to earth as the sole survivor after an alien life form had killed her entire crew in an earlier adventure. The action begins when she reluctantly agrees to return to the same planet where, twenty years before (while she slept and drifted in space), a new colony of humans was established to exploit its natural resources on behalf of a commercial corporation. When earth loses contact with that colony it is feared the same aliens may have attacked it. The plan is to dispatch a contingent of tough combat marines, with Ripley going along as adviser. With their great shooters, tough talk, and macho stances, the marines are the epitome of patriarchal phallic masculinity. The number sent is of course twelve, the magic number representing patriarchal values. Who is the symbolic thirteenth, left out of patriarchy and needed to bring human identity around to cultural and spiritual incarnation of the feminine yang principle? This function is shared by three characters, all of whom are outcasts from patriarchy in one way or another.

First, Ripley, who departs from the patriarchal story and creates a new heroine in the postpatriarchal plot that develops. Second, little Newt, the only survivor from the families sent to colonize the planet, who has been living in isolation from human contact and at first flees both the marines and Ripley. Finally, the Alien herself, nightmare personification of gestative femininity gone to extremes. Patriarchy has glorified the sentimentalized ideal of gestative femininity and at the same time has required the subordination of the feminine gender for many centuries. The Alien represents the dangerous backlash of this long-repressed human potential, against which phallic measures of even the most extreme sort are no longer effective. She destroys all the marines except Hicks, who is transformed by his relationship to the new hero*ine* and thus lives to enter the postpatriarchal era. This new heroine deals effectively with the Alien not through phallic firepower, but by pushing mightily from the womb. She represents the newly possible human, whose central determining archetype will be the exertive, transforming womb rather than the triumphant phallus.

Early in the mission Ripley characterizes herself as a fifth wheel and asks the marine sergeant, "Is there anything I can do?" He responds, "I don't know, is there anything you can do?" He is impressed when she then demonstrates her skill operating a "loader," a massive steel exoskeleton activated by her physical movements within it. The answer to "Is there anything you can do?" is in effect "Yes, I can supply initiating energy that pushes from within, like the womb giving birth, and can move mountains." This is in contrast to the female marines, who function out of assertive *masculine* energy. One is a pilot, another takes the point position whenever her squad moves in to explore an area. Both are good at what they do; both have departed from the stereotype of the subordinate woman by becoming very good in a man's world, but without transforming the system in which heroism is always masculine in quality. A male marine puts his finger on their predicament when he teasingly asks one of them, "Hey, Vasquez. You ever been mistaken for a man?" Her reply, "No. Have you?" targets the reciprocal predicament for men within patriarchal culture: the fear that any orientation but a clearly phallic one will be construed as effeminate and inferior.

When they land on the alien world, they find the colony seemingly deserted. Soon they discover a little girl who has survived by hiding in a ventilation tunnel. She reports that her entire family, in fact all the families in the colony, have been killed by the Alien. Ripley's relationship to the child shows that she comfortably expresses the nurturant side of femininity, neither rejecting it nor succumbing to exaggerated or sentimentalized expression of it. This style of no-nonsense tenderness was first demonstrated in Ripley's relationship to her cat. Early in the movie she was shown affectionately cuddling and stroking her cat as she reflected aloud upon her dread decision to return to the alien planet, concluding with, "As for you, you little shithead, you're staying here." She relates to the child with similar unsentimental warmth. Ripley holds and rocks the terrified little girl after cornering her in her lair in the ventilation shaft. At various times, she washes the child's face, gives her hot cocoa, tucks her into bed, promises to take care of her, all without becoming "nothing but" a nurturer. She is motherly and nurturant while maintaining her primary orientation within the plot as a strongly yang woman. It is her nurturant love for the little girl that ultimately motivates her assertive confrontation with the Alien, symbol of gestative-nurturant maternalism carried to extremes.

The little girl is Rebecca Jordan, affectionately known as Newt. Her formal name hints at origins in Old Testament patriarchy. There, Rebecca was wife of the great patriarch Isaac, chosen for him because she so abundantly exemplified nurturant femininity, spon-

taneously volunteering to fetch water not only for Isaac's anony-
mous emissary but also for all his camels (Gen. 24:1-53). The Jordan
is the river the Israelites crossed to enter the promised land, there
to establish the patriarchal religion of the Lord, supplanting the
indigenous worship of the Mother-Goddess. As "Newt" Jordan, she
indicates that humankind has reached a new crossing, at the brink
of a new promised land. Her nickname shows that she augurs the
transformation of humankind into the postpatriarchal Age. A newt
is a kind of salamander.[5] Since antiquity, a rich mythology has been
woven about the salamander.[6] It is said to frolic unharmed within
the flames (*Fig. 32*) and sometimes represents the alchemical fire
itself, or the mercurial spirit of transformation. In scientific classi-
fication, salamanders belong to the order Mutabilis, meaning
changeable or mutable. According to alchemical lore, to have a
vision of a salamander within the coals of a fire is a sign of major
transformation or metamorphosis within the psyche or soul. Newt's
presence in the story is such a sign, presaging transformation of the
species' psyche from phallic to exertive-womb allegiance. The salamander is symbolic cognate of both dragon and serpent.

The snake devouring its own tail, the sea monster swallowing Jonah,
and the serpent in the Garden of Eden mark the matrical origins of this
evolving symbol. Other symbolic cognates are Melusina, the water
nymph who is half woman, half snake; and Lilith, a beautiful woman
whose body below the navel consists of dancing flames. When Ripley
saves Newt from the Alien she is delivering womankind from its old
identity, accomplishing the return of exiled Lilith, and launching the
ancient serpent-salamander on its next turn of the spiral.

The nature of the Alien is revealed in bits and pieces and fleeting
glimpses in the movie. That we never do see her clearly and up close
is true to life, for she represents what members of good standing in
the patriarch's kingdom fear *unconsciously*, subliminally. The effects
of this creature upon her human victims dramatizes what is hurtful
about the place assigned to femininity within patriarchy. Like patriarchy's ideal woman, the adult female Alien is abundantly receptive and
gestative. As the Alien shows, when these valued qualities are carried to
extremes, yin-femininity becomes monstrous.

The Alien unendingly produces eggs and sticky hyper-receptive
webs. She turns her human victims into involuntary replicas of her
completely yin style of functioning. Humans caught within her
exclusively gestative orb are turned into passive gestation chambers
for incubating her young. They never actively give birth, for to be
infected with the Alien's yin-femininity is to function as a solely

Figure 32 - Left: An adult red newt.   Right: Fire salamander emblem on the chimney piece in the Guard Room of Henri III, Chateau de Blois, France.

gestative, never exertive, womb. The incubated larva eventually hatches by exploding open its passive host's (hostess') chest wall, with no exertive birthing labor on the carrier's part.

Although yang elements do contribute to the creature's life cycle, these functions are depicted as more phallic than birthing-transformative in nature, and are not discharged by the great egg-laying female. She does not herself implant her young in human hosts. She simply lays her ripened eggs one after another in pods, and creates a hyper-receptive environment for passively snaring human victims. The egg pods later split open to release larval creatures. These are the ones who actively implant embryos within human hosts for the next stage of development. While older development stages also are actively aggressive against the marines, the Alien herself continues quietly laying eggs in her lair.

To experience horror at the specter of humans made involuntarily receptive, to recognize the evil of a creature that forcibly impregnates by overpowering its host (hostess), helps the viewer know from the gut what is harmful about the patriarchal superior-subordinate, yang-over-yin pattern, which is the essence of the system that defines half its members as subordinate and identifies their very nature as unremittingly receptive. Therefore this is a salutary horror, making evident the need for the system to change, for the Age to turn.

The initial reaction within the plot is an attempt to overpower the Alien with phallus-like shooters. Ultimately, this cannot work because it further perpetuates the phallic-dominance style that has created this monster in the first place. What is needed is for someone to bring the long-exiled yang-femininity into the picture. This is what Ripley finally succeeds in doing.

First, she learns from Hicks, the one marine who survives, how to use the entire arsenal of phallic weaponry: guns, blasters, flamethrowers, grenade launchers. She will use these effectively but without the sort of relish displayed by the marines. She is not that sort of hero even when shooting that sort of weapon. When Hicks would omit the most potent weapons, intimating that they would be too much for her to handle, Ripley insists that he teach it all to her. "You started this—show me everything. I can handle myself." In other words, she must thoroughly assimilate phallic values and patriarchal human identity, as instigated by men on behalf of humankind, before she can pass on toward a human identity oriented to the exertive womb. Like Vasquez and the other female marines, Ripley is a woman who is no longer determined by patriarchal definitions of femininity. She, too, functions as well as any man in a man's world. Unlike the female marines, however, her underlying motive for fighting the Alien is her maternal love for Newt, who has been captured by the Alien and is in danger of being irrevocably taken over by a yin-only style of femininity. This, of course, is the plight of all womankind within a patriarchal context.

When Ripley assimilates phallic power without eschewing her yin femininity she begins to have an effect. Although this combination is not sufficient to neutralize the Alien, it does dislodge her from her lair. The front half of this huge creature disconnects from the egg-laying end in order to pursue Ripley and Newt. The Alien is thus moved out of the passively snaring mode toward a more active style. The transformation has begun.

After Ripley has exhausted all her phallic weapons, the Alien still threatens to overwhelm Newt. "Get away from her, you bitch!" Ripley screams as she dons the steel exoskeleton of the same "loader" she had operated in response to the sergeant's taunt, "Is there anything you can do?" From within it, she supplies assertive feminine initiative. When she moves her arm or her leg, the electronically powered exoskeleton moves with it. This is a visual portrayal of the moment-by-moment, dynamic connection between context and movement that characterizes yang-femininity. Ripley and the Alien engage in "hand to hand" combat, yang-femininity at odds with yin-femininity. Unlike the prototypical phallic battle between opposites, where one must triumph over the other, this is a confrontation between two aspects of the feminine principle. If Ripley succeeds, it will be not because yang has triumphed over yin, but because yang-femininity has pushed the old ways toward new expressions, transforming the cultural context within which both yang and yin express themselves. It is a battle to the death—the death both of the Alien creature and of the alien status of yang-femininity within patriarchy. This death relates to the gift of the thirteenth God-Mother and is part of a birth process. As slayer, Ripley is also birth maker.

The final battle is staged within an orbiting space station. Struggling mightily, Ripley and the Alien tumble into an exit shaft. Ripley disentangles herself from the exoskeleton, wedged now in the shaft. She pushes the controls that open the chute. A powerful current sweeps through the canal, thrusting everything outward. This denouement is actually a monumental birth scene, the exit shaft a birth canal, the slaying of the Alien simultaneously a birthing. We witness the exertive, out-thrusting power of yang-femininity laboring to deliver forth the new Age. The Alien, representing the back side of patriarchal values, clings tenaciously, refusing to participate in the deathing-birthing drama. She knows only yin-feminine ways. In this final struggle between the two females we see dramatized the clinging, snarling, hyper-yin energy of the Alien pitted against the assertive feminine force that brings to birth and ejects. This push-toward-birth has been the real alien of the patriarchal story, now at last to become available as a basis for human culture.

Ripley's role as bringer of yang-femininity into a formerly all-yin context is prefigured earlier in the movie when she rescues Newt from internment in the slimy, gummy webs at Sublevel Three, deep within the chambers of the Alien's lair. As she peels the sticky bands away to free Newt, this scene superficially resembles the rescue of the damsel in distress by the phallic hero. However, when female sets free female the superior-subordinate dichotomy is not activated, there are no romantic undertones based on the attraction of opposites, and the maiden does not become the rescuer's reward. Rescuer, rescued, and captor alike are female. The interplay of opposites as the force that makes the world go round is replaced by a different archetype.

Romantic love, based on polarization of male and female as opposites reconnecting through the tension of mutual projections between lovers, is notably absent from this movie. In the postpatriarchal story line, union of male and female is no longer the prime metaphor for spiritual fulfillment and wholeness. Such questions as "Will they fall in love? Will he win her heart and her hand? Will all separations be overcome by the triumph of true love so that they live happily every after?" are simply irrelevant because a different archetypal pattern energizes the plot. By way of contrast, consider how the relationship between Ripley and Hicks differs from that between Princess Leia and Han Solo in the *Star Wars* saga.

Living "happily ever after" is code language for finding your identity in the image of God. In the patriarchal pattern, the "sacred marriage" or "royal *coniunctio*" represents the fulfillment of humankind's yearning for reunion between correctly differentiated opposites, be they male and female, or heaven and earth. The postpatriarchal adventure takes for granted the differentiation of opposites and beckons the soul to follow the next turn of the spiral: toward becoming the heroine who as slayer-birther realigns the feminine trinity around the Crone as image of the Divine for both women and men in the Age to come. Just as both men and women have had to be the "hero" of the patriarchal version of the Story in order to assimilate in their own lives the cultural and spiritual expression of the pattern prefigured in the Y chromosome and phallus, so a person of either sex must become the "heroine" in the new version of the Story, in order personally to assimilate the cultural and spiritual expression of the pattern prefigured in the $X^M X^P$ chromosomes and the birth-pushing womb.

The male characters in *Aliens* show various sorts of adjustment to the challenges presented by the shifting alignment. Of all the marines, probably Hudson has the most phallic persona. In one scene he fires away at wave after wave of the Alien's offspring, shouting wildly, "Come on, you motherfuckers! Here, you want some too? Fuck you! Fuck you!" Whenever the deteriorating situation requires other sorts of response, however, he reacts to the possibility of defeat by whining petulantly. "That's great, just fuckin' great. Now what the fuck are we supposed to do? ...We're in some pretty shit now, man. That's it, game over man. Game over. What we gonna do now, huh? What are we gonna do? ...Count me out." In terms of the four body metaphors, such testiness is the negative expression of his poorly integrated testicular side.

Ripley firmly tells him, "Why don't you just start dealing with it, Hudson, because we need you." Then she outlines a specific task for him. Given a concrete objective to aim for, he is able to shift once again into his better-developed phallic mode, focusing on the goal she has identified for him. Because Hudson functions adequately only within a patriarchally shaped framework, he does not survive the transition to a new alignment.

Hudson and the other marines who fail to make the crossing are portrayed as heroic, albeit in an outmoded style. The sinister expression of patriarchal values is portrayed by Carter Burke, the "company man." The guiding objective and stabilizing goal for his phallicism is "the bottom line." His company is in the business of exploiting the natural resources of various planets. Burke carries that exploitive ethic to extremes of expression. He purposefully turns loose two larval creatures in the med-lab where Ripley and Newt are bunked. His plan is for them to be impregnated so that he can smuggle "valuable samples" of these creatures past customs, within the bodies of the two females. He plans to sell the hatchlings to the company's biological weapons research department. He is not deterred by the fact that Ripley and Newt would be horribly killed when the gestated larvae eventually explode their bodies open.

None other than Burke himself was responsible for sending dozens of families of unsuspecting colonists to the planet in the first place, neglecting to warn them of possible danger from the Alien. When confronted by Ripley, he justifies this act by explaining that interjecting security considerations would have gotten in the way of efficient pursuit of the company's objective. Furiously angry, like the princess who finally threw the frog against the wall with all her might, Ripley grabs him by the front of his shirt, slams him against the wall, and tells him that when they get back she's going to see to it that "they nail you to the wall" for the deaths of all those colonists. Burke does not survive to return to earth, however. After several additional villainous acts he comes face to face with the monster that his perverted devotion to phallic values has helped generate and is presumably carried away to be cocooned and impregnated.

One of the quaternity who does survive to depart for earth at tale's end is Bishop, an android, or "artificial person," pegged from the beginning as a likely traitor, but faithful to the end and perhaps symbolic of the role of testicular masculinity for the new humanity. The fact that he is not fully human corresponds to the likelihood that the testicular traits he represents are still another eon away from becoming the basis of human culture and the essence of the divine image through whom humanity knows its own identity. That Ripley's opinion of him changes from suspicion to distaste to respect and admiration by the end of the picture, and that she gathers up his dismembered pieces for the return trip to earth, suggest an enhanced importance for testicular masculinity in the Age of the Transformative Womb.

In the final battle-birth scene, Bishop has been literally torn in two by the Alien. His upper torso continues to function. When Ripley opens the loading hatch, the great expulsive force thus set in motion would sweep everything down that cosmic birth canal. Everything does need to undergo this deathing-birthing. However, if all the players were swept away along with the Alien, it would signify that humankind had lost continuity with its history and its heritage. As Newt is propelled toward the exit shaft, Bishop reaches out and grabs her, holding her securely in place. Thus Bishop, the faithful, steady, testicular masculine provides the continuing point of connection so that rebirth need not be at the expense of continuity.

The character who demonstrates the correct and graceful realignment of a male from phallic to exertive-womb values is Corporal Hicks. At the outset Hicks is as straightforwardly phallic as the rest of the marines. There is one clue early on that he is to participate in a special way in the awakening catalyzed by Ripley. During the rough transit by space shuttle from the carrier to the planet's surface, while everyone else is gritting their teeth against the violent vibration, Hicks falls asleep! As they touch down, the drill sergeant barks, "Somebody wake up Hicks." The real awakening is to a new cosmos centered upon a new central archetype. Because Hicks is able to sustain the necessary transformation, he survives the cataclysmic events on the alien planet and is one of the four—two males, two females—who make the return trip to earth.

When both commissioned officer and drill sergeant are lost during the initial engagement with the Alien, Hicks and Ripley immediately collaborate to carry forth the mission, with no need of formal consultation to establish a chain of command. The relationship that develops between them is marked by spontaneity, sincerity, mutual respect, and admiration. There are no romantic undercurrents between them. No charged pauses as their hands touch, or their eyes suddenly lock; no smoldering looks or suggestive remarks; no sprightly animosity veiling secret attraction. No hints that "when this is all over" they will get married and thus live happily ever after. Such subplots would be legitimate and entertaining in an adventure story in the patriarchal model, where man and woman represent the ultimate pair of opposites. Ripley and Hicks relate less as "opposites," more as coequal partners, like the two centers of an ellipse.

When just the two of them are alone for a quiet moment, Hicks gives Ripley the electronic locater bracelet he has himself been wearing, so that if she is captured he will be able to find her—not to rescue her, for once enshrouded in the yin-feminine cocoon and involuntarily nurturing an alien larva in her own body she will be beyond such help. The only rescue he could then provide would be to kill her—a yang-feminine action typical of the Death Crone—which he promises to do. As Hicks buckles the bracelet on her arm he says, "This doesn't mean we're engaged or anything." When Ripley nods as if to say "I know," we sense they are being direct and honest, not coy and flirtatious.

Little Newt, about eight years old, is too young for romantic relationships with men to be an issue. What is noteworthy is that with all those males around, she relates to none of them as "father." The Father figure, so important symbolically in the Age of the Patriarch, plays no part here. Neither does a traditional Mother figure. Although Newt relates warmly to Ripley, only once—in the supercharged moments just after the ejection of the Alien—does she call Ripley "Mommy."

At no time in the movie is any reference made to a male consort of the Alien. We learn a lot about both the successive larval stages and the egg-laying adult, but nothing about a mate for her. If he exists at all, perhaps she is so hyper-receptive that he is simply absorbed into her after mating. Or perhaps she harks back to the Great Mother of the prepatriarchal matrix, when the deity in whose image humankind found identity was exclusively female, and there were neither sons nor lovers in the pantheon.

What's most terrible about the Alien and her brood is that they *don't* kill you. Both birth and death are transformative acts of yang-femininity; pure yin-femininity can bring about neither. The contextual value of death, and our species' readiness to reclaim the lost gift of the thirteenth God-Mother, are expressed in Ripley's observation after Newt is taken: "They don't kill you—she's alive. She's alive!" That statement expresses horror rather than hope because Newt seems beyond even the rescue of timely death. This is just the sort of predicament modern life-prolonging technologies sometimes bring about, by artificially maintaining the semblance of life even when it has become a horror for all concerned.

One central motif of this story is the value of sometimes choosing death. As the situation deteriorates, Ripley and Hicks make a death pact. Each will kill the other if snared by the Alien. To do so is to choose the way of yang-femininity as antidote for the Alien's excessive yin-femininity. After valiantly fending off a pursuing larval monster using all available phallic fire power, Vasquez and another marine finally huddle within a tunnel, suggestive of a birth canal, together clutching an activated grenade. As the creature is upon them, together they release the detonator and all three dissolve in flame. Only the mythical salamander could possibly emerge from such a fire, or from the final nuclear conflagration that eventually vaporizes the planet. Again and again through the film, the screen is filled with images of the Alien or her offspring immersed in fire. The subliminal message of the salamander is there amidst the destruction: transformation is at hand!

Part of the legend of the salamander is that it is a fatally dangerous animal. Although it has neither fangs nor stinger, when molested it does secrete a poisonous milky fluid from pores just behind the eyes. This venom does no harm to humans unless rubbed into the eyes or an open cut, or taken into the mouth. Even then it is unpleasant rather than fatal. Nevertheless, popular lore says that death inevitably follows from a salamander's bite.[7] In some newts a potent nerve poison similar to that of the puffer fish is found in the skin, muscles, and blood. This causes a burning sensation and produces paralysis by blocking neural impulses. A secret identity between the Alien and Newt is intimated by the fact that each resembles the deadly mythical salamander in some way. Like salamanders and newts, the Alien's body fluids are a concentrated acid that burns whatever it touches. This is also reminiscent of the deadly blood from the left vein of the Medusa (*see Fig. 30*). Part of the significance of Newt's unusual name is that she is the promise of new life *within the context of the exertive womb*, which brings *death* and transformation as surely and correctly as it brings birth.

So Ripley, Newt, and the Alien might be thought of as a new version of the ancient triple Goddess, to be oriented henceforth in reference to the yang-feminine Crone rather than the Mother. Despite her young appearance, like Persephone, Ripley is the Crone, a true slayer-birther. Newt is the Daughter, the novice, the new convert, full of promise for New Age humankind.[8] The Alien is the Mother, temporarily deformed because unnaturally disconnected from the slayer-birther mode of the trinity. As with the Demeter-Kore-Persephone trio, the three are really one and cannot function wholesomely in isolation from one another. This is why the fight to the death between Ripley and the Alien is not a vanquishment of one by the other, but a reconnection between yin and yang modes of femininity, having saving and transforming effects for all three and for humankind.

Like "Sleeping Beauty," this is a story about sleeping and awakening. Ripley has slept within the glass coffin on board ship nearly six decades. Early in the film, after the salvage team finds her, she is hospitalized and has terrible nightmares about the larval aliens and the death of her crew. Again and again she awakens in her hospital bed drenched in sweat, panting in fear. The voice of the night nurse asks through the monitor, "Want something to help you sleep?" Ripley replies, "No, I've slept enough." Exactly so. It is time for the yang-feminine potential of humankind to awaken from its long, long dormancy.

Later, in the besieged colony, Newt is afraid to go to sleep because she will dream of the Alien. Ripley affirms that it is right to fear the Alien. She passes on to Newt the tracer bracelet and promises to watch over her on the monitor. Significantly, their quarters are in the medical wing of the deserted colony complex, so once again the issue of sleeping-waking is linked to healing. When Ripley returns a few hours later, she finds Newt asleep under the bed. She joins her there, and from that low vantage point notices the scurrying movement of one of the larval aliens in time to avert the fatal impregnation that has been planned by Burke. Many close calls later, as the great Alien egg-layer closes in on them, Newt clings to Ripley, wrapping her arms and legs tightly around her. As the creature approaches, Ripley presses Newt's head to her breast, saying, "Close your eyes, baby." This dramatizes that if the Alien wins, feminine-yang potential must again go unconscious, eclipsed by monstrously exaggerated gestative femininity.

After deliverance has finally been accomplished and both Hicks and Bishop have been installed in their glass-covered berths, Ripley helps Newt into one of the ship's glass coffins to enter hypersleep for the journey home. Newt asks, "Can I dream?" Ripley smiles. "Yes, honey. I think we both can."

The final frames of the film recapitulate the opening scene. We see a closeup of the two of them sleeping sweetly. The difference is that now we know they are not "sleeping beauties" awaiting rescue by a phallic male hero. They are themselves the new culture heroes, prefiguring the emergence of cultural patterns, personal values, and a style of consciousness metaphorically like the assertive, trans-forming womb. Humankind has yet to awaken to that cosmos, but the early signs of its coming are even now emerging all about us.

Chapter Twelve

Developing Devotion to God-Feminine

God-Feminine. God-Masculine. Two expressions of one divinity, masculine and feminine each giving a distinctive cast to the divine mystery in the same manner that alternate lighting on a single stage set can produce startlingly different effects even though the elements so illuminated remain the same. The lighting shifts and we see a different drama, a different cosmos, a different face of God.

On the one hand, this movement in the species' psyche from an order based on the phallic metaphor toward one based on the exertive-womb metaphor is taking place with or without the individual's awareness and assent. As was the shift out of the Matrical into the Patriarchal Age, it is a collective and cosmic transformation, rather than a matter of individual volition. In the language of fairytales, it is a gift from the transpersonal God-Mother rather than the result of personal wisdom. In the language of the Old Testament, once again God does a new thing for God's own sake (Ezek.36:22-23). All the same, in such a period of collective transformation it lies with each individual to align the personal life either with or against the rhythm of the time. Nowhere is this individual responsibility more significant than for developing both personal and liturgical celebrations of life that resonate with God-Feminine as well as with the phallic Lord God—while recognizing that these are complementary facets of the Divine Mystery who actually lies beyond all gender distinctions.

To make progress in encountering and experiencing the yang-feminine dimension of Deity entails cultivating nontraditional devotional practices not readily undertaken within the patriarchally toned confines of church or synagogue. The examples here are offered to stimulate the reader's own liturgical creativity. These are some of the ways I have personally found helpful, in the company of other women and men intent on knowing God-Feminine.

Of course women's bodily womb rhythms give clues to what we may expect to encounter when we depart from established religious forms to seek experiences of God-Feminine: both life and death; both boundless grace and salutary undoing; both absolute acceptance and timely demand for new birth; periodicity; momentary unexpectedness with a larger cyclic order. Simply paying attention to female body experience is an excellent means of becoming experientially attuned to the ways of God-Feminine.

As the moon correlates well with women's cyclicity, so it also provides a tangible means for connecting with the feminine dimension of the Deity. When the waxing, full, waning, and new quarterpoints of the moon are plotted on a longitudinally arranged calendar, the moon dates seem to spiral or twine serpentlike through the year (*see page 178*). Tracing the moon's phases weekly can enhance awareness of the eternal feminine Wisdom-Serpent.[1] To meditate or worship on nights marking the moon's quarterpoints is an effective way of seeking communion with God-Feminine. The moon itself is not the object of worship. It helps orient us toward the invisible God, who in some ways resembles the moon. Each phase of the moon brings to attention a different aspect of God-Feminine.

Unlike weekly worship in church or synagogue, these moon dates do not fall on the same day each week. If a person makes a commitment to observing moon points as worship occasions, it quickly becomes apparent that the practice does not fit neatly into the secular calendar. It is not simply a matter of setting aside time regularly on Mondays or Thursdays or Sundays. Because moon quarters continually shift to fall throughout the week, attentiveness to moon rhythm means a different schedule each week. This in itself models the quality of momentary spontaneity within a larger orderliness, so characteristic of the way in which God-Feminine is experienced.

The idea is to take time to sit quietly, either alone or with friends who also seek to know God-Feminine, on the nights of each quarter moon. Allow the core of yourself to focus on the moon as she is that night. If the sky is clear, gaze at the moon itself; or use a Moon Bowl (described below) as focal point. Allow your thoughts to circle around that moon image. Censor nothing. Allow a rich web of associations to shape itself around the moon in that phase. Whom does she reveal? Which aspect(s) of the ancient triple Goddess come to mind? Does this phase "feel" more yin or more yang to you? In what ways are you created in this image?

Bring the moon into the room symbolically by creating a Moon Bowl (*see box, page 197*). To use the bowl within worship as a focal point representing the Full Moon, place a low, fat white candle in the

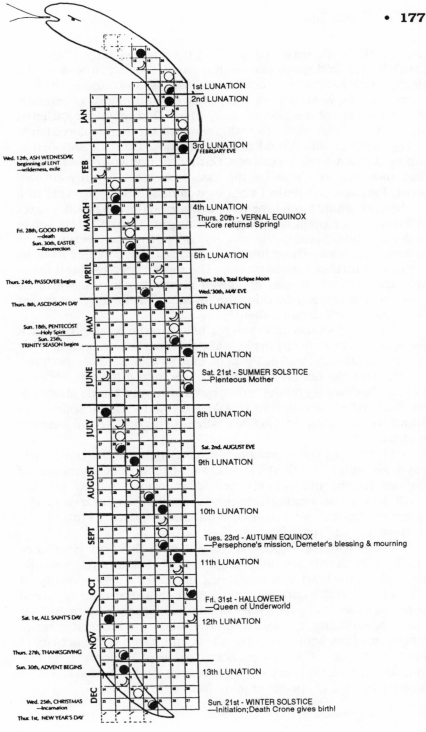

center of the bowl. In a darkened room, the bowl perfectly reflects the candle's light and glows like the full moon. The brightness from a single candle set low in the bowl is astonishing, and suggestive of the connection between perfect receptivity and abundant generosity. Other symbols of the bountiful, motherly God might be gathered around the bowl to make a worship centerpiece: richly colored fruits or vegetables, a small bowl or goblet of milk. Don't be satisfied to simply duplicate my experience. Gather around your bowl tokens that make concretely visible the associations arising in your own heart. Perhaps one perfect egg...or a photograph or drawing of a mother...or what? Each time you meditate on the full moon, expect different associations, meanings, and insights. Trust God Herself to evolve within you exactly the imagery needed to know Her nurturing nature. And honor those images by giving them concrete form as objects for further contemplation. The more concretely and faithfully these inner images are given substance in the world as symbols, the more truly does the invisible, ineffable, unmanifest Deity show Itself through them.

When the moon is dark, you might swath the bowl with a black silk scarf and use a deep purple, midnight blue, or black candle. Play with the shadow, as well as the light, cast by the candle. Experience the positive presence of shadows as the center of attention. Perhaps make a shadow play on the ceiling by moving your hands above the candle. Maybe look over your shoulder at your own great shadow on the wall behind you and imagine it is She, giving birth to you this very moment.

To represent the waxing moon, you might fill the bowl partway with water and float blossoms on the surface, symbolic of virginal femininity. What other ideas occur to you as you meditate on the waxing crescent moon? What images of the Virgin or Maiden come to you? What bodily postures might you assume, to "be" Her?

For the waning moon, experiment with different heights of candles and choose one tall enough to brightly illuminate only the upper rim of the bowl, leaving the rest shadowed. Or for an unusual effect place a votive candle within a partially submerged spherical glass "fishbowl," to light up the water from beneath. You might float tokens of "undoing" one by one on the water, producing a gradual darkening of the light that is not a loss, but a sign of the activity of She Who Brings to Completion. Some tokens of "undoing" might be an autumn leaf, an apple core, an orange rind, a traffic ticket, a tampon, the ace of spades or joker from a deck of cards.

Do not be too cerebral about planning your tokens and centerpiece design. Trust the uncanny wisdom of the Feminine Snake. Be willing to experiment. Remember that the Feminine Spirit loves spontaneity and transformation. Dare to do a new thing when the moment moves toward birthing.

Before attempting any sort of worship or meditation that falls outside of the containment of the traditional rites of your own religious heritage, it is of utmost importance to establish an alternative transpersonal container to protect yourself from possible ill effects. Acknowledge that you lack sufficient personal wisdom to discern what is salutary, what is harmful to you in the spiritual realm. Realize that the true and eternal Deity poses as much danger to the unprotected ego as does a demonic power. This truth is expressed in the scriptural warnings, "It is a fearful thing to fall into the hands of the living God" (Heb.10: 31) and "No one can see God and live" (Exod.33:20). Only God can protect you from God. And that protection is not automatic. This is why Jesus taught his followers to pray to the Father that God would not lead them into temptation and the clutches of the evil one (Matt.6:13). And indeed, it was God-the-Holy-Spirit who drove Jesus into the wilderness at the start of his ministry, requiring him to resolve the tempting illusion that the limited power of the human ego is capable of negotiating directly with the Holy One. One great value of the established rites of traditional religions is that they are tried-and-true vessels to contain spiritual power that might otherwise overwhelm and destroy the naked ego of a lone worshiper. Those who would commune with God-Feminine have no choice but to move outside the traditional patriarchal forms. When we do so, we must find ways to seek "God's protection from God."

One way is to invoke the protective presence of the least masculine representative of holiness in your faith tradition. Historically, the Holy Spirit and Shekina sometimes have been described as feminine by Christian and Jewish faithful.

State clearly to yourself and to God your intention of relinquishing trust in ego-wisdom and of placing complete trust in the Divine Spirit to mediate to you only that which is for your ultimate good. It is important to visualize entrusting yourself to that greater Divine Wisdom in some concrete way. Those who have been taught meditative practices may already be used to imagining a white Light surrounding them, which they can trust to protect them from all dark, evil influences. This is the right idea, but that particular imagery is problematic if we wish to remain open to the positive dark dimension of God-Feminine. To clothe ourselves in Light is to screen out not only evil, but also yang-femininity. A number of people have shared with me alternative imagery they have personally developed and used:

•Picture a semipermeable transparent birth caul, completely enclosing you and letting in whatever is good for you, keeping out whatever would harm you; and at the end of your meditation, delivering you "newly born" into your everyday life.

•Imagine a clear, flexible balloon or bubble filled with wonderfully fresh air that serves to collect and hold near you whatever spiritual influences are for your good, and deflects whatever would do you harm. It changes shape to follow the moving of your body and can be "worn" as you go about daily life as well as while meditating.

•Picture a head-to-toe veil of finest silk, woven exactly to complement your body and soul at this moment, perfectly designed to screen out whatever would harm you at this time and allow to pass through whatever is good for you. Perhaps it has changing colors or textures corresponding to your aura.

•Visualize Christ pouring holy water over you so that it flows over your entire body like a protective garment.

•Imagine a spring of water arising within you at the center point and welling up to flow like a fountain out of the top of your head, bathing you from head to toe in a protective and refreshing wash.

•Imagine fragrant oil smoothed over your entire body like a second skin that allows only what is good for you to pass through.

•Picture beneficial sonic vibrations or music originating at your center point, permeating every cell of your body, permitting entry only to influences ultimately harmonious with your spiritual well-being.

•See a deep blue flame at the heart of your center place, which radiates "dark light" or "bright darkness" throughout your body.

Use whatever variation seems most authentic to you. **Take time to visualize it vividly.** Then trust God to honor your sincere intention to turn over the screening task to that Protector. Only the Deity Itself can protect you from the potentially shattering effect of devotional communion with God-Feminine. Do not omit to invoke this protection before engaging in the kinds of devotional practices described here, whether alone or in the company of others who seek to know Her.

I have noticed some common factors in my experiences in various devotional groups ranging from two to thirteen women and men.[2] The nighttime hours seem better suited than daylight. Nearly always there is a spontaneous tendency to sit on the floor rather than in chairs, in a circular configuration with a focal point at the center. God-Feminine is most often experienced as either a surroundment or a withinness, rather than a high or distant Other. Devotional energy is drawn down, in, and around—rather than upward or outward. This seems to be so not by conscious choice or design, but as a phenomenological pattern.

Even more basic than these generalizations is the tendency for God-Feminine to manifest in unrepeatable ways, no two times alike. She delights in surprise and spontaneity. Within patriarchal religion, rites and ritual, liturgies and ceremonies and sacraments, tend to take the form of rules and set sequences, whose spiritual power inheres in faithful observation of the prescribed pattern. The experience of ritual in groups orienting toward the Divine Womb rather than the Great Father is so different that perhaps a new term is needed to convey simultaneously the ideas of *sacred enactment* and *spontaneity*. An entry from my personal journal describes the phenomenon, and suggests a descriptive phrase for it:

There is no set form to follow. What we do is not prescribed by law, custom, or outer authority. Only after-the-fact can we begin to extract from the experiences common denominators, which then can be seen as "form." Thus the sense of form that we discover is descriptive, not prescriptive.

We have found that the forms these experiences take have in common the marking of the Center—often by a candle. Sometimes by a bowl filled with sand, or by the Moon Bowl; sometimes by a representation of the Goddess/Womanly One; sometimes by implication through marking the four cardinal points that generate a sense of their central vertex whether or not it is itself marked.

We ourselves enter into that structured forcefield, arranged around the Center, balanced in some way around it. Held, supported, encompassed—as in a womb?

A primary element is our trust. We trust without knowing the form, without an advance clue as to what is required of us or what is in store for us. In trust we both initiate and wait, respond and wait again. It is like a dance. Like a conversation without words between ourselves and God-Herself.

There is a playfulness. Reverence without solemnity. Silence and laughter equally appropriate. Earthy laughter sometimes. Silence that becomes comfortably pregnant, then brings forth something or other—and whatever that is, is just right! There is a simple resource-fulness in the process, which receives every Given and weaves it into the emerging fabric. We are weavers. Or at least witnesses of the Weaving. It unfolds with surprising designs. We feel awe at each, yet it is all so natural, automatic, matter-of-fact. Without plan or premeditation, the fluted candle casts a scalloped shadow on this bowl of sand, precisely filling it to the rim, dancing as if alive among the shells in the sand; like water, like a seaflower. Our four hands join the dance. Without premeditation, just following the flow of the energy around the Center, showing its shape; now they are a flower; now a womb; now moths circling the flame; the electron shell around the glowing center of the Atom-One; now plunged to earth. Without premeditation, perfectly coordinated and single and whole.

Without premeditation. This kind of meditation is not premeditated. What I am doing now in writing out these thoughts might be called postmeditation: reflecting after the fact on the event itself.

Perhaps instead of ritual we should use the phrase "sacred coming together". The two or five or thirteen of us come together; all the random "givens" come together and cohere into a meaningful Whole; and we experience the Present One being together with us. Such is the nature of God-Feminine ritual, the moment-by-moment "coming together."

In such circles it seems natural to trust contextually rooted spontaneity, appreciating the random silences and spaces, the welling up of playfulness and laughter. Since there is no premeditation, no set routine, it becomes essential to value silence and waiting as intrinsic elements in the unfolding of God-Feminine "ritual." Cues are given as we wait and watch.

Without sacrificing openness to spontaneity, there are ways we can prepare ourselves for experiencing the presence of God-Feminine. The women in one ongoing group have made themselves "Goddess Gowns" to be worn when the circle gathers. These are loose, flowing, graceful, simple. They permit ease of movement and are comfortable for sitting on the floor. Unlike usual religious vestments, they are not for the purpose of signifying authority or distinguishing clergy from laity. Every woman who chooses to, wears one. Wearing them marks the time as sacred. To put on the Goddess Gown is to enact readiness to know Her and to affirm ourselves in Her image. The same group collectively owns several liturgical stoles decorated with patterns representing various aspects of God-Feminine as they have been experienced within that Circle. These may be used in dance enactments, as part of a worship centerpiece, or worn for an evening

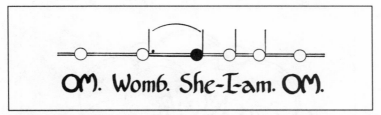

OM. Womb. She-I-am. OM.

Figure 33 - If chanting alone, choose the lowest note comfortable for your voice. For group chants, various harmonic tones may be chosen by individuals. Speak the entire line slowly on one exhalation, all on one tone. Inhale evenly. Repeat line again. Notice vibrations your voice makes in various parts of your body—chest, back, abdomen, feet, head. OM represents the original creative word encompassing in itself all potential. The Divine Womb first gestates every potentiality, then brings each to birth at its right time. "She I Am" affirms the mystery that each woman, each person, bears the image of God-Feminine in her being; moreover, it affirms that the OM has brought forth in actuality the person who is chanting now.

by a woman who either feels a special connection with the aspect of the Goddess represented on a particular stole, or feels a special need of Her presence in that guise. In other words, as beautifully crafted as these stoles are, functionally they are but *raw materials* available to be used sometimes one way, sometimes another, sometimes not at all, depending on the needs of the moment, rather than formal vestments with prescribed uses and meanings.

Chanting is a mode of worship included in the practice of virtually every religion. Such repeating of vocal patterns over and over mimics the cyclicity of God-Feminine. Two sorts of chanting have been used effectively within groups I have known.

The first type consists of a brief chorus that is learned by all and sung repeatedly without alteration for ten minutes to an hour. (Examples are given in Figures 33 and 34.) Once engaged, this sort of chanting can suspend the mind's usual chatter and help consciousness shift into an acceptant witnessing mode. In that frame of mind, feelings, images, thoughts, and impressions of the Deity normally screened out by ego designs may be experienced.

The second type is illustrated on page 185. Here a repeating traditional melody has its usual words replaced by various names of God-Feminine. The first three verses are sung in unison. Thereafter each person sings words of her (or his) own choosing, either from the assortment of suggested alternatives or whatever names of God-Feminine well up in the heart at the moment. (And, of course, names of God-Masculine might be intermixed, as well.) I especially

Figure 34 - Speak the three words in this mandala evenly and rapidly, with no breaks, so that the meanings "I Am She" and "She I Am" are sensed simultaneously.

commend this kind of chanting because it holds in balance the repetitive cyclicity and the free spontaneity of the Feminine way. At first the intellect chooses the words. Soon a more spontaneous creativity from the heart is bringing unpremeditated names of God-Feminine to the lips. The result is not chaos and babble, but an interweaving of the many independent voices in a manner that suggests that a suprapersonal power is orchestrating the process. More than one person has been amazed to notice that spontaneous nodes of meaning emerge, magical moments when many simultaneously speak variations of the same name—as though describing in various terms a single object of contemplation, a single facet of God-Feminine. One man said it reminded him of the biblical description of the apostles speaking in many tongues, yet one meaning, when the fiery Spirit inspired them at Pentecost (Acts 2:1-21). A woman confided to me that she had actually begun "speaking in tongues"[3] midway through the chant as the Spirit gave her utterance.

Sonic meditation is a somewhat chantlike procedure that emphasizes spontaneity. Each person places a hand on another's back, chest, or head. Beginning with any random sound, each person

begins to vocalize, noticing the vibrations produced, both within their own body and that of their partner. When a group does this, soon beautiful harmonies and unusual rhythms take shape out of the chaos. The sounds produced may range from melodious to harsh, groaning to laughter, animal sounds to angelic. A variation is to begin with a reading from Scripture, then express through sonic meditation interpretive resonances that lie beyond language.

A group that meets regularly will soon develop its own wealth of resources—tangible, ideational, and actional—on which to draw. Some of these will require careful crafting in advance, such as the stoles and Moon Bowl, or tuned percussion chimes that ring harmoniously in any combination (*below*), or new words to old songs (*pages 187 & 202*). Others will emerge in the spontaneity of the moment to become thereafter a part of the repertoire of shared experience available for recycling in new combinations—such unpremeditated activities as dancing; shadow play, rhythmic beating, stamping, or clapping; sonic meditation.

TUNED MUSICAL CHIMES

Two or more players may strike any notes, and the sound is always harmonious. Make two or more sets for multiple players. Accompany with drums or other rhythm instruments.

MATERIALS NEEDED:
   8' electrical conduit pipe, 3/4" diameter
   2" thick foam rubber, as from
      square molded pillow;
      (or use 2" rigid foam insulating board)

TOOLS:
   ruler
   hack saw
   large scissors
   (or sharp knife if using rigid foam)

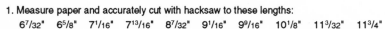

1. Measure paper and accurately cut with hacksaw to these lengths:
   6^7/32" 6^5/8" 7^1/16" 7^{13}/16" 8^7/32" 9^1/16" 9^9/16" 10^1/8" 11^3/32" 11^3/4"

2. Using scissors, cut a 3" wide strip of 2" thick foam rubber, 15"-18" long. (Or cut rigid foam insulation with sharp knife.)

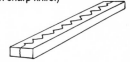

Split in two using a zig-zag cut to make about ten even notches in each piece. Arrange both pieces, points upward, so they are about 6" apart at one end, 12" apart at the other.

3. Arrange metal pipes so each is supported just at ends in foam notches.

4. Play by striking with various object for varied tones. Good strikers are: handle end of scissors; ballpoint pen; wooden spoon; teaspoon; a scrap of pipe. Experiment!

5. If desired, pipes may also be drilled to be hung from cords as windchimes.

THE DANCER

Genia Pauli Haddon

Traditional Shaker Tune, ca. 1850

1   "I danced in the eve-ning When the world was be-gun.
2   "I am moth-er, I am daugh-ter, I am sis - ter, crone.
3   "I am found in the fire And the dark of the womb.

I danced in the moon, In the sta-rs, in the sun.
I am witch, bitch, whore; I am vir-gin: one a - lone.
I am known in wo-men's cy-cles, In the phas-es of the moon.

I came from the de-pths and I danced on earth,
I am spir-it, I am bod-y, I am pow-er from with - in,
I give in - it - i - a - tion in - to death and then

The dance of death, And the dance of birth."
I am con-text, I am ma-trix, I am cy-cle, I am spin."
Bring trans - for - ma-tion To new life a - gain."

Dance, dance! Who - ev - er you may be:

Rec - og - nize your ho - ly i - dent - i - ty.

Know the One in the man-y, know the One in the Three,

For She is the One, and you are She!

Resist the temptation of trying to repeat a configuration that was wonderful the first time. The Feminine way is to create, destroy, and create again out of the pieces. From each experience garner additional elements for the mix, out of which to discover always the new form awaiting birth.

Yet other pieces in the group's fund of resources may grow out of serious research into historical Goddess worship and mythology. If the purpose is to undergird personal devotion to God-Feminine, something more than intellectual knowledge is wanted. When one person in the group has engaged personally and deeply with a particular myth, he or she can then mediate that meaning to others, perhaps by retelling the story, or dancing it, or drawing or sculpting from it. The story in the box below is an example of this kind of retelling. It is based on one woman's research on the Hindu Goddess Kali. Instead of reporting factual details about Kali's classical forms as both Destroyer and Great Mother, this woman shared with the group a re-creation that communicated the essence of Kali's nature, as she now understood it in her own heart.[4]

FEARSOME, PLAYFUL KALI — OUR MOTHER

When you were a little girl, did you ever sit on your mother's lap and play peek-a-boo? When you shut your eyes, Mother disappeared. You opened them, and there she was! Then her eyes shut again and you watched closely every moment until suddenly they opened again, and—"Peek-a-boo!"

Sometimes God is like that. God is such a great-great Mother, the whole world is Her baby. God is playing with Her world, and She shuts Her eyes. Then all our lives we try to catch the great Mother peeking at us. And if any of us do look into the eyes of God, in that moment we recognize Her and know for sure that we are in Her image, strong, loving and wise.

Does a mother love her baby when she is hiding from her? Why of course! Why else play at hiding? Though her eyes are long shut, we need never be afraid, for She is laughing and enjoying the play all the while. Sometimes we do feel frightened. Sometimes it seems that She has abandoned us altogether, and that Her eyes will stay shut forever. In truth it is we who have tired of playing and have looked away too soon. In Her own good time God will end this play and we will be able to look into Her eyes deeply and forever.

Our great Mother is everywhere. Even when She seems to be far away, it is only that you cannot see Her eyes. But really She is always there, always loving, and always ready to play with Her children. There is another game of hide-and-seek that the great Mother plays. She hides sometimes in other people. She hides in anything! Any day you might see Her eyes, just by looking into the eyes of a sister or brother. While hiding in someone, She herself once said (he spoke the words for Her), "Who is my mother and who are my brothers and my sisters? Inasmuch as you have done it to one of the least of these, you have done it to me." Truly, She is everywhere. Did you ever lift a stone or break open a piece of wood to see what was inside? Did you recognize God there at the heart of things? "Lift the stone and thou shalt find Me. Cleave the wood, and there am I!"

Oh, how beautifully She plays! Why, you might find Her anywhere.

Whether alone or in a group a good way of connecting non-academically with a goddess story is to draw or sculpt the Goddess as you imagine her to be in the wake of having heard the story. The same group that wears the Goddess Gowns gradually accumulated among themselves a large number of pictorial representations of the Great Woman Deity, collected by the women at various times over several years. Some were photographs of classical artworks, some drawn by the women themselves under widely varying circumstances. When we displayed them all around the walls of our room the bounteous power generated by these gathered pictures surprised us. It was almost physically palpable, filling the entire room, filling ourselves. The room served as a reverberation chamber, where the notes sounded by each picture were held, amplified, sorted and resorted into harmonics, augmenting one another.

All of these drawings of ours are at one level expressive of our personal psyches. Taken one at a time, they reveal more about our individual psychology than they do about the transpersonal Feminine. Taken one at a time, chronological order and the life context in which each was produced are important. Taken as a group, something other than those personal idiosyncrasies shines through. Our experience was that the deeper common denominators became visible, became the predominant notes, sounding through all of them. The idiosyncratic elements were seen to be mere embellishments on the fundamental underlying images.

In the same way, any of the ancient goddess stories that come to life for a person today do so because they strike a note in that person that is a harmonic of the deepest archetypal level, the root and source of all images and experiences of God-Feminine. When the deep archetypal source is stirred by such resonance it delivers forth additional concretions, illustrating itself through new pictures, stories, movements, sacramental enactments.

Having been stirred by the story of Persephone's mission to initiate those who were passing through death to a different condition, a friend and I decided to eat a pomegranate together, to see what initiational meaning such a sacramental act might have for us. I had never seen a pomegranate before and was astonished at how full to bursting this tough-looking fruit is with juicy, tightly packed, faceted, pea-sized "rubies," each containing one seed. This fruit seemed *pregnant*, and in breaking open the leathery outer skin we were in the role of midwives. Each seed-jewel carefully removed and eaten seemed to represent willingness to carry within us for incubation some facet of our unrealized selves, to be brought forth in due time. Some segments inevitably broke in the handling, blood-red juices running over our fingers. This pomegranate-womb bleeds as a woman's womb does in both its yang expressions, birthing and menstruating. This juice is the blood of the birthgiving, menstruating, initiating Dark Goddess Persephone. And we find it not disgusting, not polluting, but very good. Our teeth crunching the seeds within the soft flesh of each bright kernel are like the teeth of Kali in her terrible mode, crushing the bones and skulls of her devotees. And this too seems no longer disgusting and horrifying, but very good. Through this sacramental eating of a pomegranate my friend and I experienced rapport with both Persephone and Kali, alternative images of the Destroyer.

Another sacramental enactment is enfoldment. Two people embrace a third between them, completely enfolding her or him in the warmth, love, security of the gestative womb. This is a satisfying experience no matter where you are in the sandwich. I know of a group that enacts enfolding at the doorway to bless each woman in the name of God-Feminine before she enters the worship place.

Doorways have always been sacred to God-Feminine, representing the birth canal through which we pass not only at the moment of physical birth, but again and again symbolically each time we are reborn into fuller actualization of the divine image. For the same reason birthing rituals, either physically enacted or vividly imaged, are profound ways to experience the living power of the Goddess. Hallie Inglehart's *Womanspirit: A Guide to Women's Wisdom*[5] gives suggestions for mentally imaging being born of the Divine Mother into the arms of our sisters, and several other deeply affective meditations. Her method is similar to Jung's technique of Active Imagination. Others have called it guided imagery. It typically entails beginning with a prescribed image that is visualized vividly. This might be a single image, such as those suggested above for invoking God's protection against God, or an entire story line, such as a journey to and return from the underworld, or being born and awakening to the first day of life. Such imaging is like dreaming while awake. In the fully asleep state, a dream simply unfolds, and consciousness is a passive watcher. In the fully awake state, a person can decide arbitrarily whether to visualize this or that, or something else. In Active Imagination neither the conscious intention nor the automatic dream takes precedence. The two states dialogue with each other, taking turns modifying the image and story line, each responding respectfully to the other's contribution by generating a next step, then watching to see what the other will do in further response. In that way a living product is generated through which we may well be touched by the Deity in ways we could not have planned.

Devotion to God-Feminine is not limited to "sacred" times, places, and actions. What I call "everyday sacraments" are actions that not only have practical value, but also symbolic power to connect us with God-Feminine. For me, composting kitchen scraps and yard refuse is a devotional act as well as a source of good, black topsoil.

To treat these discarded materials no longer as garbage but as valuable ingredients for new creation is to look at the world through the eyes of God-Feminine. Any kind of recycling partakes of the cyclicity of the feminine principle, and the compost pile offers an especially rich mix of symbols. At every step, composting interweaves Destroyer and nurturant femininity. The raw materials placed in the compost pile provide nourishment for the bacteria, molds, and insects that decay them. The resultant topsoil nourishes the vegetables in the garden, which in turn are destroyed to nourish the gardener's family. Like the teeth of Kali, organic processes in the compost pile break down everything to fine particles. In composting we can see that this disintegrative process is not merely a necessary prelude to a subsequent creative act that makes rich soil; rather, the disintegration itself is the creative act thorough which transformed substance comes into being. That which is despised and rejected is not worthless after all, but is the ingredient for a new reality. Furthermore, in composting, the patriarchal equation *black = evil* is shown false, for the ideal result of this decomposition is good black humus.

The word *compost* comes from two Latin roots meaning "together" and "bring." In composting, a little of this, a little of that, a bit of something else is brought together and transformed into a single end product: rich, black soil as crumbly and fragrant as the bagged potting soil sold in garden shops. All sorts of organic materials—kitchen scraps, grass clippings, ashes from the fireplace, a dead robin, the entire contents of the kitty-litter tray, uprooted weeds, and sawdust, to name only a few—may be brought together in this way. Just as in God-Feminine rituals where every new "given" is woven into the whole and we experience a *sacred coming together*, in the compost pile, whatever the mix, it *comes together* through the dark, creative forces of decomposition.

I make compost in a freestanding four-by-six-foot oval ring of two-by-four-inch mesh wire fencing, about thirty inches high. To best *bring together* the various kinds of materials, I try to spread out each addition in a thin layer. When I add materials that might be smelly as they decompose, I sprinkle on a bit of earth. This not only keeps any odor contained, but also adds microorganisms to the pile to speed the decomposition process. As decomposition accelerates,

Elements for a Sacramental Coming-Together

What's Needed

•VEGETABLE MATTER
for carbon & nutrients

•ANIMAL MATTER
for concentrated nitrogen

•BACTERIA, MOLDS, INSECTS
to decompose materials

•AIR
so pile won't get slimy & smelly

•MOISTURE
so microbes work effectively

•INTERMIXING OF ELEMENTS
so they "come together"
into compost

•OTHER optional ingredients

How to Provide for It

•Fruit and vegetable parings, kitchen scraps (but not fats), moldy bread, weeds, grass clippings, hedge clippings, wilted bouquets, old plant stalks from vegetable and flower garden at end of season, dry leaves (chop with lawnmower), sawdust, wood shavings, coffee grounds, pure cotton or wool rags.

•Manure from pets or any animals; dead mice, birds, or other small critters; hair, nail parings; bonemeal; lean meat scraps; feathers; scraps from cleaning fish; sour milk.

•Add some topsoil or fully ripened compost every few layers.

•Intersperse coarser, dryer materials (like chopped dry leaves, pine needles, twigs, or dried plant stalks) between succulent layers (like grass clippings and freshly pulled weeds.) Turn over pile every 2-3 months to aerate. Don't build pile more than 5' high, 5' wide so that air can penetrate.

•Green vegetation, such as grass clippings, add moisture. Gently water the pile as you build it, every few layers, if it seems dry. Too much water makes pile smelly; too little slows down decomposition.

•Grind or chop coarse materials; spread in layers; alternate types of materials; turn pile over every 2-3 months until finished. *HINTS: Use food processor to grind citrus rinds, egg shells, melon rinds, etc. Use lawnmower to chop dry leaves.*

•Ashes from fireplace or ashtray; old soil from potted plants; dust from vacuum cleaner bag; fertilizers.

AVOID: mud, sand, gravel, lumps of charcoal, insecticides, pesticides, animal fats or grease, coarse twigs or branches, synthetic fibers.

An excellent sourcebook is Stu Campbell's *Let It Rot! The Home Gardener's Guide to Composting* (Charlotte, Vermont: Garden Way Publishing, 1983).

GENERAL HINTS:

•*Size of pile:* Height & width, between 3 ½' and 5'; length, as long as you want. For very small yards, a vertical column of wire fencing 3' in diameter and 5' high works well, according to Campbell. If you have very limited space, special fully-enclosed composting containers are available for use in dooryard, garage, or basement. See Campbell for descriptions and addresses of manufacturers.

•*Alternate* moist and absorbent materials; fine and coarse; vegetable and animal products. Intersperse some topsoil or fully ripened compost every few layers.

Depending on the 'coming together' of all these variables, composting may take six months to two years to produce finished soil.

the pile becomes warm, then hot enough in the center to steam when forked open. I like to think of this as emblematic of the dark yang energy of God-Feminine, fully as valuable and awesome as the divine light of God-Masculine.

When the oval enclosure is heaped high, I slip the ring of fencing up off the pile and reposition it to begin filling again. Sometimes I enjoy turning over a half-composted pile with a pitchfork, repiling it into the ring. This helps insure that the different layers are brought together thoroughly and promotes efficient decomposition. Eventually the transformation is complete. Out of garbage and weeds, out of death and disintegration, comes the stuff from which new life will grow. When I delight in the flowers in my windowbox, taste the tomatoes and squash for dinner, I am experiencing another part of the same cycle I connected with when I added a wilted bouquet and some vegetable parings to the compost pile a year before. Participating without partiality in both halves of the natural cycle of life, death, and re-creation gives me joy and deep peace. It teaches me much about the ways of God-Feminine.

Quilting from scraps likewise enacts the creativity of the womb. It is most satisfying symbolically to use actual scraps, rather than buying new fabric off the bolt. What would otherwise become a rag or be thrown away can become a unit in a colorful patchwork quilt, and thereby pass from death to new life. Braiding old-fashioned rag rugs from strips of outworn clothing gives the same sort of experience, teaching that feminine creativity is not "out of nothing," but out of what has died.

The kitchen is a natural place for participating in such transformative processes. Both bowl and oven are like the womb: containers where ingredients are transformed into new substances. For this reason I have installed in my kitchen a mantel-like shelf that functions as an altar. There I ripen individual pieces of fruit; aromatize pinches of kitchen spices in an incense burner; display figurines representing God-Feminine; offer beautiful flowers, leaves, dried grasses; burn a candle while preparing a meal; display attractive samples of lentils, nuts, dried beans, and peas; place striking found items, such as a bird's egg, unusual rock, seashell, or piece of lichen. All of this in celebration of God-Feminine in the midst of everyday life.

I began to do this before my research on ancient Goddesses turned up the fact that offerings to Demeter Ploutos typically were natural products of the fields. In view of this, perhaps one way to integrate God-Feminine into established church rites might be to consecrate unprocessed grapes and wheat grains along with the wine and bread (or wafer) for the sacrament of Holy Communion. On the several occasions on which I have done so, no communicants have objected and a number have commented that it was extraordinarily meaningful to them.

Only in private Eucharist celebrations have I described the bread as baked in Mother Mary's womb for the life of the world, and the wine as symbolic of the bleeding of the Divine Womb in its labors of transformation, death, and birth. Such a notion may be startling, unaccustomed as we are to noticing and naming the feminine dimension of the divine mystery. To articulate these womb-meanings enlarges rather than negates the familiar formulation that the bread is the body of Christ broken for the life of the world and that the cup pours out his blood for the salvation and deliverance of the faithful into new life.

My personal vision is that newly emerging experiences and insights of God-Feminine be interwoven with existing rites and ceremonies wherever there are authentic points of connection. For example, it is no accident that the Christian festivals that are traditionally *celebrated at night* are the ones that most relate to the dark yang energy of the Divine Womb: Maundy Thursday, the Easter Vigil, and Christmas Eve. On Christmas Eve the faithful keep watch at the manger, awaiting the delivery of the Deliverer into the world out of the Divine Womb, as actualized in the body of Mary. Maundy Thursday celebrates initiation into the process of dying, entombment, and entering the womb a second time. The Easter Vigil is like keeping watch for Christ to be born anew from the tomb-womb as midnight turns to Easter morning, when he is resurrected in an act of feminine-divine creation—not creation *ex nihilo*, but creation anew from the discarded remains of the one who had been despised, rejected, spit on, mocked, executed as a despicable criminal.

As I became attuned to both the God-Feminine dimension of Maundy Thursday and the symbolic meanings of the moon phases, I intuited that this holy day would fall on the dark of the moon, signifying the centrality of the aspect of God-Feminine that both destroys and gives birth. I was taken aback to find that instead it is timed to fall always on the *full* moon. How can this be?

Jesus' last supper with his disciples before being arrested is described as a Passover meal in the Bible.[6] Thus this Christian holy day corresponds originally to the first day of the Jewish festival of Passover, which "commemorates the deliverance of Israel's firstborn" (note *birthing* imagery) from the scourge of death that God brought upon the firstborn of the Egyptians to force them to release the people of Israel from bondage and permit their exodus.[7] Death, deliverance, firstborn, exodus (meaning "going out")—all these seem to relate well to the yang-Goddess as symbolized by the new moon. Why, then, does Jewish tradition link Passover to the full moon? Are my instincts mistaken, or is there some overriding consideration that results in Passover being celebrated during a phase of the moon that seems symbolically so ill suited?

The answer lies in the fact that originally Passover *was celebrated at the dark of the moon,* in the month of Abib ("green shoots") of the ancient Hebrew calendar.[8] At some later time, the calendar was revised to change the name of that month to Nisan, and at that time the celebration of Passover was shifted to fall thenceforth on the full moon. I have been unable to document the official reasons for this change. I conjecture that it may have been in the interest of disengaging thoroughly from all links to God-Feminine symbolism, thus securely establishing the exclusively God-Masculine religion. So long as the authentic connection between Passover and the dark moon remained intact, worshipers would continue to experience at some level of awareness the presence of God-Feminine. Throughout the Old Testament period great energy was devoted to eradicating practices that in any way kept alive the old Goddess religion. These efforts included the destruction of groves and sacred trees where the Goddess had been worshiped; the prohibition against eating pork, the flesh of an animal sacred to the Goddess; the rejection of the Golden Calf, an image of the Goddess, in order to receive the Ten Commandments of Yahweh mediated by the great patriarch Moses. In view of such efforts, it might make sense that the intrinsic link between Passover and the dark new moon be deliberately countermanded. Both Jewish Passover and Christian Holy Week thus no longer fall at the phase of the moon to which they best correspond symbolically, but instead at the phase that is most valued by patriarchy, the full moon.

More than once I have rediscovered the God-Feminine origins of now thoroughly masculinized practices or doctrines, not through book research but through experiential understanding growing out of my devotion to God-Feminine. In this way I determined that the Holy Spirit acts in my life as a *feminine* force. Subsequent library research confirmed my experience as consonant with people's experiences through the Ages. What I name *Holy Spirit,* the Hebrew faith knows as *Shekina,* Eastern Orthodox Christians as *Sophia,* and Hindu tradition as *Shakti*—all three of whom are feminine personifications of the Deity.

The Hebrew word *Shekina,* from *sheken,* "dwelling place," means the indwelling presence of the Deity.[9] In Jewish cabalistic theology, Shekina is the supernal Mother of God and all being; She is both the "soul of God" and the source of all soul in the universe. She is the Indwelling One, the deity within. Her outer garment is Torah, Holy Law. The one who studies Torah is gradually indwelled by Shekina and given wisdom. Not only does humankind require Shekina for spiritual wisdom; She is the wisdom and creativity of Godself.

In Torah, in the Old Testament, in Eastern orthodox Christianity, and most explicitly in Gnostic tradition, Wisdom or Sophia or Sapientia is the living soul, the active mind of the Deity. Gnostic tradition called her both God's Mother and God's vitality. She is the Origin out of whom were born not only all universes, but also the sevenfold power of God. Sophia as spirit of feminine-divine wisdom was symbolized by both the dove and the serpent. According to the Gnostics, the serpent in the Garden of Eden was an alternative form of Christ, both forms being incarnations of Her spirit. It was that same Spirit who entered Mary to conceive Jesus. In the form of a dove, the same Spirit came upon Jesus at his baptism. It is in reference to Wisdom herself, therefore, that Jesus admonished his followers to be "wise as serpents, innocent as doves" (Matt. 10:16).

The Goddess Shakti of Hindu devotion likewise is both a cosmic female principle, creating universes and enlivening God himself, and the intimate indwelling divine presence in the Heart/Self/Center of the individual. She is vital energy in all its forms and actions, the essence of "power, ability, faculty, strength, prowess; the power of composition, poetic power, genius; the power or signification of a word or term."[10] She is the active power of Divinity. She herself awakens the individual to truth and leads the devotee toward wisdom and eventual reunion with Godself.

Despite the fact that clergy and theologians have all this information, as well as personal testimonies of modern Christians who spontaneously use the feminine pronoun to describe this Presence,[11] doctrinally Christians continue to use exclusively the male pronoun for the Holy Spirit. What kinds of shifts, not only in theology, but also in liturgical and devotional practices, might flow from simply reaffirming the feminine orientation of one member of the Trinity?

According to Hasting's *Dictionary of the Bible*, the Holy Spirit is "the mysterious creative power of God, possessing and inspiring men [sic], manifested especially in ecstatic conditions, prophesying, and special gifts and abilities such as strength, leadership, wisdom, judgement, and skill; the personal activity of God Himself [sic]...the inner principle of the new life 'in Christ'...the fully personal mode of the Divine operating in creation and recreation."[12] Though this article fails to use the feminine pronoun, it seems clear it is describing the same phenomenon that in Hebrew is called Shekina; and in Greek, Sophia; and in Sanskrit, Shakti. The article goes on to document Old Testament/Torah usage of the term as the creative spirit, the "living energy of a personal God"; brooding over the waters at creation; inspiring heroes and mighty men; manifesting itself in artistic genius, insight, and wisdom; "active in the wisdom and judgement of lawgivers and prophets."

The anointing of God's chosen representatives with oil signifies their intimate bonding with the Holy Spirit. In the New Testament the Holy Spirit appears as a dove at the watery baptism of Jesus, who speaks of bringing to the faithful a baptism in fire. She pours herself forth in tongues of flame at Pentecost, clothing the faithful in power. As paraclete ("one to call on") She is perpetually present, guiding the faithful into all wisdom and holy knowledge. As pneuma/breath/spirit, the Holy Spirit pervades and fills all things.

She is both above, as dove, and below, as serpent. Her symbolism embraces all four elements: fire, air (wind/breath), water, and earth (as oil). She makes holy by washing, burning, anointing, illuminating. She is "God in action, the presence of God, the power or love of God," vitality, dynamics, power.[13] She both creates the manifest universe and makes possible reunion of the creation with its Creator.

It is She who calls forth our nascent devotion to Godself as *both* God-Masculine and God-Feminine. It is She who wakens in us dissatisfaction with liturgical practices that inadequately honor the Deity, and She who leaps up within us in recognition of authentic innovations in our worship rites. It is She who initiates us into whatever devotional practices are authentic, for the delight of God and the good of our souls.

HOW TO MAKE A MOON BOWL

Buy a 16" (10-quart) stainless steel bowl. Wash and dry thoroughly. Using a #8-Bright artists' brush, apply irridescent white acrylic artist's paint (such as Grumbacher Hyplar #H214) to inside of bowl in short overlapping strokes, like hundreds of petals. For each short stroke, draw the brush from edge toward center. Begin at the outer edge and work round and round toward the center, covering the inner surface entirely. This paint is translucent, giving a glowing pearlized effect as light gleams through each "petal" from the silvery surface beneath. Paint dries in 10-20 minutes. Apply a second layer overlapping the first around the upper inch or two of inner surface, to build up slightly more opaque rim.

Chapter Thirteen

You Are She

Once every month or six weeks I meet with a group of women for several hours of connecting and meditation with awareness of God-Feminine. Sometimes the feminine presence of the Holy Spirit is strongly felt within our circle. One may speak in tongues, another may break into song or even dance, or there may be periods of profound silence as we commune with the Divine One. One evening I was moved to open my eyes and look at the faces of each woman around the circle. As my gaze came to rest on one of them, I was given the spiritual vision to realize, "You are the Christ! You are She, the living Christ."

This was a startling perception. I was familiar with the idea that we "meet Christ" whenever we respond with compassion to someone in need, whether by offering a cup of water to the thirsty or housing for the homeless (Matt.25:31-45). However, I had taken that as but a lovely figure of speech. Now, here I was seeing as the Christ, not the needy stranger, but my friend; and not figuratively, but actually; and with the words "Christ, she" coming naturally to my lips in that moment, even though until then I had equated Christ with the man Jesus.

Since that time I have come to understand such experiences as glimpses of the fact that we each bear the image and likeness of God as our true identity. This is who we are, as God conceives us to be in the Divine Mind and Womb. If we were to live up to this conception, if we were to be our real selves, we would literally incarnate God in our physical, mental, emotional, and spiritual being. The Christ is the incarnate form of God: God in human flesh. In Jesus—and in any person who lives out his or her true identity in the image of God. Jesus was fully and perfectly Christ because he was perfectly and fully himself. Exactly as such, he incarnated God.

It is the patriarchal way to set Jesus apart from and above all other human beings. Having done so, the church through the centuries has struggled to maintain a clear sense of his humanity.

198

The various creeds, asserting that he is both "fully human" and "fully divine" are examples of this tension, and of the challenge the incarnation presents to the patriarchal mind-set. In contrast, the way of the womb furthers an egalitarian understanding of Jesus, inevitably recognizing both his humanity and his deity in common with us. Having said of Jesus, "Thou art the Christ," it is then no diminishment of him to also say of my friend, "You are She." From the God-Feminine perspective, his worth is not contingent upon his being superior to all others, but upon his being authentically human within his unique, actual life, and *in that way* incarnating God.

My friend has not fulfilled her identity in so complete a manner as Jesus; she does not consistently incarnate the image and likeness of God as herself, has not fully been born of the Divine Womb. Nevertheless, to be so is her calling, and every person's. All creation groans in travail (Rom.8:19-23), along with the Divine Womb, pushing toward the fulfillment of human nature, which in fact does accomplish incarnation of God.

Just as the disintegrative process of composting is not merely a necessary prelude to a subsequent creative act making rich soil, but is itself the means through which transformed substance comes into being; so the creation of the human species is not merely a necessary prelude to a subsequent creative act making Jesus alone divine, but is itself the means through which God-self wills to actualize in beings of flesh and blood. To the eyes of faith, Jesus Christ is the epitome of that actualization. Such a perception of Jesus is not automatic and inevitable, any more than is the perception of my friend's God-nature. In both cases, the moment of perception is the moment when the Holy Spirit-Shekina-Shakti looks through my eyes and recognizes Herself in the other.[1] "Thou art the Christ." "You are She."

This is what happened when I perceived my friend, in the fullness of her being, as the Christ. And since that experience I have been gifted to glimpse this truth in person after person. At odd moments right in the thick of life suddenly I recognize the God-nature of another person. It may be the stranger in line ahead of me at the supermarket checkout, someone I have never met and most likely will never see again; my elderly father, struggling up out of a chair onto legs no longer steady; the person sitting across from me in my counseling office. It is no longer hard for me to believe Jesus' words, that as Christ and the Father are one, so each of these and Christ are one being. That this unity be actualized in our lives was his prayer on the eve of his death: "May they all be one. Father, may they be one in us, as you are in me and I am in you....With me in them and you in me, may they be so completely one that the world will realize that it was you who sent me...so that the love with which you loved me may be in them, and so that I may be in them" (John 18:21-26, JB).

Not long ago I was guest minister for a Communion service at a large urban church. Toward the end of the coffee hour following the service an older man from the congregation drew me aside for a few words. With simple sincerity he said, "I want you to know that during Communion I looked at you and I saw the face of Christ in your face." I was very moved to know that he had been graced to witness with his own eyes that I too am She, I am the embodiment of Christ, just as Jesus prayed I would be. Churches that refuse to ordain women priests and ministers on the grounds that Jesus was male have not yet grasped what this man witnessed: the Christ is *the Divine One incarnating*, not solely in Jesus, but at any moment and wherever revealed to us in human form.

All the major faiths affirm that we are in God's image. Scriptures common to Christian, Muslim, and Jew specify that both the male and female are created in the image of God (Gen. 1:27). We have not really absorbed that truth until we become able to name the Holy One in ways that can also appropriately name ourselves, whichever sex we are: God-She, Mother, Great Woman, as well as God-He, Father, and Lord. Not as a contrived exercise, but as language that simply reflects such spiritual experiences as those just described.

The primal male experience of identity is "I am different than my source," which translates to the spiritual insight "I am not like God" and leads to an emphasis on the transcendence of God as the Absolute Other. This is a valid and profound theology.

The primal female experience of identity is "I am like my source." The gestative mode of femininity translates this awareness to the spiritual insight "God is everywhere roundabout me," or "I live in God." This is a theology of immanence of the sort that sees all of nature as charged with various degrees of numinosity, mana, divine energy. This too is a valid and profound theology, although commonly held in low esteem by patriarchally attuned minds. It may, of course, deteriorate into either sentimentality (taking exaggerated delight in the beauties of Nature while ignoring Her starkness) or superstition (the notion that we can control God through manipulation of natural objects).

The exertive mode of femininity translates the awareness "I am like my source" into the spiritual insight "God is the Birther perpetually bringing forth likenesses of God-self." Each "likeness" is of course a birther in its turn, too, breaking itself open to reveal God anew. This is *sacramental immanence*. Precisely at the moment we most clearly see an element *as itself* is the moment it fulfills its birthing function and delivers forth an experience of the divine.

Both this sacramental way and the phallic-transcendent approach to the Holy One are valid. However, depending on which orientation predominates, we will experience either the God-Feminine or God-Masculine identity of that One in daily spiritual life. Washing dishes, for example, might be experienced either way. (Of course, washing dishes might *sometimes* be simply a secular act, undertaken to satisfy the expectations of my social group or my internalized notion of what I ought to do, to get a necessary chore out of the way, or even for the sense of accomplishment in a job well done.) If I am religious in the phallic manner I might sacralize washing dishes by considering myself to be dong them "for the Lord" or "to the glory of God." The task becomes sacred by consecration to an exterior "Other" who is known aside from the task. If I am religious in accordance with the exertive womb, then it is within the task itself—being done for itself and no other motive—that all at once I may experience God. Washing this cup or that plate becomes a sacramental act at the moment I engage intimately and solely with it. There is no need to dedicate it to an extrinsic Lord, for the Slayer-Birther is intrinsically present.

Such a sense of sacramental immanence results in every moment becoming sacred, every act liturgical. The distinction between secular and religious becomes irrelevant. One practical result for me of beginning to live this way is that every little chore of the day is potentially a sacrament, and so engages me as deeply and joyfully as does receiving the Bread or Cup of the Eucharist. Another practical result is that virtually every room in my house has quite naturally developed an altar place. There is the shelf in the kitchen where I ripen fruit and aromatize spices. Whenever I set to work in the kitchen, I light a candle there. Just now on the wall above that shelf is a plaque to remind me of the importance of remaining aware of the death side of the Deity as I chop vegetables for the pot and place the parings in a bowl for the compost pile. Made years ago from the worship bulletin used at the funeral of my eight-year-old nephew and six-year-old niece, this plaque says, "Unless a grain of wheat falls to the ground and dies, it remains alone; but if it dies, it bears much fruit" (John 12:24). In the room where I do my writing, I have created a glowing, transparent mandala on one window, using pieces cut from brightly colored plastic page protectors, simulating stained glass. Beneath the window, on an extra typing table, are the two halves of a cleft rock, a miniature terrarium, a small figurine of a pregnant woman, and an incense burner. In the bedroom, a tray on one dresser holds a bowl of fresh blossoms and a candle. It is near the dressing table mirror and helps remind me to watch for glimpses of God-Feminine in myself as well as in others. Tending these sacramental nooks daily, changing their symbolic objects often, lighting a candle or incense as my first act when I enter that room to work, helps me cultivate as fully as I am able each day my capacity for engaging sacramentally with each little task.

The sacramental experience of seeing God by seeing each thing *as Itself* leads to a sense of the singleness of God, self, and world. Every object, action, and event, including myself, is discovered to be a likeness of God, a birther of the Divine Presence here and now. The confession of faith issuing from the sacramental immanence of the exertive womb is not only "Thou art the Christ" and "You are She," but also "I am She"; not only "This sacramental element marks the real and actual presence of God," but also "I am That."

AMAZING GRACE [2]

A-maz-ing grace! How sweet the voice
That named and set me free!
I once was name-less; Now, re-joice:
I know God — I am She!

Her grace is pres-ent every-where.
She's here in you and me.
Com-pas-sion, wis-dom, pe-ace, and care
De-fine ou-r dig-ni-ty.

Be-fore Go-d formed me in Her Womb,
I was al-read-y known.
My li-fe is wo-ven on Her Loom.
By name She calls me home.

By grace, I learn to know my strength.
By grace, no more to fear
The Light and Dark, the heights and depths
Of Love in-car-nate here.

A-maz-ing grace! How sweet the voice
That named and set me free!
I once was name-less; Now, re-joice:
I know Her — I am She!

Out of such awareness grows an ethical "therefore" and a way of living that celebrates both the uniqueness of each expression of the Slayer-Birther and the unity of them all. In commitment to the exertive womb we best honor the Deity by recognizing the dignity, wonder, beauty, and unique God-likeness of each individual, whether human, animal, or inanimate. True compassion arises from realizing that I am one with every other likeness of God. To love my neighbor is to love myself is to love God—not as an amorphous confusion of identity or regression to immersion in the undifferentiated Matrix, but through the paradox that when we are most truly our particular selves, we are also most fully incarnating the One God. Alienation from both God and neighbor, the inevitable curse of patriarchal spirituality with its emphasis on separation and transcendence, is overcome in Christ the incarnate One. Knowing "You are She" and "I am She" is the basis of profound atonement, the essence of the holy, healing work of Jesus Christ.

For those who share the womb perspective, the person who can say, "It is no longer I who lives, but Christ in me" (Gal.2:20) is not talking about submitting to an outside power, but of becoming his or her true self. The "I" that I imagine myself to be, that limited "I" must be broken open, must die, enter the Womb of God again and come forth anew incarnating more clearly the image of God *as myself.*

Being that self is not the same as having your own way, doing whatever you please. It is not the same as being good according to anyone else's standards, nor hitting the mark in accordance with extrinsic ethical goals. It is doing, moment by moment, what pleases God-in-you—She whose purpose is to bring to birth the fullness of your unique incarnation of Herself. Those are the times when our actual lives come into congruence with God's conception of us; times when God lives in you *as you;* times when Jesus Christ's prayer for you comes true.

When we live out of the awareness that God is the Birther perpetually bringing forth likenesses of God-self, we name as sin failure to come to birth in likeness to God and failure to perceive that likeness both in oneself and all others. Then the phallic virtue of seeing God as wholly other than yourself and superior in every way seems less awesome than the awareness of how you are *like* God. In a life of faith modeled on the exertive womb, to contemplate some attribute of the Deity, knowing simultaneously that this characteristic is supernally divine and yet that you yourself are a likeness of That, is the source of greatest joy and awe. Therefore, the more fully we know the breadth of our own human nature, all four of the metaphorical modes described in this book, the more authentic can be our reverence for the Deity. If we are excluding one or more modes from our own development, at that point we are blocked from worshiping God in the sacramental, incarnational way modeled by the womb.

God-Feminine is not so much an object of veneration as She is the universal Subject; not so much a Thou to relate to as a Self to be. She cannot be known by you apart from yourself. She manifests in each moment when you recognize "I am She; I am That." Such recognition is not merely a mental affirmation, but is experienced by your whole being.

For many people the word *goddess* suggests instead a distantly revered feminine figure, either an actual woman (as in "Hollywood sex goddess") or an ideal image of unattainable femininity, as distant as the patriarchal God but of feminine gender. Such a "goddess" is not God-Feminine as revealed from the perspective of the Divine Womb. God-Feminine is loved and revered close up; "goddesses" are venerated from afar. This is why the contemporary tendency to greatly value large breasts does *not* signify reverence for God-Feminine, even though it superficially resembles ancient worship of many-breasted deities. Present-day male fascination with the female breast differs from religious veneration of God-Feminine in the same way that infatuation differs from reverent awe. Infatuation is obsessional longing for a lost part of oneself that has become projected onto another—whether onto another person or even onto one's idea of God. Reverent awe arises when we contemplate some characteristic of God and, without inflation, acknowledge ourselves to be in that likeness, rather than projecting that attribute solely onto God.

What is the meaning of male infatuation with large breasts? Ostensibly it has to do with their being sex objects. Yet, physiologically, breasts are but third-order expressions of sexual differentiation. First-order sexual differences are the chromosomes (XX or XY) and the gonads themselves: ovaries or testicles, each producing sex-specific reproductive cells and hormones. Second-order differences are the structurally differentiated genital organs, designed for mating and gestating, and shaped during embryological development: vulva, vagina, and uterus; or testicles and penis. Third-order

Next page

The first two verses of this hymn beautifully express the traditional (phallic) understanding of the incarnation as an extraordinary earthing of the supremely high, transcendent God. The final two lines emphasize the value of watching for "God-with-us," both in Jesus and in every human being, including oneself.

COMMUNION HYMN

Liturgy of St James, vs. 1 & 2
Tr. Gerard Moultrie, 1829-1885
Genia Pauli Haddon, vs. 3 & 4

PICARDY 8.7.8.7.8.7.
Traditional French melody, 17th century

1 Let all mor - tal flesh keep si - lence, And with fear and
2 Ful - ly God, yet born of Ma - ry. As of old on
3 Bread is bro - ken, Christ is with us, "This my bo - dy:
4 Christ in - car - nate, Christ e - ter - nal, Christ the ho - ly,

trem - bling stand; Pon - der noth - ing earth - ly mind - ed,
earth he stood, Word di - vine in hu - man ves - ture,
Take and eat." In the cup poured out we dis - cern him
Christ the whole. Christ the heal - er, Christ res - ur - rect - ed,

For with bless - ings In both hands, Christ our God to
In the bod - y and the blood, He will give to
Ho - ly, emp - tied, pres - ent, com - plete. Turn and see the
Christ ful - fill - ing all fore - told. Al - le - lu - ia,

earth de - scend - eth, Our full hom-age to de - mand.
all the faith - ful His own self for heav-enly food.
Christ before, beside, behind you; Christ in ev' - ry - one you meet.
Al - le - lu - ia, Christ my ver-y Self, my soul!

differences are later modifications of body features that until puberty are *identical* for the two sexes. Both the enlargement of the woman's breasts and the altered texture and length of a man's facial hair are tertiary gender differences.[3] Theoretically, therefore, breasts should be no more emphasized as objects of sexual attention or sexual identity than are full, bushy beards. Were we not thoroughly conditioned to consider women's breasts as so central to their sexual identity and attractiveness, we would find this fixation odd and would look for its special meaning. Another strange attitude toward breasts is the widespread erroneous belief that large-breasted women can suckle infants more successfully than small-breasted women.[4] Since not a physiological reality, what is the reason for this cultural emphasis on the large breast as signifying both sexual attraction and womanly effectiveness?

From the point of view of the suckling infant, the breast looms large regardless of its physical size, as the source of perfect nurturance. In this function it carries on the gestative work of the yin-womb. In patriarchal culture the female breast is accentuated and prized as the visible carrier of all yin by the female gender. The bigger the breast, the greater the symbolic evidence of the woman's yin-nature. The adult male (the normative human being within patriarchy) no longer seeks from the breast the physical nurturance of milk. Rather, as the symbolic repository of his projected yin energies, the breast becomes an object of intense attraction or sentimental adoration. That this is due to more than simply memories of the breast from infancy is clear from the fact that generally women do not similarly sentimentalize the breast, even though they too suckled at it in infancy. The sight of the infant at the breast is for many men embarrassing. What excites is the full-looking breast as symbolic carrier of their own projected yin energy. For the female breast to become for the man revelatory of God-Feminine, he must relinquish it as an object of fascination and longing and discover, paradoxically, "I, too, am That. I am She."

The phallic-patriarchal system by its very nature plays up the differences between self and other, human and divine, God and Satan. The exertive-contextual orientation of the womb emphasizes likeness without conflation. In our patriarchally-determined world, where the common viewpoint remains phallic, it is not surprising if many hear the affirmation "I am She" as either nonsensical or blasphemous, for it not only names God as other than Lord, but implies both likeness and reciprocity between Deity and person. This is in fact the blasphemy for which Jesus was condemned by the religious council of elders.

When religious sensitivities modeled on the exertive womb awaken, the Holy Spirit-Shekina-Shakti is readily recognized as She. Then both Dove and Serpent, both Birther and Slayer expressions, are found equally worthy of veneration. The affirmation "I am She" is as ridiculous for women as for men, until that quickening has occurred; it is as salutary for men as for women once the Holy Spirit has been recognized as the Exertive Womb deep in the soul.

When religious sensibilities modeled on the phallus arose at the turning of the last Age, it was their nature to overpower and depose the former matrical religions. Because of the multivalent, contextual style of the exertive womb, it is not in its nature to wage a war of extermination against phallic religious impulses. As God-Feminine becomes the central ordering principle for the human species in the coming Age, the phallic religions need not be destroyed or replaced, but will be *recontexted* within the new cosmos and thereby reborn of the Divine Womb. Then even the Lord in His utter transcendence will be loved as you love yourself. The phallic dimension of the new spirituality will express through penetrating deeply into each given moment with great trust, anticipation, and reverence.[5] The primary religious impulse will be the sense of sacramental immanence, celebrated moment by moment within a life that gives thanks.

Chapter Fourteen

Uniting Sex, Self, & Spirit

Based on careful attention to sexual differences, the body metaphors have provided a frame of reference for envisioning the journey out of the Patriarchal scenario into a New Story. Oriented now by that story-line, we can look anew at sexuality, this time as prime vehicle of sacramental immanence.

The relationship between sexuality and spirituality has evolved through the Ages, apace with the evolution of human consciousness. In the Matrical Age, the instinctual forces of sexuality were revered for their creative power. To be carried away on waves of natural sexual ecstasy allows participation in the divine creative matrix. In common fertility rites the generative mating of man and woman served as metaphor of the regenerative effect of immersion in the Divine Matrix, where consciousness itself is a state of participational inclusion.

The Patriarchal Age brought a new mode of consciousness, and a revised view of sexuality. This consciousness is based on clear distinctions rather than immersion. God is known as the ultimate Other. Sexuality is seen as the antithesis of spirituality, since physical merging reactivates the state of immersion in the divine womb. To be swept away by instinctual energies into sexual union is no longer an apt metaphor for the ideal relationship to the Divine, and does not advance consciousness.

To grow in patriarchal-style consciousness requires becoming able to resist the natural urges. Sexual energies are to be sublimated—harnessed and transformed—in the interest of enhanced consciousness and spirituality. Thus, celibacy is a great virtue, since it protects the celibate from the undertow of sexual urges toward merging, and makes available a quantum of energy to be repatterned for spiritual rather than sexual uses. Nonphysical spiritual communion, rather than sexual union, is the patriarchal religious ideal.

An alternative motif in Patriarchal mythologies exalts the joining of male and female as an enactment of the union of opposites, thereby giving sexuality symbolic significance. Indeed, the central spiritual dilemma in the patriarchal system is how the opposites (male, female; heaven, earth; divine, human) can be reunited without destroying their distinctness. The *coniunctio oppositorum* of alchemical lore represents this paradox. It pictures the creation of the spiritual Self as the end product of a process of separating and distinguishing the opposites, then reuniting them through a Royal Marriage, in which King and Queen, Sun and Moon—representing all such opposites—come together. It was common for the alchemical adept to have a female partner, or soror, in the great Work. Whether in the alchemical flask or the conjugal bed, the coming together of oppositional physical elements is symbolic of the union of opposites as a spiritual achievement.

In the emerging Age, the nature of consciousness undergoes another shift. Oppositions are no longer central, and spirituality no longer is summed up in the mystery of the Royal Marriage. The emerging symbol is the hologram.

Holograms could be produced only after techniques had been perfected for focusing light into laser beams. The diffuse quality of ordinary light is characterized by non-ordered patterns of waves and photons. In a laser beam, the waves/photons are aligned in an orderly, coherent arrangement. This kind of light can be so sharply focused as to serve as a scalpel. It is an apt analog of the keenly focused nature of the patriarchal style of consciousness. Just as the hologram could be created only after the invention of the laser beam, so the new mode of consciousness can emerge only after an eon of patriarchal focusing.

A hologram is a fully three dimensional image produced by a photographic process using laser light. Through a series of prisms and mirrors, a single laser beam is split into two beams sharing the identical wave/photon pattern (*Fig. 36*). Note that the two beams are not a "pair of opposites"; their *alikeness* is crucial to the holographic process.

Figure 35 - The Royal Wedding

Beam A is diffused through a lens to illuminate the object being photographed. It is reflected from the object's surface in a pattern specifically determined by the shape, colors, and textures of the object. Beam B is focused so as to intersect A precisely at the photographic plate. The intersection of the two beams produces an effect much like the intersection of ripple patterns from two pebbles dropped in still water (*See Fig. 21, p.92*). It is this interference pattern, rather than a direct image of the object, which is captured on the photographic plate.

Examined in ordinary light, a holographic plate shows a moire field of grays, not resembling in the slightest the object photographed. Those dappled patterns, however, contain the record of the complicated interaction of the two beams. When a beam *of the same orderedness as B* is shone through this plate, the light waves become rearranged to exactly match the pattern of beam A as it was originally reflected from the surface of the object. The eye perceives that intricate pattern just as it would perceive light reflecting directly from the object. Thus a fully three-dimensional image of the object is recreated in empty space.

Note that the image is created neither through a merging of the two beams (which would resemble the matrical/participational system) nor through the use of beams that are unlike ("opposites," as in the patriarchal worldview), but through the creation of a meaningful pattern by the intersection of two alike, yet discrete, beams.

In the emergent Age, the central paradox is not the union of opposites, but the simultaneous coexistence of multiple orders of "wholes" (*as described on pp. 91-96*). The hologram is an exquisite illustration of this mystery. If the holographic plate is broken into several pieces, *each piece* contains all the information needed to recreate the three dimensional image of the original object when a beam identical to B is shone through it. There is no need to reunite the several pieces. The whole inheres in each.

This suggests a new way of appreciating the significance of sexual union. In Matrical terms, it is an experience of immersion in the generative/regenerative Divine Matrix. In Patriarchal understanding, it is the paradoxical coming together of opposites, reconstituting a whole from separated parts and representing the reunion of human and Divine. In the emergent Age, sexual union can be thought of as mutual activation of one another's holographic plates. Partner A already contains the Whole; partner B's presence reveals it. And visa versa.

In the conventional view, the highest purpose of sexual union is the procreating of new life. The new consciousness sees sexual union as the optimum opportunity to allow ourselves and our partner to serve as holographic mediators of the Holy.

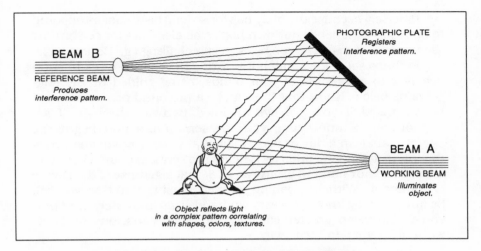

BEAM B

REFERENCE BEAM
*Produces
interference pattern.*

PHOTOGRAPHIC PLATE
*Registers
Interference pattern.*

BEAM A

WORKING BEAM
*Illuminates
object.*

*Object reflects light
in a complex pattern correlating
with shapes, colors, textures.*

Figure 36 - Diagram of holographic photography.

The holographic model illustrates that the Holy can be seen in every fragment. This is the essence of sacramental immanence, where each object, by being itself, when illuminated by the beam of your consciousness can suddenly reveal a glimpse of reality exceeding in vividness your usual awareness as breathtakingly as the three-dimensional holographic image transcends the gray mistiness of the holographic plate.

The finite world (including your embodied self) can be thought of as a holographic plate, the solidified record of the intersection of two "beams of divine consciousness." (In Hindu mythology, these are Shiva and Shakti. In Western thought, they are the immanent and transcendent modes of divinity.)[1] Your individual consciousness can serve as the reference beam to activate the hologram *only because it is alike to the divine consciousness.*

Those elements which have been deemed unholy in the patriarchal system are especially valuable teachers of this new order of consciousness, since the transcending of old truths is what confirms the new. Hence, the great value of developing the holy potential of the body and—especially—of sexuality.

In the patriarchal system, sexual union and spiritual communion are seen as incompatible modes for satisfying the human craving for connection. As we enter the emergent Age, where such constructs of opposites will have less power, the new test of spiritual sincerity and maturity will be, not celibacy, but the capacity to discern Spirit within the sexual sphere.

Precisely because the body has for so long been cast as opposed to spirit, to experience our own bodies as elements for celebrating sacramental immanence can be especially challenging. Begin small.

Perhaps set aside a half hour during the coming week to enter deeply into awareness of your hands, being guided by the suggestions below. Know that this can be a profound process. Do not be surprised if you feel overwhelmed partway through. If so, supportively acknowledge your present limits and begin the exercise anew in a day or two. Know that what overwhelms you is the intensity of perception as it nears that critical point where you are seeing your hand so clearly as *itself* that a glimpse of the Divine is imminent. Without pushing yourself, trust that in time you will be able to enjoy knowing your own hands this intimately, and that you will develop greater capacity for being conscious of Spirit without needing to turn away.

Sacramental Hands[2]

First, review the centering and protecting practices described on pages 193-194. Then begin this exercise by looking closely at your hands for several minutes. Study their shape, their color, the patterns of lines and whorls. Then touch one hand with the other, noticing carefully how the texture and temperature varies from place to place. Try closing your eyes as you continue to touch and massage one hand with the other. Is there any difference between your tactile perceptions with eyes open, eyes closed? With your fingertips, trace the lines of the bones, tendons, veins. Feel how these structures shift as you make a fist; as you flex your fingers; as you spread them wide. Spend at least three minutes just playfully observing these movements. How many different hand postures can you invent?

Bring one hand near your face. Sniff the surface of the skin, all over, front and back. Does it increase or decrease your sensitivity to allow your nose to actually touch the skin? Can you notice nuances of different odors at various places? Can you recognize the residue of recent activities still clinging there? Perhaps the fragrance of the aftershave lotion you put on hours ago, or the persistent pungency of the orange you peeled for lunch, or the metallic tang on your fingertips from the paperclips you have been handling. If you washed your hands right before beginning, notice whether the lingering odor of the soap is uniform. (Next time, try this exercise without washing first.) Take your time, then repeat with the other hand.

Touch the tip of your tongue to the back of one hand. Do you taste anything? What does your tongue reveal about the texture of this part of your skin? What does it feel like to have this part of your body touched by your tongue? Explore the palm, the fingers, between the fingers, the entire surface of your hand. What memories or thoughts stir in response? Repeat with your other hand.

Bring one hand near your ear. Rub your thumb and forefinger together. What do you hear? Can you snap your fingers? Carefully notice how you do that. Can you discern what makes the sound? Now rub your palms together near your ear, first in a back-and-forth, then in a circular pattern, then at various speeds. Can you hear the differences? Flex and extend your fingers, like a baby waving bye-bye, and see if you can hear the whispers of sound this movement creates. Playfully experiment to see how many different sounds you can create with just your hands.

Now relax with your hands held up comfortably in front of you. With eyes opened or closed, whichever works better for you, *pull your awareness of your hands into the core of your being.* Invite an intuitive sensing of these very hands as they were when you were born...as you grew...as they are right now...as they will be on the day you die. Feel the whole history and future of these hands, condensed to a single moment of awareness. Savor as long as comfortable, then release the awareness and return to ordinary consciousness.

Finally, with loving attentiveness, wash and dry your hands in exactly the routine you usually follow. Do this while maintaining close awareness. Notice whether your mind wanders. Can you do this ordinary thing while maintaining extraordinary awareness?

❖ ❖ ❖

Most of the time our awareness is diverted. The mind "protects us" from too-intense glimpses of reality to insure that we will function effectively in the world as defined by ordinary waking consciousness. So the mind is conditioned to partially close down or to wander away whenever the intensity of perception nears that critical point where the object of our attention reveals itself to be God in disguise. This protective mechanism was instrumental in devleoping discriminating consciousness. Having become established in that style of consciousness, we are now called to venture beyond its confines.

> You are being called to come forth.
> You are being called to appear.
> See-er, Name-er, Sacramentalizer.
> You are being called to come forth.[3]

Once you can maintain consciousness while relating to your hands, create a similar ritual with your feet, and eventually with your genitals.

Reclaiming pristine awareness of your genitals may be especially difficult. There are many taboos against looking, touching, experiencing this part of the body; many preconceptions about how we *ought to* feel and what we *ought not* do.

In the emergent age, our organs of sexuality become organs of spirituality, not by repressing or sublimating sexual libido, but by perceiving sexuality as an instance of sacramental immanence. With sexuality as with anything, we find the Divine there not by looking for "something additional," but by seeing and experiencing the object of attention *as itself.*

One heritage of the patriarchal mode of consciousness, wherein the Divine is by definition Other and distant, is a deep yearning for connection. When our yearning for the Divine is displaced, whether on money, food, sex, alcohol, success or whatever, addictive behavior is the result. We fixate on the "fix", as though it were the Divine/Self/God. We can never get enough, because what we really want is God.

One valid solution is to discard the substitutes. "If thy right hand offend thee, cut it off."[4] If sexual union interferes with spiritual communion, choose celibacy. The new consciousness permits an even more excellent solution—*sacramental awareness,* which is the way of unconditional appreciation.[5] Instead of calling our addictions evil, this kind of nonjudgmental awareness transforms them from God-substitutes to true channels of divine grace.

Sexual union becomes sacramental communion through enhanced powers of awareness. Recall the peak of conscious awareness when your observations of your own hands became so acute, so clear, that simple sensory acuity spilled over into ecstatic recognition of the Divine. To maintain that sort of conscious awareness during sexual arousal and orgasm is rare. Since purely physical, instinctual forces are adequate to carry the process along without benefit of conscious discernment, lapses of full awareness can go unnoticed. The patriarchal ideal is to banish, or at least master, the instinctual powers, for the purpose of insuring greater consciousness. In the emergent age, the ideal is to neither master instinctual forces nor be swept into lesser consciousness by them, but to *maintain full consciousness while being carried away.*

If we practice sacramental awareness, any fragment of daily reality can serve as a holographic plate, revealing its richness and depth when we shine our focused consciousness through it. The ultimate challenge is to realize that *we ourselves* are holographic fragments. This can happen when we experience another viewing us holographically.

The following simple exercise to be done with a partner offers that possibility and can help develop greater capacity for maintaining awareness while communing with another. Your partner need not be a potential sexual mate, although what you learn can carry over into sexual practice.[6] Before beginning this exercise, remember to do the centering and protecting practices described in Chapter 8. At first, limit the intense phase of the gazing to 3-5 minutes, *gradually* extending the time as you become fully comfortable in the practice.

Sacramental Gazing with a Partner[7]

Sit comfortably facing one another, quite close. For the first minute or so, just look at each other in any manner that seems natural. Then form the intention of making and sustaining eye-contact. As you settle into the stillness of these moments, allow all expression to gradually melt from your face.

At first, you may find that sustained eye-contact is so intense you become uncomfortable or afraid. You may find yourself blinking a great deal, or compulsively glancing away, or allowing your eyes to close for a long moment. Be patient with yourself. Know that with practice it will become possible to sit for fifteen minutes or more without breaking connection.

When you are able comfortably to maintain your focus on your partner's eyes for some moments, notice whether it is her left or her right eye that has engaged you. Take time to savor what that eye "feels like," then shift your focus to the other side and compare. Experiment also with focusing primarily first through one of your eyes, then the other.

All this shifting back and forth can provide respite from the intensity of gazing. When you feel ready, let your focus come to rest at a point midway between your partner's eyes, above the root of the nose. Allow a profound stillness to develop. Notice that while focused on this point you can see the entire face. As you continue thus, you may be amazed when suddenly your partner's face begins to lose its familiar features. Its proportions may change; parts of it may temporarily go void, as though dematerializing; you may recognize a succession of various animals or the visages of many different people, of both sexes and many ages and racial types; some happy and benevolent, others angry, sad, or malicious, and sometimes bringing to your mind uncanny impressions of whole personalities and lives. Such a magic show comes about only as you relax into the intention of simply taking in the reality of *this* particular person sitting before you. If you are looking for a sideshow, the effect will elude you.

When it does begin, you may again feel overwhelmed and need to break off the practice, just as you may have needed to stop partway through your first sacramental exercises with your own hands, feet, or genitals. Remain patient with yourself, and begin again another time.

✤ ✤ ✤

Regardless of whether you reach that holographic moment when clear perception reveals the "face of God" in the face of your partner, you will likely feel salutary effects of these sessions. For awhile afterward, both inner and outer worlds may seem to have shifted subtly on some invisible axis, giving rise to fresh perceptions of everything in your universe.

Whether practiced with a partner or by gazing at your own reflection in a mirror, to see and be seen holographically is to enter the new Story, where Patriarchal hierarchies are replaced by multivalent interconnections and where the interplay of integers succeeds the separation of opposites as the primary structural pattern of reality.

When the reunion of opposites is no longer the universal theme, then sexual *union* need not be the only valued mode of sexual expression. Thereafter, sexuality can be thought of in terms of energy exchanges, rather than as genital contacts.[8]

Language such as "foreplay" and "climax" loses its significance once the linearity of the Patriarchal view shifts to the multivalent simultaneity of the emerging Age, where each moment is potentially as valuable as any other for revealing the Divine. Then, sexual success is no longer equated with either orgasm or procreation, but with the degree to which the sexual experience actualizes the holographic potential of the individual. Being able to achieve orgasm becomes less pertinent than being able to build and hold a composite energy charge as intensely conscious as it is intensely physical. And whether or not a new being is conceived is less primary than whether or not the beating of the Divine heart is perceived.

In this new Story, we find our true selves by uniting sex and spirit in this way. Realizing our alikeness to the Divine lover, we, too, become lovers of all life. We awaken to our calling as Seers, recognizing the Divine likeness everywhere we look.

❦

Each plan is oriented toward one of the four body metaphors. Materials are drawn mostly from the Protestant-Congregational tradition, rounded out from other sources. All are brief, taking under a half hour. They are designed to be celebrated in a large room with movable chairs that can be set up differently for each. With some advance preparation by a small planning committee plus coaching of designated readers immediately before the service, a group of six to fifty people can enact each service smoothly without rehearsal or elaborate printed programs.

Boldface type indicates material to be spoken aloud. Materials needed by every worshiper have been collected onto handout sheets, at the end of the Appendix, for easy duplicating.

Worshiping God in the PHALLIC Style

Set up the room to reflect the hierarchical emphasis of the phallic mode. Arrange the chairs in rows, all facing toward the front of the room, where a wooden cross ringed by a jeweled crown is to be erected as a focus for worship. It is to be lifted high above the worshipers, for as God is above all, so the upward direction is holy and shows honor. In accordance with this principle, a few special chairs are brought forward from the rest as places of honor for those chosen to represent Elders/Deacons.

DESIGNATE THESE ROLES:
(Note that as used here such words as *Priest* or *Deacon* signify merely functional roles to be played, not the participation of bonafide ecclesiastical officers of any denomination.)

> *Priest*—Wearing clerical robes as sign of divinely granted authority; elevated by standing on a stepstool.

> *Elders/Deacons*—Designate one to read Scripture (reproduced from these pages) and a second to lead singing. Might wear choir robes or liturgical stoles or chest ribbons as signifiers of their special status, since hierarchical ranking is important in the phallic system.

> *Standard-bearer*—Carries and holds up before the congregation the focal point for worship: a cross with a beautiful jeweled crown. This might either be a three-to-five-foot wooden cross with a gold-foil paper crown, or a large banner or poster with the same design.

GENERAL GUIDELINES FOR ALL

> **Remember that upward is holy and honored; God is above all. We kneel in his presence to emphasize our smallness, his greatness. Christ is recognized as King, reigning in glory over all creation. Always stand to sing, kneel to pray.**

When all is ready, a procession of the honorary dignitaries carries the cross to its place of honor. If desired, recorded trumpet fanfares, such as "The Grand March" from Verdi's *Aida*, would be appropriate accompaniment. The *Standard-bearer* lifts the crowned cross above the congregation.

The *Priest*, in robes signifying the dignity and authority of his office, stands on a stepstool and begins the service with the words:

> **Let us worship Almighty God.**

ALL STAND and look upward in adoration at the crowned cross, singing together this HYMN. (For music refer to LYONS 10.10.11.11., found in most hymnals.)

O Worship the King, All Glorious Above
Words by Robert Grant, 1779-1838, altered

> 1. O worship the King, all glorious above,
> O gratefully sing his power and his love;
> Our Shield and Defender, the Ancient of Days,
> Pavilioned in splendor, and girded with praise.

2. O tell of his might, O sing of his grace,
   Whose robe is the light; whose canopy, space.
   The earth with its riches of wonders untold,
   His almighty power has founded of old.

3. O worship the King, all glorious above,
   O gratefully sing his power and his love;
   Our Shield and Defender, the Ancient of Days,
   Pavilioned in splendor, and girded with praise.

ALL ARE SEATED.

Elder/Deacon stands and reads SCRIPTURE:

This is the word of the Lord through Paul, foremost Apostle:

Fight the good fight of the faith and win for yourself the eternal life to which you were called when you made your confession and spoke up for the truth in front of many witnesses. Now, before God, the source of all life and before Jesus Christ, who spoke up as a witness for the truth in front of Pontius Pilate, I put to you the duty of doing all that you have been told, with no faults or failures, until the appearing of our Lord Jesus Christ, who at the due time will be revealed by God, the blessed and only Ruler of all, the King of kings and Lord of lords, who alone is immortal, whose home is in inaccessible light, whom no man has seen and no man is able to see: to him be honor and everlasting power! Amen.
   1 Tim. 6:12-16, JB

ALL KNEEL when the *Priest* says:

Let us pray . . .

Praised be Thou, O Lord our God, King of the Universe!
   We kneel before you
      awed by your glory and power and wisdom.
We can scarcely believe that you invite us into your presence.
   We thank you and praise you that you care about us
      and have made us, of all your creatures,
         "a little lower than the angels."
      Help us be worthy of your trust.
   Fill us with passion for your holy purposes.
Set our hearts afire with commitment to your Kingdom,
   that we might go forth to serve with gladness. Amen.

After the prayer, everyone *STANDS* for the BENEDICTION and to sing together the closing HYMN (found in most hymnals):

Onward, Christian Soldiers !

Worshiping God in the GESTATIVE Style

Set up the room to reflect the enclosing circularity of the womb. Arrange chairs in a circle with a small, low table at center holding a specially prepared BOWL as symbolic focal point.

A very large, deep bowl is either painted black inside or lined with a black scarf. Encircle the outside with a long strip of white poster cardboard cut to fit, with modified words of the Doxology lettered around it three times so it can be read easily from all sides:

ONE GOD FROM WHOM ALL BLESSINGS FLOW
PRAISE GOD ALL CREATURES HERE BELOW.
PRAISE GOD ABOVE YE HEAVENLY HOST.
CREATOR, CHRIST, AND HOLY GHOST. AMEN.

In center of bowl place circle of black paper with a copy of this design centered on it:

HAVE READY AT HAND

For *each dozen* worshipers: an apple, paring knife, and napkin on a plate or tray to pass around circle.

DESIGNATE SIX PEOPLE as *Aides:*
- One to call the group to worship; later, to begin Apple Rite
- Three to read Scriptures reprinted from this book
- One to start hymns
- One to read prayer, and later to suggest closing greetings

GENERAL GUIDELINES FOR ALL

The chairs form a womblike vessel and our focus is on God as the Center. God is within both self and circle; experienced as in the depths rather than the heights. Intervals of silent resting in God are to be savored as well as the more active portions.

All present contribute equally to the circle; none has elevated rank or authority. The *Aides* are distributed evenly around the circle to avoid generating any focal point other than the Center.

When all are *SEATED*, an Aide announces:

We join hands around the circle and silently invite God's presence from the depths. When we have developed a sense of God's care surrounding us like a mother's loving arms, someone will start us singing the first hymn many of us learned as little children, *Jesus Loves Me.*

After several moments of *SILENCE*, musical *Aide* begins HYMN:

Jesus Loves Me
Words by Anna B. Warner, 1895, *altered*

Jesus loves me! This I know, For the Bible tells me so.
Little ones to him belong, Enfolded in his arms so strong.

Yes, Jesus loves me. Yes, Jesus loves me.
Yes, Jesus loves me. The Bible tells me so.

Allow comfortable silence a few moments more, then *DROP HANDS*. One by one *Aides* around circle read SCRIPTURES, allowing brief silences between successive readings.

(PAUSE)
SCRIPTURE 1

[God said,] "I have seen the affliction of my people who are in Egypt, and have heard their cry because of their taskmasters; I know their sufferings, and I have come to deliver them out of the

hand of the Egyptians, and to bring them up out of that land to a
good and broad land flowing with milk and honey..."

Exod. 3:7-8, RSV

(PAUSE)
SCRIPTURE 2

[The people were saying] "God has forsaken me, my God has
forgotten me."

[God responds,] "Can a woman forget the infant at her breast,
or a loving mother the child of her womb? Even these might
forget; yet I will not forget you. Behold, I have graven you on the
palms of my hands."

Isa. 49:14-16, RSV

(PAUSE)
SCRIPTURE 3

"Comfort, comfort my people"—it is the voice of your God.
"Speak tenderly to Jerusalem, and tell her this, that her term of
bondage is ended, that her iniquity is pardoned..."

Behold your God! He*/she will feed his/her flock like a shepherd; he/she will gather the lambs in his/her arms; he/she will
carry them in his/her bosom, and gently lead those that are with
young.

Isa. 2:1-2, 11, RSV

*If desired, substitute feminine pronouns.

All Aides *STAND* and move closer to center, inviting rest to follow so that
the design at center of bowl can be seen by all.

An *Aide* reads the PRAYER:

As we pray now, focus all attention into the depths, knowing that
God is there...

Gracious and loving One,
help us to know your presence at the center of things:
both in the deeps of our own souls
and within the circles we generate
whenever we gather face to face and side by side.
Help us to know that you are both
the invisible Center holding all things together
and the surrounding circumference,
embracing us securely.
We turn to you as to a good Mother
who tenderly cares for us:
welcoming us,
actively drawing us to yourself,
embracing and enclosing us
in the safe haven of your loving arms.

**We are your little children.
You nurture and nourish us.
All blessings flow from you
as flows milk to the suckling babe.**

**Now in the silence we ask that you bring to awareness of each one
a specific way in which we have experienced your nurturing care
flowing to us during this past week. Hear us, as we name these to
ourselves.**

(PAUSE AWHILE)

**Within the stillness and safety of this moment, let each one of us
bring to mind a specific burden or problem—and when we have it
in mind, visualize placing it in the bowl at the center. Take time
to do this, and as you finish, quietly say "Amen" aloud and be
seated.**

After all are *SEATED*, an *Aide* explains the APPLE RITE and begins it.

**We can enact for one another the nurturing care of God by offering
each other a slice of this token of God's bounteous fruitfulness.**
(CUT APPLE IN HALF.) **As the tray passes to you, cut off a slice and give
it to the person on your left; then pass the tray on to the right, where
that person will cut a slice and serve you; and so on. We serve one
another in the name of God, who provides every good thing.**

*(SERVE THE PERSON TO YOUR LEFT AND BEGIN PASSING APPLE TRAY TO RIGHT,
RECEIVING OWN PORTION FROM NEXT PERSON AND EATING IMMEDIATELY.
Note: If the group is larger than twelve, begin TWO apples at opposite sides of circle.)*

**As we do this for one another, let's sing in praise of God from
whom all blessings flow, using the words printed around the
bowl at the center.** *(MAY BE SUNG REPEATEDLY UNTIL ALL HAVE
BEEN SERVED.)*

When all have received, an *Aide* starts the group singing last HYMN. (For
music refer to "We Plow the Fields," WIR PFLUGEN 7.6.7.6.D., in any hymnal.)

All Good Gifts Around Us

Words by Matthias Claudius, 1740-1815
Trans. by Jane M. Campbell, 1817-1878
Modified by Genia Pauli Haddon

1. We plow the fields and scatter the good seed on the land,
   But it is fed and watered by God's all-loving hand.
   Who sends the snows in winter, the warmth to swell the grain,
   The breezes and the sunshine and soft, refreshing rain.

   REFRAIN:
   All good gifts around us, Show God's hand everywhere.
   We thank thee, God; We thank thee, God,
   For all thy loving care.

2. God only is the maker of all things near and far;
   Who paints the wayside flower and lights the evening star.
   All life is in good keeping. By God the birds are fed.
   Much more to us, like children, is given daily bread.

3. We thank thee then, great Giver, for all things bright and good,
   The seed-time and the harvest, our life, our health, our food.
   Accept the gifts we offer, for all thy love imparts,
   And what thou most desirest, our humble, thankful hearts.

An *Aide* suggests that the group close by GREETING one another in Christian love, with handshakes, hugs, or whatever seems authentic between each two people.

Worshiping God in the TESTICULAR Style

Set up the room with four equal lines of chairs arranged to form a closed square, as in the diagram at the right. The ends of each line have the chair reversed, as place holders at the corners.

On the floor in the center, place a ring of clean fist-sized ROCKS, several more than the number of worshipers. In the very center, place either a GEODE, cut side down, or a SPLIT ROCK fitted together as though whole.

DESIGNATE FOUR TO SIX PEOPLE as *Anchors*:
- Two to read Scriptures.
- Several to learn the sung prayer in advance, perhaps even tape-recording it as a resource for introducing it to the group.
- One to invite all to choose rocks; later, to lift the central rock and speak the words.
- One to signal end of repeating sung prayer (after ten to fifteen minutes) by singing "Amen"; and later to start the closing hymn.

GENERAL GUIDELINES FOR ALL

The testicular qualities are solidity and steadfastness, constancy rather than change. God is the same yesterday, today, and forever.

Worship in this mode is through reverent repetition. The main part of the service will be a Sung Prayer, repeated many, many times.

When all are *SEATED*, begin with this UNISON READING:

Let the words of my mouth
and the meditation of my heart
be acceptable in thy sight,
O God, my Rock and my Redeemer.

For God alone my soul waits in silence
from him comes my salvation.
He is my only Rock and salvation.

Ps. 19:14 and 64:1-2, RSV

Anchors read SCRIPTURES in sequence:

SCRIPTURE 1

My heart exults in Yahweh,...
for I rejoice in your power of saving.
There is none as holy as Yahweh,
(indeed, there is no one but you)
no rock like our God.

I Sam. 2:1-2

SCRIPTURE 2

[Jesus said,] "Every one then who hears these words of mine and does them will be like a wise man who built his house upon the rock; and the rain fell and the floods came, and the winds blew and beat upon that house, but it did not fall, because it had been founded on the rock. And every one who hears these words of mine and does not do them will be like a foolish man who built his house upon the sand; and the rain fell, and the floods came, and the winds blew and beat against that house, and it fell; and great was the fall of it.

Matt. 7:24-27, RSV

An *Anchor* invites all to choose a rock from the center to hold while SINGING THE PRAYER. Explains how to join in singing it:

Several of us have learned a repeating prayer-song. The tune is very simple and pitched low enough to be in your regular speaking range. Follow the tune, but use your speaking voice

rather than singing in the usual sense. As you sing along, notice where your voice is coming from—your mouth, your throat, chest, belly, etc. Holding your stone in both hands, lift it to the level at which your voice is originating. As the prayer continues, allow your voice to come from deeper and deeper, always holding the stone at the corresponding level as it changes, up or down. At first you may need to read the words; allow your eyes to close as soon as you are comfortable singing along from memory. Several of us who have already learned this prayer will begin, and the rest join in as soon as you get the gist. We'll sing for about fifteen minutes—quite a long time! I will signal when it's time to stop, by singing "Amen" instead of beginning another round. I'll repeat the "Amen" twice more, for you to sing it with me as our communal ending.

SUNG PRAYER (words and music on page 235), repeated for about fifteen minutes: "O-o-o-o my God. Only One. Spiritus Sanctus."

Allow a few moments of *SILENCE* after completing the sung prayer. Then *Anchor* asks that all return their stones to the center.

When all are *SEATED* again, *Anchor* lifts special rock from the very center, either showing to all the cut side of geode or opening the split rick, saying:

> **God says:**   **"Cleave the Stone and thou shalt find me.**
> **Lift the Rock and there am I."**

Musical *Anchor* begins closing HYMN. (For music refer to AUSTRIAN HYMN 8.7.8.7.D., found in most hymnals.)

Glorious Things of Thee are Spoken

Words by John Newton, 1725-1807, altered

Glorious things of thee are spoken, Zion, city of our God;
One whose word cannot be broken formed thee for a blest abode.
On the Rock of Ages founded, what can shake thy sure repose?
With salvation's walls surrounded, rest secure from all thy foes.

As BENEDICTION, again repeat *IN UNISON:*

> **Let the words of my mouth**
> **and the meditation of my heart**
> **be acceptable in thy sight,**
> **O God, my Rock and my Redeemer.**

Worshiping God in the EXERTIVE WOMB Style

Set up the room in circular, womblike configuration, this time with chairs placed around a large table. Use a round table if available. (Use more than one setup if group is to be large.)

In the center of the table, place a bowl filled with Easter grass, in which are egg-shaped lumps of Play-Doh in many colors:

Preparing this centerpiece takes some time. Buy several packages of Play-Doh in assorted colors. Blend as directed on package to make many beautiful colors. Shape like eggs and wrap smoothly in plastic film. Have more eggs than worshipers, so everyone has a choice of colors.

DESIGNATE four to five *Initiators:*
- Two or three to read Scripture
- One to initiate singing of hymns
- One to read prayer

GENERAL GUIDELINES FOR ALL

The exertive womb represents creative and recreative push; destruction in the service of transformation; breaking open of the old to reveal the new; being surprised by God; and also knowing that it is a fearful thing to fall into the hands of the living God.

When all are *SEATED* around the table, an *Initiator* reads the first SCRIPTURE:

"I am GOD, your Holy One, the Creator of Israel...."
Thus says the One who makes a way in the sea, a path in the mighty waters, who brings forth... "Remember not the former things, nor consider the things of old. Behold, I am doing a new thing; now it springs forth—do you not perceive it?"
Isa. 43:15-19, RSV

Another *Initiator* invites each to *CHOOSE* an egg:

Choose an egg from the bowl, picking one in a color you especially like at the moment.

Unwrap it and knead it a bit to soften up the dough. . . *(Let all begin handling the dough.)* **Go ahead and squish it into strange shapes.**

(WAIT AWHILE)

Now STOP! Don't change the shape of your dough! Pass it on carefully to the person at your left.

Look at the new piece of dough you receive. What does it resemble? Can you discern the shape of something almost there, just waiting for you to bring it into being? Is it meant to be an animal, or a person, or a food, or what else? Go ahead and finish

the new creation that has been handed to you. Don't worry about it being a masterpiece; shape it just enough to make its nature visible to others. Then place it at the center of the table. *(There will probably be much laughter and delight. Allow some time for sharing.)*

Another *Initiator* reads SCRIPTURES:

As I read the Easter story from the gospels according to Matthew and Luke, listen for exertive-womb imagery—the darkly divine power, tomb-womb meanings, things breaking open, surprise after surprise from God:

Now from the sixth hour there was darkness over all the land until the ninth hour. And about the ninth hour Jesus cried with a loud voice, "Eli, Eli, lama sabachthani?" that is, "My God, my God, why hast thou forsaken me?" And some of the bystanders hearing it said, "This man is calling Elijah." And one of them at once ran and took a sponge, filled it with vinegar, and put it on a reed, and gave it to him to drink. But the others said, "Wait, let us see whether Elijah will come to save him." And Jesus cried again with a loud voice and yielded up his spirit.

And behold, the curtain of the temple was torn in two, from top to bottom; and the earth shook, and the rocks were split; the tombs also were opened, and many bodies of the saints who had fallen asleep were raised, and coming out of the tombs after his resurrection they went into the holy city and appeared to many. When the centurion and those who were with him, keeping watch over Jesus, saw the earthquake and what took place, they were filled with awe, and said, "Truly this was the Son of God!"

Now there was a man named Joseph from the Jewish town of Arimathea. He was a member of the council, a good and righteous man, who had not consented to their purpose and deed, and he was looking for the kingdom of God. This man went to Pilate and asked for the body of Jesus. Then he took it down and wrapped it in a linen shroud, and laid him in a rock-hewn tomb, where no one had ever yet been laid. It was the day of Preparation, and the sabbath was beginning. The women who had come with him from Galilee followed, and saw the tomb, and how his body was laid; then they returned, and prepared spices and ointments.

On the sabbath they rested according to the commandment. But on the first day of the week, at early dawn, they went to the tomb, taking the spices which they had prepared. And they found the stone rolled away from the tomb, but when they went in they did not find the body. While they were perplexed about this behold, two men stood by them in dazzling apparel; and as they were frightened and bowed their faces to the ground, the men said to them, "Why do you seek the living among the dead? Remember how he told you while he was still in Galilee, that the Son of man must be delivered into the hands of sinful men, and be crucified and on the third day rise." And they remembered his words, and returning from the tomb they told all this to the eleven and to all the rest. Now it was Mary Magdalene and Joanna and Mary the mother of James and the other women with them who told this to the apostles; but these words seemed to them an idle tale, and they did not believe them.

That very day two of them were going to a village named Emmaus, about seven miles from Jerusalem, and talking with each other about all these things that had happened. While they were talking and discussing together, Jesus himself drew near and went with them. But their eyes were kept from recognizing him. ...[They went together to an inn for the evening meal.] When he was at table with them, he took the bread and blessed, and broke it, and gave it to them and their eyes were opened and they recognized him; and he vanished out of their sight....And they rose that same hour and returned to Jerusalem; and they found the eleven gathered together and those who were with them, who said, "The Lord has risen indeed and has appeared to Simon!" Then they told what had happened on the road, and how he was known to them in the breaking of the bread.

As they were saying this, Jesus himself stood among them. But they were startled and frightened, and supposed that they saw a spirit. And he said to them, "Why are you troubled, and why do questionings rise in your hearts? See my hands and feet, that it is I myself; handle me, and see; for a spirit has not flesh and bones as you see that I have." And while they still disbelieved for joy, and wondered, he said to them, "Have you anything to eat?"

Matt.27:45-54; Luke 23:50--24:41 RSV, excerpts

Music *Initiator* begins HYMN.
(For music refer to REDHEAD NO.76 7.7.7.7.7.7., found in most hymnals.)

Go to Dark Gethsemane

Words by James Montgomery, 1771-1854
Modified by Genia Pauli Haddon

1. Go to dark Gethsemane, Ye that feel the tempter's power;
   Your Redeemer's conflict see; Watch and pray one bitter hour.
   Turn not from such griefs away. Learn of Jesus Christ to pray.

2. Calvary's mournful mountain climb; See Christ dying on the tree.
   Mark that miracle of time, Turning point of history.
   "It is finished!" hear the cry. Learn of Jesus Christ to die.

An *Initiator* reads the PRAYER:

Please concentrate from your heart as I speak words of prayer on behalf of the group.

O Gracious and Divine One:
We don't like the idea of dying in order to be born.
We find it hard to picture you
as the One who destroys
in order to bring forth a new thing,the one of whom it is said,
"It is a fearful thing to fall into the hands of the living God."
Yet, we know we are unfinished creations
until we bear your divine image fully
in our bodies, our minds, and our spirits.
So we do place ourselves in your hands.
Carry on your creative labor.
Push us toward new life.
Push us—as the womb that has
embraced and shaped and nurtured us
and knows intimately who we are
and how we are to be.
We trust your timing.
We accept the pain and effort of being born.
So push us, gracious One,
into the new life you envision for us.
Surprise us with the new thing you have in mind.
Birth us and re-birth us,
until we are all you need us to be,
and are truly in your image. Amen.

Musical *Initiator* begins closing HYMN. (For music refer to "Come, Ye Faithful, Raise the Strain," ST KEVIN 7.6.7.6.D., found in most hymnals.)

Poured Forth!

Words by Genia Pauli Haddon

1. Sing the joyous heart's true refrain, pouring forth your gladness.
God makes all things new again, birthing joy from sadness;
Resurrecting through the tomb every son and daughter.
Praise we God's eternal Womb, source of living water.

2. "Can we enter a second time the Womb of God our Mother?"
"If ye would be born again," answers Christ, our brother.
Birthing power of God brings forth what is least expected.
Tomb of death is womb of birth: Christ is resurrected!

3. All creation groans in travail, Christ's New Age to enter.
Old foundations and structures fail. Life yearns toward its Center.
Christians, having received new birth, in the Spirit confessing,
Bring that love to all the earth; multiply the blessing.

4. Join the jubilant, free refrain, all life sings with gladness.
   God makes all things new again, birthing joy from sadness.
   Saving from the brink of doom, human civilization.
   Praise we God's eternal Womb, source of new creation.

All join hands and repeat together as BENEDICTION:

> **It is a fearful thing**
> **to fall into the hands of the living God.**
> **Nevertheless, into thy hands**
> **I commit my spirit. Amen.**

Unison Materials for Worship Service 1

ALL STAND and look upward in adoration at the crowned cross, singing together:

O Worship the King, All Glorious Above

Words by Robert Grant, 1779-1838, altered

1. O worship the King, all glorious above,
   O gratefully sing his power and his love;
   Our Shield and Defender, the Ancient of Days,
   Pavilioned in splendor, and girded with praise.

2. O tell of his might, O sing of his grace,
   Whose robe is the light; whose canopy, space.
   The earth with its riches of wonders untold,
   His almighty power has founded of old.

3. O worship the King, all glorious above,
   O gratefully sing his power and his love;
   Our Shield and Defender, the Ancient of Days,
   Pavilioned in splendor, and girded with praise.

ALL ARE SEATED

Onward Christian Soldiers, as in traditional hymnal, first and last verses.

Unison Materials for Worship Service 2

Jesus Loves Me

Words by Anna B. Warner, 1869, altered

Jesus loves me! This I know. For the Bible tells me so.
Little ones to him belong, Enfolded in his arms so strong.
Yes, Jesus loves me. Yes, Jesus loves me.
Yes, Jesus loves me. The Bible tells me so.

All Good Gifts Around Us

Words by Matthias Claudius, 1740-1815
Trans. by Jane M. Campbell, 1817-1878
Modified by Genia Pauli Haddon

1. We plow the fields and scatter the good seed on the land,
   But it is fed and watered by God's all-loving hand.
   Who sends the snows in winter, the warmth to swell
      the grain,
   The breezes and the sunshine and soft, refreshing rain.

   > REFRAIN:
   > All good gifts around us
   > Show God's hand everywhere.
   > We thank thee, God;
   > We thank thee, God,
   > For all thy loving care.

2. God only is the maker of all things near and far;
   Who paints the wayside flower and lights the evening star.
   All life is in good keeping. By God the birds are fed.
   Much more to us, like children, is given daily bread.

3. We thank thee then, great Giver, for all things bright
      and good,
   The seed-time and the harvest, our life, our health, our food.
   Accept the gifts we offer, for all thy love imparts,
   And what thou most desirest, our humble, thankful hearts.

Unison Materials for Worship Service 3

UNISON READING:

Let the words of my mouth
and the meditation of my heart
be acceptable in thy sight,
O God, my Rock and my Redeemer.

For God alone my soul waits in silence
from him comes my salvation.
He is my only Rock and salvation.

Ps. 19:14 and 64:1-2, RSV

SUNG PRAYER, as printed on next page.

HYMN:

Glorious Things of Thee are Spoken

Words by John Newton, 1725-1807, altered

Glorious things of thee are spoken, Zion, city of our God;
One whose word cannot be broken formed thee for a
   blest abode.
On the Rock of Ages founded, what can shake thy sure repose?
With salvation's walls surrounded, rest secure from all thy foes.

UNISON BENEDICTION:

Let the words of my mouth
and the meditation of my heart
be acceptable in thy sight,
O God, my Rock and my Redeemer.

For God alone my soul waits in silence
from him comes my salvation.
He is my only Rock and salvation.

Ps. 19:14 and 64:1-2, RSV

Spiritus Sanctus
A Sung Prayer

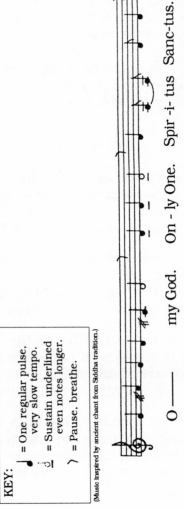

KEY:

♩ = One regular pulse,
very slow tempo.

𝅗𝅥 = Sustain underlined
even notes longer.

⌐ = Pause, breathe.

(Music inspired by ancient chant from Siddha tradition.)

O——— my God.   On - ly One.   Spir -i- tus Sanc-tus.

Keep repeating slowly and with feeling,
using natural speaking tone. (Raise or
lower starting pitch if necessary.)

Unison Materials for Worship Service 4

Go to Dark Gethsemane

Words by James Montgomery, 1771-1854
Modified by Genia Pauli Haddon

Go to dark Gethsemane, Ye that feel the tempter's power;
Your Redeemer's conflict see; Watch and pray one bitter hour.
Turn not from such griefs away. Learn of Jesus Christ to pray.

Calvary's mournful mountain climb; See Christ dying on the tree.
Mark that miracle of time, Turning point of history.
"It is finished!" hear the cry. Learn of Jesus Christ to die.

Poured Forth!

Words by Genia Pauli Haddon

Sing the joyous heart's true refrain, pouring forth your gladness.
God makes all things new again, birthing joy from sadness;
Resurrecting through the tomb ev'ry son and daughter.
Praise we God's eternal Womb, source of living water.

"Can we enter a second time the Womb of God our Mother?"
"If ye would be born again," answers Christ, our brother.
Birthing power of God brings forth what is least expected.
Tomb of death is womb of birth: Christ is resurrected!

All creation groans in travail, Christ's New Age to enter.
Old foundations and structures fail. Life yearns toward its Center.
Christians, having received new birth, in the Spirit confessing,
Bring that love to all the earth; Multiply the blessing.

Join the jubilant, free refrain all life sings with gladness.
God makes all things new again, birthing joy from sadness.
Saving from the brink of doom, human civilization.
Praise we God's eternal Womb, source of new creation.

Stand together in a circle. Place this sheet on floor at your feet so that you can read it without holding it.

All join hands and repeat the following together as BENEDICTION:

It is a fearful thing to fall into the hands of the living God.

Nevertheless, into thy hands I commit my spirit. Amen.

Appendix B ❦ *A Sample Living Will*[1]

Directions for My Care

To my family, physician, clergy, attorney, or medical facility:

I _____, want to participate in my own medical care as long as I am able. To this end, I instruct all those responsible for my care and knowledgeable of my condition to be completely honest with me in the event of a serious and possibly terminal illness, that I may make my own decisions and preparations as much as possible. I recognize that an accident or illness may someday make me unable to do so. Should this come to be the case, this document is intended to direct those who make choices on my behalf. I have prepared it while in good health and spirits. Even if this document be not binding legally, I implore those who care for me to honor its intent. If these instructions create a conflict with the desires of my relatives, or with hospital policies or with the principles of those providing my care, I ask that my instructions prevail.

I wish to live a full and long life, but not at all costs. If I have lost the ability to interact with others and have no reasonable chance of regaining this ability, or if my suffering is intense and irreversible, I do not want to have my life prolonged. I would then ask not be be subjected to surgery or resuscitation. Nor would I then wish to have life support from mechanical ventilators, intensive care services, or other life prolonging procedures, including the administration of anti-cancer chemicals or radiation, antibiotics, and blood products. I would wish, rather, to have care which gives comfort and support, which facilitates my interaction with others to the extent that this is possible, and which brings peace. If at all possible, I would choose to spend my last days at home, surrounded by those I love.

In order to carry out these instructions
and to interpret them, I authorize _____
to accept, plan, and refuse treatment on my behalf in cooperation with attending physicians and health personnel. This person knows how I value the experience of living, and how I would weigh incompetence, suffering, and dying. Should it be impossible to reach this person, I authorize the following persons to make such choices for me:

_____   _____

I have discussed my desires concerning terminal care with them, and I trust their judgment on my behalf.

Date_____   Signed_____

Witnesses_____   _____

Notes

Chapter One
Departing from the Patriarchal Story

1. Merlin Stone, *When God Was a Woman* (New York: Dial Press, 1976).

2. Ibid., p. 11.

3. Carolyn G. Heilbrun, *Reinventing Womanhood* (New York: Norton, 1979), p. 29: "In the past those women who have made their way successfully into the male-dominated worlds of business, the arts, or the professions, have done so as honorary men, neither admiring nor bonding with other women, offering no encouragement to those who might come after them,...sacrificing their womanhood."

4. As uncommon as it is for individual women to escape this scenario, it is much less likely for men to do so. Despite eventual benefits to men from moving beyond patriarchal patterns, as members of the dominant cultural group they tend to have a stake in maintaining the status quo, because the present system is structured in ways that satisfy certain of their basic needs and tendencies. This makes the "wild man" groups as pioneered by Robert Bly especially significant, for here we find men seeking to claim as their own emotional attributes traditionally considered unmasculine.

5. Archetypes are unlearned, typical patterns of likely behavior in response to common human experiences. These basic patterns of universal human behavior are general templates or forms, which are fleshed out in various ways in actual lives and situations, expressing themselves as emotions, mental imagery, thought processes, or actions. "Human nature" is our species' psychological makeup, consisting of all the archetypal patterns we have in common as human beings. Jung himself seemed to leave open the question of whether or not the archetypes evolve, although he tended to emphasize their stability and longevity. In comparing the archetypal basis of the psyche to the genetic basis of the body, he suggested that at bottom both rest on unchanging substrates. Just as certain proteins and DNA molecules continue as the single basis for bodily life, so it is likely that the most basic foundation of the psyche remains unchanged. On the other hand, as Jung pointed out in *Psychology and Religion: East and West (Collected Works*, 12:149n) just as the manifestations of that basic biological blueprint change over the course of time in the evolution of the species, so we can expect a similar degree of evolution of the archetypes.

6. Jung did study ancient materials in an effort to get beyond conventional ideals about masculinity and femininity. Much of this material bore the patriarchal stamp, and all of it was viewed with the inevitable bias of a Victorian patriarch. The result was that Jung's ideas of masculinity and femininity did not depart significantly from the prevailing stereotypes, although he did develop his anima/animus theory as a way of escaping the confines of the stereotypes.

239

7. In actual practice the tendency has been to look at man's life and experience to learn about masculinity, and man's unconscious anima to learn about femininity.

8. The derivative status of his animus concept is easily documented by a survey of the *General Index* to Jung's *Collected Works*, compiled by Barbara Forryan and Janet M. Glover (Princeton, NJ: Bollingen/Princeton University Press, 1979), pp. 51-54, 75-76. More than three times as many column-inches are devoted to the anima as to the animus. By actual measurement, 32.5 centimeters of column space are devoted to the animus as a feature of women's psyches. (If generic references to animus as "spirit" are included, the total is 33 centimeters.) The listing of references to the anima as a feature of men's psyches fills 101 centimeters. (If generic references to anima as "soul" are included, the total swells to 130 centimeters.) The ratio is thus either one-to-three or one-to-four, depending on whether generic references are included. Recently Jungians have themselves been questioning this simple reversal, pointing out that women's psychology is neither derived from nor a direct mirror image of masculine psychology. In fact, some Jungian analysts and authors are calling into question the whole anima/animus theory and working to redefine masculinity and femininity in other ways. See, e.g., Jean Shinoda Bolen, *Goddesses in Everywoman: A New Psychology of Women* (San Francisco: Harper & Row, 1984); Mary Ann Matoon and Jennette Jones, "Is the Animus Obsolete?" *Quadrant* 20, no. 1 (Fall 1987):5-21; and Edward C. Whitmont, "Reassessing Femininity and Masculinity: A Critique of Some Traditional Assumptions," *Quadrant* 13, no. 2 (Fall 1980):109-22.

9. See Carol Gilligan, *In a Different Voice: Psychological Theory and Women's Development* (Cambridge, MA: Harvard University Press, 1982).

10. In reality, of course, it is not possible to escape to an Archimedean point. As I make clear in Chapter 6, even the "objective facts" of anatomy and physiology are not objective after all, but have been discovered and defined by researchers whose world view may have excluded some phenomena from consideration.

11. Charlene Spretnak, *Lost Goddesses of Early Greece: A Collection of Pre-Hellenic Myths* (Boston: Beacon Press, 1989), pp. 31-37.

12. See Bolen, *Goddesses in Everywoman.*

13. For example, Marija Gimbutas, Sylvia Perrera, Charlene Spretnak, Merlin Stone, and Beverley Zabriskie.

14. See Jean Baker Miller, *Toward a New Psychology of Women* (Boston: Beacon Press, 1976), p. 70. She cites Robert J. Stoller, *Sex and Gender* (New York: Science House, 1968); "Facts and Fancies: An Examination of Freud's Concept of Bisexuality," in Jean Strouse, ed., *Women and Psychoanalysis* (New York: Grossman, 1974), pp. 343-62; and J. Money and A. Ehrhardt, *Man and Woman, Boy and Girl* (Baltimore, MD: Johns Hopkins University Press, 1973).

Chapter Two
Letting the Body be your Guide

1. Although I have chosen the word *testicular* to designate the large anatomical feature commonly known as "the balls," that configuration actually includes,

in addition to the testicle proper, the epididymus and other associated structures.

2. The breasts, although not strictly genital organs, are considered metaphorically in Chapter 13.

3. Richard Wilhelm, in his "Introduction" to the *I Ching or Book of Changes* (Princeton, NJ: Princeton University Press, 1967), p. lvi.

4. I have chosen to use the word *phallus* to name the yang-masculine organ. This term differs from the simple anatomical designation, *penis*, in that it signifies specifically the erect organ, especially as an object of veneration or symbolic significance. There are no equivalently dignified names for the testicles, nor for the female genitals. (Not surprising, since we do live in a world oriented to give greatest honor to yang-masculinity.) For the yin-masculine gonad the choice is between various slang terms—some of which are picturesque, but all somewhat crude—and the formal anatomical nomenclature, *testicle*. I have chosen the latter. Instead of either slang (all of which has a derogatory flavor) or the anatomical, clinical-sounding *uterus*, I have chosen the more old-fashioned but respectable word *womb*.

Chapter Three
Body Clues to Fuller Manhood

1. The prevailing patriarchal system, with its characteristic style of consciousness, requires clear differentiation of masculine from feminine, self from other. In such a system, even though the contents of each gender formula might change, the role of the contrasexual "other" will remain much as Jung described: whatever is typically human, but not typically one's own gender, will cohere as a subpersonality corresponding to the other gender. Therefore, in developing a body-based model of masculinity and femininity, I continue to speak of animus and anima, although redefining the features of each. As humankind moves out of the patriarchal pattern, with its system of clear opposites, new ways of imaging and actualizing the interplay of masculine and feminine within the psyche will emerge.

2. Edward F. Edinger, *Ego and Archetype: Individuation and the Religious Function of the Psyche* (New York: Putnam, 1972), pp. 62-69.

3. By the Rev. Dr. Kenneth W. Taylor, Associate Conference Minister of the Connecticut Conference, United Church of Christ. See also his "Family and Sex—A Christian Refocusing," *Family Album* (United Church Board for Homeland Ministries, 1984).

4. Identities of all individuals are disguised, and in some instance composite descriptions combine material from two or more people.

5. See "What 100,000 Women Told Ann Landers," *Family Circle* (June 11, 1985).

6. Barbara G. Walker, *The Woman's Encyclopedia of Myths and Secrets* (San Francisco: Harper & Roe, 1983), p. 541. In *Hebrew Myths: The Book of Genesis* (Garden City, NY: Doubleday & Co., 1963), Robert Graves and Raphael Patai write: "It is characteristic of civilizations where women are treated as chattels that they must adopt the

recumbent position during intercourse, which Lilith refused....Melanesian girls ridicule what they call 'the missionary position,' which demands that they lie passive and recumbent." (pp.68-69).

7. Allen Edwardes, *The Jewel in the Lotus: A Historical Survey of the Sexual Culture of the East* (New York: Doubleday, 1959), p. 7. Variants of this Islamic tradition are: "Men are ruined when they place women above them." (Sayyid Ahmad al-Hashimi, *Mukhtar al-Ahadith al-Nabawiyah* [Cairo, undated], p. 155); and "The Prophet cursed the femininity in men and the masculinity in women" (*Rasa'il al-Jahiz*, ed. Harun [Cairo, 1965], 2:101).

8. A traditional structural linguist might disagree that *testis* and *testum* are related in any way but phonetically. However, even in the event that the two could be proved not to share a common historical derivation, the nascent science of archetypal linguistics offers a rationale for seeking to discern "the semantic relationship between various meanings that have become attached to one phonetic pattern." Paul Kugler, *The Alchemy of Discourse: An Archetypal Approach to Language* (Lewisburg, PA: Bucknell University Press, 1982), as quoted in the book review by Richard W. Thurn in *Quadrant* 16, no. 2 (Fall 1983).

9. So far as is known, Aesop's fables date from about 600 B.C.E. "The Hare and the Tortoise," *Aesop's Fables*, transl. V.S. Vernon (New York: Avenel Books, 1912), pp. 92-95.

10. Prior to the differentiation of the yin-masculine from the feminine (upon which it tends to be projected), the tortoise is associated with the "terrible mother," the moon, and the earth. (See Erich Neumann, *The Great Mother: An Analysis of the Archetype*, (Princeton, NJ: Bollingen/Princeton University Press, 1963), pp. 164, 180, 235, 310, 334-45.) Yet there are hints of its authentic connection with the masculine. The infant Hermes made a lyre from the shell of a tortoise fitted with string. He gave this to his brother Apollo, who in exchange gave him "the [phallic] gold wishing rod of good luck." Katherine A. Raleigh, *The Gods of Olympos*, trans. and ed. from the twentieth edition of A.H. Petiscus (London: T. Fisher Unwin, 1892), p. 43.

Chapter Four
Womanhood Delivered

1. As retold by Barbara Black Koltuv, "Lilith," *Quadrant* 16, no. 1 (Spring 1983):63-86.

2. Walker, *Woman's Encyclopedia*, "Lilith."

3. Patricia Monaghan, *The Book of Goddesses and Heroines* (New York: E.P. Dutton, 1981), "Lilith."

4. *Zohar I*, 16b-17b, cited by Koltuv, "Lilith," p. 59.

5. Monaghan, "Lilith."

6. Gilligan's recent research (*Different Voice*) on the distinct moral perspectives of males and females corroborates this image.

7. "The Frog-King, or Iron Henry," *The Complete Grimm's Fairy Tales* (New York: Random House, 1972).

8. This resolution is couched in terms of patriarchal values. The masculine ideal is still a "king," whom the maiden will wed. The reunion of opposites in the male-female *coniunctio* is still the symbol of ultimate fulfillment.

9. Active Imagination involves allowing a fantasy to unfold to the mind's eye. It differs from daydreaming in two ways. First, an active effort is exerted to suspend censoring and to receive "whatever comes," even if it is nonsensical or disturbing by ego standards. Second, the conscious mind enters into active dialogue with the fantasy, perhaps asking questions, and then seeing how the fantasy responds.

10. "Mother Holle," *Grimm's*. The development of the exertive womb is represented by the maiden taking bread from the oven when done, shaking apples from the tree when ripe, industriously shaking things out, and taking initiative to move to the next stage of the journey: all vigorous, contextually appropriate initiative, at just the right time.

11. But note that, through her interviews with women, Gilligan (*Different Voice*) has uncovered the underlying *positive* meaning of *web*, from the woman's point of view.

12. "If she pursues the [yang] virtues...she is to be avoided with fear and loathing as a mutant, a denier of [her feminine] destiny. If she fails to take up these values and pursues others [exclusively yin]—she is weak, vacuous, and superficial." Linda Singer, "Nietzschean Mythologies: The Inversion of Value and the War Against Woman," *Soundings: An Interdisciplinary Journal* 66 no. 3 (Fall 1983):283.

Chapter Five
Sorting Religious Practices

1. I write as a retired Christian minister whose denominational home is the United Church of Christ, through its New England Congregational heritage.

2. From "Be Thou My Vision"; words from the ancient Irish, transl. Mary E. Byrne (1880-1931), versified by Eleanor H. Holl (1860-1935).

3. From "Abide with Me"; words by Henry F. Lyte (1793-1847).

4. From "Praise to the Lord, the Almighty"; words by Joachim Heander (1650-1680), transl. Catherine Winkworth (1827-1878).

5. "Praise My Soul the King of Heaven" modified from original verses by Henry F. Lyte (1793-1847), based on Psalm 103.

6. For two dozen hymns rewritten inclusively, see Genia Pauli Haddon, *One God, Many Names: Praise Him! Praise Her!* (Scotland, CT: Plus Publications, 1993). Ordering information at back of this book.

7. Using the four gender metaphors, I analyzed the imagery in hymns used during January and February in the regular worship services of three congregations: a large, metropolitan UCC-Congregational church; an Episcopal church in a rural setting; a Methodist church in a suburban community. I chose those eight weeks to avoid such

seasonal emphases as Advent and Easter, so that hymns would have been freely selected from the full range available to each congregation. A definite pattern emerged in common across the three (rounded to nearest whole percent):

	Phallic	Gestative	Testicular	Exertive
UCC	60%	17%	18%	5%
Episcopal	63	18	12	5
Methodist	65	16	16	4

Although this is an informal survey, based on my subjective evaluation of each hymn and without sophisticated controls, it indicates both the presence of all four gender motifs within actual church usage, and also the predominance of the phallic mode.

8. The Doxology is a piece of liturgical music sung regularly by many Protestant and Catholic congregations.

9. This version was introduced to the Connecticut Conference Office by Amy Beveridge, of the secretarial staff at that time. The recently published *Book of Worship* (New York: United Church of Christ Office for Church Life and Leadership, 1986), which is recommended for use in UCC churches nationwide, offers both the traditional Doxology and this alternative:

> Praise God from whom all blessings flow;
> Praise Christ the Word in flesh born low;
> Praise Holy Spirit evermore;
> One God, Triune, whom we adore.

Although it is significant that such material is generated at the national level, the reality is that it may be decades before local congregations of the denomination actually begin using this Doxology in Sunday services. Unlike the Episcopal Book of Common Prayer or the Methodist Worship Book, for example, this book of liturgy is *recommended* rather than mandated. Until it enters the actual worship life of the people it has no real impact.

Chapter Six
Genes, Embryos, and the Turning of the Ages

1. Jolande Jacobi, *The Psychology of C.G. Jung* (New Haven, CT: Yale University Press, 1968), p. 10; also C.G. Jung. *Man and His Symbols* (Garden City, NY: Doubleday, 1964), p. 67.

2. Similarities and differences between physical and psychological evolution are worth noting. *Physical* inheritance and evolution is through genes, which are very stable but sometimes undergo random mutation as a result of various physical factors. Physical evolution is said to come about by natural selection of beneficial changes from among all those occurring. Those changes that do not increase chances of survival and procreation literally die out, whereas those that promote survival and procreation are passed on to succeeding generations, eventually to become specieswide traits. According to this theory, characteristics acquired during the lifetime of a parent cannot be passed on to the offspring, because an individual's experience has no effect on the genes. *Psychologically*, however, such experience is precisely the issue. Although thoughts and ideas *about* the archetypes are not

heritable, *new human experiences* resulting from the interplay of archetype and consciousness in all likelihood are.

3. Rupert Sheldrake, *A New Science of Life: The Hypothesis of Formative Causation* (Tarcher,
1981); and a series of four articles on "Morphic Resonance and the Collective Unconscious"
in *Psychological Perspectives* beginning with 18, no. 1 (Spring 1987):1-25.

4. Jean Shinoda Bolen, "Healing the Psyche," *Psychological Perspectives* 18, no. 1 (Spring
1987):26-27. Having focused on the cumulative experience of those who actively
envision world peace, she continues (p. 36), "In our prayer, meditation, or contemplating
we are truly constellating this new archetype....By contributing to this change, we may
contribute to a shift in the outcome of the history of humankind."

5. In the West, consciousness is defined as whatever the waking ego is aware of; all else
is considered *unconscious*. In contrast, in yogic thought consciousness is transpersonal
and transcendental, far exceeding the grasp of ego knowledge.

6. This gardening technique is based on principles described by Derald G. Langham,
Circle Gardening (Old Greenwich, CT: Devin-Adair, 1978). Only the circles themselves
(not the walkways) are spaded, cultivated, fertilized, weeded, watered—reducing labor.
Benefits include pleasant appearance, efficient watering, even distribution of sunlight,
fewer weeds, convenient planting of successive crops, ready rotation of crops year to
year, ease of harvesting.

7. Angela Taylor, *Practical Human Cytogenetics* (London: Baillier Tindall, 1974), p. 14. Until
1956, it was thought that the human chromosome number was forty-eight. In that year,
refined techniques permitted accurate counting, establishing that there are twenty-three
pairs of human chromosomes. The chromosomes, each with its characteristic pattern of
light and dark bands, can be seen under a highpower microscope. Even at such
magnifications individual genes are too small to be physically seen. The locations and
degrees of variation of many genes have been determined indirectly through sophisticated
technique and procedures. Chromosomes are literally "colorful bodies," so named because
when cells are treated with a certain dyes for microscope study these parts stain most vividly.

8. This describes the most fundamental method of reproduction. Under certain circumstances even such simple organisms as bacteria and algae engage in *conjugation*, which
entails the temporary merging of pairs and swapping of chromosomes.

9. In all mammals and many other animal and plants, it is the Y chromosome that
determines sex. In other organisms different mechanisms are responsible. Eeva
Therman, *Human Chromosomes: Structure, Behavior, Effects* (New York: Springer-Verlag,
1980), p. 113.

10. In some species, including frogs and rabbits, parthenogenesis (literally, "virgin births")
can be induced under certain conditions. In species with an XX/XY pattern of sex
determination, because there is no sperm involved to introduce the deviant Y
chromosome, all such offspring will be female—again emphasizing the female as the
basic sex, the male as differentiated from it.

11. Jean D. Wilson, James E. Griffin, and Fredrick W. George, "The Mechanism of
Phenotypic Sex Differentiation," *Arthritis and Rheumatism* 22, no. 11 (1979):1275; and
Milo Herrick Spaulding, "The Development of the External Genitalia in the Human
Embryo," *Contributions to Embryology* 13, no 61 (1921):72.

12. Ronan O'Rahilly, "The Timing of Sequence of Events in the Development of the Human Reproductive System During the Embryonic Period Proper," *Anatomy and Embryology* 166, no. 2 (1983):258.

13. Wilson, "Phenotypic Differentiation," p. 1275.

14. Ibid., p. 1279; also R.V. Short, "Sex Determination and Differentiation," *British Medical Bulletin* 35, no. 2 (May 1979):121. Note that without any hormones a female-appearing body develops, not a completely normal female.

15. Esther Greisheimer, *Anatomy and Physiology* (Philadelphia: Lippincott, 1955), p. 793. Three sets of embryonic kidneys develop in succession. The wolffian ducts function for the first four weeks. A second set connects to the wolffian ducts and functions the fifth through ninth weeks. This is replaced by the final kidney.

16. Wilson, "Phenotypic Differentiation," p. 1277.

17. O'Rahilly, "Timing," p. 253, quoting W. Felix, "The Development of the Urogential Organs," in *Manual of Human Evolution*, ed. F. Kreibel (Philadelphia: Lippincott, 1912), 2:752-979.

18. A gene on the short arm of the Y chromosome induces the production of H-Y antigen, which triggers the neutral gonad to become a testicle. Therman, *Human Chromosomes*, p. 114; and Paul Saenger, "Abnormal Sex Differentiation," *Journal of Pediatrics* (Jan. 1981):2.

19. Saenger, "Abnormal Sex Differentiation," p.3.

20. Wilson, "Phenotypic Differentiation," p. 1277.

21. Ibid., pp. 1277, 1280; also W.E. Ellenwood et al., "Control of Steroidogenesis in Rhesus Fetal Testes," *Twelfth Annual Meeting of Society of Reproduction* 20, suppl.1.

22. Short, "Sex Determination," p. 123.

23. T.C. Hsu, *Human and Mammalian Cytogenetics: An Historical Perspective* (New York: Springer-Verlag, 1979), p. 77.

24. Ibid., p. 56. This process is called *lyonization*, after its discoverer, genetic researcher Mary S. Lyon of Great Britain.

25. The simultaneous broadcasting of "We Are the World" on more than five thousand stations worldwide took place on Good Friday in 1985 (*New York Times*, April 5, 1985). "Live Aid" concerts were staged simultaneously in London and Philadelphia on July 13. As later chapters explain, both Good Friday and the number 13 relate symbolically to the yang-dimension of femininity and the exertive womblike Death Goddess who both slays and gives birth. Although surely not by conscious design, it is eerily appropriate that these events auguring the style of the coming "Age of the Yang Womb" took place on dates that reverberate with yang-feminine significance. This is what Jung would call a *synchronicity*.

Chapter Eight
Conversion to the Divine Womb

1. Jean Shinoda Bolen, *Goddesses in Everywoman.*

2. Charlene Spretnak has researched the pre-Olympian myths, drawing on the work of Jane Ellen Harrison, Marija Gimbutas, Lewis Farnell, Robert Graves, E.O.

James, Carl Kerenyi, Martin Nilsson, George Thompson, and R.F. Willetts. She collected fragments from many sources to reconstruct the prepatriarchal stories of eleven goddesses, among them Demeter and Persephone. My retelling of this story is closely based on Spretnak's "Demeter and Persephone," in *Lost Goddesses of Early Greece*, pp. 105-18.

3. Walker, *Women's Encyclopedia*, "Demeter."

4. Monaghan, *The Book of Goddesses and Heroines*, "Demeter."

5. Walker, *Woman's Encyclopedia*, "Kore."

6. Through Dutch *kronje* and *karonje*, "crone" connects to both "carcass" and "hag." "Hag" may also be related to Greek *hagio*, meaning "holy." The death-crone is wise and holy, as well as ugly.

7. This common but picturesque term for menopause hints at the transforming potential of the Crone.

8. "God is light and in him there is no darkness at all" (1 John 1:5). "Cast off the works of darkness and put on the armor of light" (Rom. 13:12).

9. The solar-patriarchal mind-set is suspicious of *all* phases of the moon. Both New Moon and Full Moon are associated with "lunacy." However, the dark of the moon is considered especially sinister, the Full Moon merely uncanny. A look at poetic language reveals that the bright Full Moon is often considered romantic and spellbinding in a favorable way. I know of no poetic praise of the dark New Moon.

10. This parallels the danger to women living under patriarchal conditions, whose only access to yang energy seems to be by identifying with the phallic animus. Having lost their own yang womb power, they become "women in pants," figuratively "carried away" by the animus.

11. John 7:6—"my time has not yet come."   John 7:8—"my time has not yet fully come." John 2:4—"my hour has not yet come."   John 7:30—"no one laid hands on him, because his hour had not yet come."   John 8:20—"no one arrested him because his hour had not yet come."   Matthew 26:18—"my time is at hand."   Matthew 26:45—"Behold, the hour is at hand."   John 12:23—"the hour has come for the Son of man to be glorified."   John 13:1—"Jesus knew that his hour had come."   John 17:1—"Father, the hour has come."

12. Jesus was arrested at night by soldiers and members of the Jewish Temple guard sent by the religious elders and priests. He was taken to Annas and Caiaphas, former and current high priests of the Temple, who presented him to the ruling council of religious teachers and elders for trial according to the religious law. He was convicted of blasphemy for claiming to be the Messiah/Son of God. According to Jewish law, the punishment for blasphemy was death. However, because Jerusalem was then under Roman rule, the Temple had no jurisdiction to execute criminals. So the next morning the religious officials took Jesus to the local Roman governor, Pontius Pilate. Pilate was not eager to handle the case, with its overlapping Jewish and civil jurisdictions. He sent the prisoner to Herod, Roman governor of neighboring Galilee, who questioned him and sent him back to Pilate. Pilate finally sentenced him to death for the political crime of setting himself up as "King of the Jews" in defiance of the Roman emperor.

13. There are several versions of the resulting god, called interchangeably Pluton, Plouton, Plutus, or Pluto. All are associated with darkness and bounty. One is the blind god of wealth. Another is said to preside over mining and precious minerals buried in the earth. The third is the lord of the underworld, realm of the dead.

14. Thus deprived of her original yang powers, Demeter$_2$ can be construed as an overly possessive mother whose daughter must be freed from her clutches by the intervention of the male. From this perspective, the rape of Persephone$_2$ is a saving act, initiating a separation necessary for her development—just as it was necessary for patriarchy to bring about separation from the matrix for the developmental good of the human species. Demeter$_2$'s anger and extreme grief can be considered as stemming from the exaggerated and neurotic overdevelopment of the gestative, nurturant, containing qualities. Further, she is pictured as subsequently withholding her one valued commodity, her nurturance, thus turning it into a tool for manipulating those more powerful than herself. The very feminine qualities most prized within the patriarchal world view are thus the cause of Demeter's "neurotic" behavior so long as she identifies exclusively with them; their negation is her only weapon for survival in a system in which she has no initiating power. According to the original story, however, Demeter's grief was not neurotic. It was portrayed as profound, but in proportion to the sacrifice—the immensity of which is parallel to the heavenly Father willingly sending his Son. She, too, willingly gives her only child.

15. Feminist theologian Fiorenza states a similar premise: "Whereas in a feminist conversion *men* must take the option of the oppressed and become women-identified, in such a conversion *women* must seek to overcome our deepest self-alienation. Since all women are socialized to respect and to identify with men, our position of advocacy must be articulated not as an 'option for the oppressed' but as self-respect and self-identification as women in a patriarchal society and religion. While feminist theology advocates for men a 'theology of relinquishment,' it articulates for women a theology of 'self-affirmation.'" Elizabeth Schussler Fiorenza, *Bread Not Stone: The Challenge of Feminist Biblical Interpretation* (Boston: Beacon Press, 1984), p. xv.

16. The woman who has already succeeded in seemingly escaping the ritual subjugation normative for her sex within patriarchy, by becoming an "honorary man" or a "female king," has yet to disidentify with the world view that predisposes her to experience mankind as the human standard and her own gender as substandard.

17. New words by Genia Pauli Haddon to traditional hymn "Come Ye Faithful, Raise the Strain." For entire hymn, see page 230 in Appendix A.

18. At a symbolic level it is significant that this act marking his "coming of age" involved transformation of water into bloodlike wine in womblike vessels—a kind of spiritual menarche marking the start of his public ministry.

19. In two accounts, the woman is nameless; the third identifies her as Mary of Bethany, sister of Martha and Lazarus. This story may be but a variant version of the one just cited, or may represent a distinct event.

20. Matthew 26:6-13; Mark 14:3-9; John 12:1-8.

21. The women at the cross are listed variously as including: Mary, the mother of Jesus; Mary's sister; Mary, the wife of Clopas; Mary Magdalene; Salome; Joanna; Mary, the mother of James and Joses (Joseph); Mary, the mother of Zebedee's sons.

Chapter Nine
The Body that Bleeds but Is Not Wounded

1. For a summary of shortcomings of research practices through the early 1980's and guidelines for future research on menstruation and menopause, see Ann M. Voda and Mona Eliasson, "Menopause: The Closure of Menstrual Life," *Women and Health* 8, nos. 2-3 (1983):137-56; Randi Daimon Koeske, "Lifting the Curse of Menstruation: Toward a Feminist Perspective on the Menstrual Cycle," *Women and Health* 8, nos. 2-3 (1983):1-16.

2. P.J. Jongbloet, "Menses and Moon Phases, Ovulation and Seasons, Vitality and Month of Birth," *Developmental Medicine and Child Neurology* 25, no. 4 (Aug. 1983):525.

3. Penelope Shuttle and Peter Redgrove, *The Wise Wound: Eve's Curse and Everywoman* (New York: Richard Marek, 1978), pp. 99-101.

4. See John Bancroft et al., "Mood, Sexuality, Hormones, and the Menstrual Cycle. III. "Sexuality and the Role of Androgens," *Psychosomatic Medicine* 45, no. 6 (Dec 1983):509-17.

5. See Paula Weidegger's interpretation of a study by Benedek in *Menstruation and Menopause: The Physiology and Psychology, the Myth and the Reality,* (New York: Knopf, 1975), pp. 122-23. Also see Shuttle and Redgrove, *Wise Wound,* pp. 89-91.

6. One reason suggested for heightened perimenstrual sensitivity is that the pelvic organs, breasts, and vulva become swollen and tumescent in response to hormone levels. In some women, this increased turgor makes further stimulation unpleasant and even painful. This, as well as negative conditioning about the nastiness of menstruation, may account for the number of women who experience decreased sexual appetite perimenstrually.

7. In addition to references in n. 5, see Bancroft et al., "Sexuality and the Role of Androgens," pp. 509-16.

8. Weidegger, *Menstruation and Menopause,* p. 120, citing Masters and Johnson study.

9. For discussion of anthropological theories about the evolution of the clitoris, see Sarah Blaffer Hrdy, *The Woman That Never Evolved* (Cambridge, MA: Harvard University Press, 1981).

10. See study by Benedek referred to by Weidegger, *Menstruation and Menopause,* p. 122-23.

11. In both men and women, progesterone is the basic steroid molecule, precursor for synthesis of all steroids by the body. (Personal interview with Ann L. Voda, R.N., Ph.D; April, 1992.)

12. Rosetta Reitz, *Menopause: A Positive Approach* (Radnor, PA: Chilton, 1977), p. 143, quotes Dr. Estelle R. Ramey from the Department of Physiology and Physics at Georgetown University School of Medicine: "Both women and men secrete the entire spectrum of steroid hormones."

13. Gloria Bachmann et al., "Sexual Expression and Its Determinants in the Postmenopausal Woman," *Maturitas* 6 (1984):19-24. Also Reitz, *Menopause,* p. 143.

14. In the human fetus this hormone is produced in the developing gonad, whether ovary or testicle. In this sense, the term "testosterone" is inappropriate. Due to the influence

of a gene on the Y chromosome (see Chapter 6), at a certain point in embryological development a greater amount is produced in the testis than in the ovary. It is the presence of increased concentrations of testosterone at this crucial developmental point that triggers the formation of male-appearing genitals. In this sense, there is some justification in calling it a "male" hormone. The problem in doing so is that its natural presence and role in female physiology is obscured.

15. Directed by Stephen Spielberg, based on the novel of the same name by Alice Walker (New York: Harcourt Brace Jovanovich, 1982).

16. See, e.g., David Hart, "The Evolution of the Feminine in Fairy Tales," *Psychological Perspectives* 9, no. 1 (1978); Marie-Louise von Franz, *Problems of the Feminine in Fairy Tales* (Zurich: Spring Publications, 1972); Philip T. Zabriskie, "The Loathly Damsel: The Motif of the Ugly Woman," *Quadrant* 12, no. 1 (1979):47-63; William O. Wolcott, "Of Stepmothers and Witches," *Psychological Perspectives* 14, no. 1 (1983).

17. Three times Jesus uses the image of "drinking the cup" to refer to his death. He asks two disciples who desire glory and honor in heaven, "Are you able to drink the cup I am to drink?" (Matt.20:22). Facing impending arrest and execution, in anguish of soul he begs God, "My Father, if it be possible, let this cup pass from me." (Matt.26:39). Later, when one of the disciples tries to fend off Jesus' captors, he says, "Put your sword into its sheath; shall I not drink the cup which the Father has given me? (John 18:11).

18. Shuttle and Redgrove, in *Wise Wound*, cite Emma Jung (p.119) and Ann Ulanov (p.113).

19. Ovulation typically does not actually begin with the first menstruation. Full cyclicity is not established for a number of months or even years.

20. Notwithstanding loving sentiments that may be attached to the unborn baby, at the purely physiological level the fetus is an alien presence in the woman's body, a living tumor or parasite, drawing its entire nourishment from its "host." The placenta acts as a filter between the mother's blood and that of the infant, for otherwise her antibodies would attack the fetus. "Leakage" across the placenta in fact can be deadly when the mother's blood type is Rh-negative and the baby's is Rh-positive. When Rh-positive red blood cells enter the woman's circulation, her immune system produces antibodies as if against disease. Blood serum bearing these antibodies in turn passes through the placenta into the baby's circulation, attacking red blood cells through-out its body. Joseph M. Hill and William Dameshek, *The Rh Factor in the Clinic and the Laboratory* (New York: Grune and Stratton, 1948).

21. See also Ann M. Voda and Jim Tucker, *Menopause, Me, & You: The Sound of Women Pausing*, publication pending, 1994.

22. Penny W. Budoff, *No More Hot Flashes and Other Good News* (New York: Putnam, 1983).

23. Voda and Eliasson, "Menopause," p.146.

24. Weidegger, *Menstruation and Menopause*, pp. 205 & 225.

25. Dena Taylor and Amber Coverdale Sumrall, eds., *Women of the 14th Moon*, (Freedom, CA: Crossing Press, 1991). Includes selection by Haddon.

26. Reitz, *Menopause*, p.165. Technically, two forms of Estrogen are produced. During the menstrual years, estradiol (E_2) predominates. Estradiol is produced in the ovaries. Post-menopausally, estrone (E_1), produced in fat cells, predominates. Thus, very lean

("stylish") women are at greater risk for osteoporosis than are women whose bodies are somewhat round.

27. Voda and Eliasson, "Menopause," p. 148.

28. Ibid., quoting R.W. Kistner, "The Menopause," in R.M. Caplan and W.J. Sweeny, eds., *Advances in Obstetrics and Gynecology* (Baltimore, Md.: Williams & Wilkins Co., 1978).

29. See references and examples in Voda and Eliasson, "Menopause".

30. Ibid., p.148.

31. Stated during personal interview by Haddon, April 1992.

32. Voda and Eliasson, p.144.

33. Multiple studies have found that although menarche has shifted earlier and earlier each generation, the average age of menopause has not changed since antiquity. Ibid., p. 146.

34. See for example the *Sutras* of Patanjali and *Vignana-bhairava*.

35. See Appendix in Lee Sanella, *The Kundalini Experience*, (Lower Lake, CA: Integral Publishing, 1987).

36. Neuromap Research SYSTEM-24, runs on IBM AT.

37. Data in graph form, on file at The Monroe Institute.

38. Sannella, *The Kundalini Experience.* Stanislav Grof and Christian Grof, eds. *Spiritual Emergency,* (New York: Tarcher, 1989). Emma Bragdon, *Helping People in Spiritual Emergency* (Los Altos, CA: Lightening Up Press, 1988). Bonnie Greenwell, *Energies of Transformation,* (Cupertino, CA: Shakti River Press, 1988).

39. See from previous note, Sanella; Grof and Grof; Bragdon.

40. Itzhak Bentov, *Stalking the Wild Pendumum: On the Mechanics of Consciousness* (Rochester, VT: Destiny Books, 1988), pp. 174-185.

Chapter Ten
Gift of the Thirteenth God-Mother

1. Numerous versions of this story have been published as children's books, and it is included in most collections of Grimm's fairy tales as well. *Synopsis of the tale:*

A king invited the whole kingdom to a great feast to celebrate the long-awaited birth of a daughter. In that kingdom were thirteen Wise Women, or Fairy God-Mothers, but since he had golden dinner plates for only twelve, one God-Mother was not invited. At the feast each used her sacred powers to bestow a gift on the baby: virtue, beauty, riches, etc. After eleven had so blessed her, the thirteenth burst in and loudly announced her gift: "On her thirteenth [some versions say fifteenth or seventeenth] birthday the princess shall prick herself with a spindle and fall down dead." All were shocked. Could nothing be done? The twelfth God-Mother, who had not yet given her gift, stepped forward now. "Although I cannot fully undo what my sister has said, yet it shall not be death, but a deep sleep of a hundred years." Determined to save his daughter from even this lesser misfortune, the king ordered that every spindle and spinning wheel in the kingdom be destroyed. Only one was spared, locked high in a tower where an old woman toiled to spin the yarn and thread needed in the kingdom. On the fated birthday the princess wandered through the palace and came upon the tower. At the top she turned the rusty key in the lock, the door sprang open, and there in a little room sat the old woman with her spindle, busily spinning. "What sort of thing is that, twirling round so merrily?" the princess asked, and took the spindle, wanting to spin too. But scarcely had she touched it when the gift of the thirteenth God-Mother was fulfilled. Upon pricking her finger she, and the entire royal court with her, fell into a deep sleep. All around the castle a dense hedge of thornbushes sprang up. From time to time princes from surrounding kingdoms tried to get through, but all perished amid the thorns. Just as the hundred years came to an end, another prince came to try his luck. As he drew near the hedge it lost its thorns and burst into bloom. He easily passed through, soon found the princess sleeping in the tower room, and bent to kiss her. That very moment she awakened and all the court with her. She and the prince went down together, celebrated their wedding, and lived happily ever after.

2. The word *fairy* derives from the same root as *fate*, confirming that the fairy God-Mother is a form of the fate-dealing Goddess. In some versions the thirteen are called "Wise Women" instead of "Fairy God-Mothers." As described in Chapter 8, the Crone is both wise and holy.

3. For description of spinning apparatus and techniques, see Marion L. Channing, *The Textile Tools of Colonial Homes* (New Bedford, MA: Reynolds-DeWalt Printing, 1969).

4. See Ken Wilbur, *Up from Eden: A transpersonal View of Human Evolution* (Boulder, CO: Shambhala, 1983).

5. See Adrienne Rich, *Of Woman Born: Motherhood as Experience and Institution* (New York: Norton, 1976).

Chapter Eleven
Delivered by the Crone

1. As David Hart has pointed out, just because a man is the hero of a story does not mean the psychological events depicted pertain only to men. "This culture hero is our ego or our consciousness of Self, and...this is a common (and uncommon) human experience regardless of sex." In "The Evolution of the Feminine in Fairy Tales."

2. A 20th Century-Fox, Brandywine Production, collaboratively written and directed by James Cameron and Gale Ann Hurd, and starring Sigourney Weaver as Ripley. (Dialogue quoted from soundtrack.)

3. All three are from the collection by the Grimm Brothers.

4. Marie-Louise von Franz, *Interpretation of Fairy Tales: An Introduction to the Psychology of Fairy Tales* (Irving, TX: Spring Publications, 1978), p. 32.

5. The words *newt* and *salamander* commonly are used interchangeably, even though two different genuses are involved. Both are amphibians (like frogs), in the order Mutabilis. Technically, salamanders of the the genus *Ambystomidae*, comprising thirteen (!) species, including the tiger salamander and marbled salamander. Newts are in the genus *Salamandridae*, which includes the American newt, crested newt, and European fire "salamander"—the ones most directly linked to the myths. Thus the name Newt

suggests transformation in two ways: the name of the order ("changeable") and the mythological meanings of the fire "salamander," which is actually a newt.

6. See in Jung's *Collected Works*: vol. 12, #404 n.8, #537 n. 581, fig 138, and #391; vol. 13, #177 and #258; vol. 14, #172 n., #264 and #632.

7. Edward Topsell, *Historie of Four-Footed Beasts*, written in 1607, cited in *The International Wildlife Encyclopedia*, ed. Maurice Burton (New York: Marshall Cavendish, 1969), p. 766.

8. In slang, a "newt" is a novice, someone new to a situation. From army and factory use, condensing "new" and "recruit." *A Dictionary of American Slang*, ed. Harold Wentworth and Stuart Flexner (New York: Thomas Crowell, 1975), p. 353.

Chapter Twelve
Developing Devotion to God-Feminine

1. The moon's quarter-points for each coming month are given in the meteorologist's report of any large newspaper. Consult an almanac to plan ahead through the year.

2. Some men and some women seem genuinely ready to engage liturgically with God-Feminine; other individuals of both genders seem very resistant to any deviation from patriarchal patterns. Within my limited experience, a greater number of women than men are yearning for devotional relationship to God-Feminine.

3. Glossolalia or "tongues" is ecstatic speech in a language other than any known by the speaker, typically praising God, and attributed to the enlivening effects of the Holy Spirit. Although in some instances witnesses have reported recognizing a known foreign language, some researchers report that linguistic analysis of a selection of tape-recorded glossolalia samples does not reveal integrated linguistic structure. Regardless, the subjective experience of glossolalics is that the Holy Spirit is speaking through them, giving them means of expressing the otherwise inexpressible joy, devotion, and thanksgiving they feel in intimacy with God.

4. By Josephine Bush, based in part on a tract written in 1897 by Sister Nivedita, *Kali the Mother*, 2d ed. (Mayavati, Himalayas: Advaita Asrama, 1983).

5. Hallie Inglehart, *Womanspirit: A Guide to Women's Wisdom*.

6. All four gospels agree that Jesus ate his last supper, was betrayed, was arrested and tried, and was crucified and buried within the twenty-four-hour period ending at sundown on a Friday. The Gospels according to Matthew, Mark, and Luke specifically name this twenty-four-hour period as the first day of Passover. The Gospel according to John claims it was the day *before* the Passover feast, but nevertheless describes the Last Supper in terms that clearly relate it to the traditional seder, as celebrated in that time. Biblical scholars continue to analyze this discrepancy, seeking ways to harmonize the two versions, but for our purposes it is sufficient that all four gospels indicate a connection of one sort or another between the Last Supper and the celebration of Passover. See Joachim Jeremias, *The Eucharistic Words of Jesus* (London: SCM Press, 1964); Norman Hook, *The Eucharist in the New Testament* (London: Epworth Press, 1964); Scott McMormick, Jr., *The Lord's Supper: A Biblical Interpretation* (Philadelphia: Westminster Press,

1966); and Eduard Schweizer, *The Lord's Supper according to the New Testament* (Philadelphia: Fortress Press, 1967).

7. *The Jewish Encyclopedia* (New York: Funk and Wagnall's, 1905), 9:548.

8. *Encyclopedia Judaica* (New York: Macmillan, 1971), 13:170; and *The Jewish Encyclopedia*, 9:548.

9. See Exodus 33:14 and 40:34, Numbers 35:34, Deuteronomy 12:5, Isaiah 60:19, and commentaries in *Pentateuch & Haftorahs: Hebrew Text, English Translation, and Commentary*, ed. J.H. Hertz, 2d ed. (London: Soncino Press, 1972), pp. 723, 801.

10. Heinrich Zimmer, *Myths and Symbols in Indian Art and Civilization* (Princeton, NJ: Princeton University Press, 1946) p. 25, as quoted in Walker, "Shakti," *Women's Encyclopedia.*

11. I personally have met many Christians who in their private devotional lives experience the Holy Spirit as Feminine-Divine Presence.

12. *Dictionary of the Bible*, ed. James Hastings, rev. ed. (New York: Scribner's, 1963), p. 389.

13. Alan Richardson, ed., *A Dictionary of Christian Theology* (Philadelphia: Westminster Press, 1969).

Chapter Thirteen
You Are She

1. When Peter first recognized Jesus as the Christ, Jesus exclaimed that this insight was not a matter of ordinary human insight, but was given by God.

2. Written by Irene Levine, Genia Pauli Haddon, and Linda DeMarco during WomanChurch-East retreat, "Birthing Mystery," Pentecost, 1988. [Copyright © Genia Pauli Haddon, 1993.] To order a collection of songs celebrating the Divine in feminine metaphors, see back of this book.

3. Both beards and breasts are later enhancements of structures that are initially gender-neutral. In the embryo and throughout childhood, there are no differences between the breasts of males and females. Not only do they look alike; the interior structure is identical for both sexes. (Carl C. Frances, *Introduction to Human Anatomy*, 3d ed. [St. Louis: C.V. Mosby, 1959], p. 466; Alexander A Maximow and William Bloom, *A Textbook of Histology*, 7th ed. [Philadelphia: W.B. Saunders, 1957], p. 551; Charles H. Best and Normal B. Tayler, *The Living Body*, 4th ed. [New York: Henry Holt, 1958], p. 653.) Before puberty, breasts of both sexes contain rudimentary glandular tissue similar in structure to sweat glands. (Greisheimer, *Anatomy and Physiology*, p. 778.) In the female, at puberty the duct system elaborates and branches out, but the glandular nodes remain rudimentary. Only upon pregnancy do the glandular follicles develop fully for the production of milk. (Best and Tayler, *Living Body*, p. 653.) The production of a beard on a man is due not to greater hairiness than the woman, but to hormonally stimulated growth of the same sort and number of hair follicles as the woman has on her face. Males and females within a family, race, or ethnic group have equal numbers of hair follicles. (Susan Brownmiller, *Femininity* [New York: Fawcett/Columbine, 1985], p. 139.)

4. The increase in size of the female breast is due mostly to deposits of fatty tissue. Contrary to popular expectation, very small-breasted women have as much glandular tissue as large-breasted women and can suckle infants as successfully. Brownmiller, *Femininity*, p. 41.

5. I am indebted to Jim Overall for this insight.

Chapter Fourteen
Uniting Sex, Self, & Spirit

1. The mystery of the Christian trinity can be re-expressed in a holographic analogy where the transcendent God and the indwelling Holy Spirit are the original intersecting beams, and Christ the beam illuminating the hologram of the Universe to reveal the essence of Being.

2. An audio cassette by the author guiding you through both "Sacramental Hands" and "Sacramental Gazing with a Partner" is available. See ordering information at back of this book.

3. From "The Calling" by Irene Levine, a song written for WomanChurch-East. See information at back of this book for ordering a collection of such music.

4. Matt. 5:30.

5. See Matt 5:38-45.

6. This practice is similar to an exercise described by Margo Anand, *The Art of Sexual Ecstasy: The Path of Sacred Sexuality for Western Lovers* (Los Angeles: Tarcher, 1989) pp. 116-120 She calls this "Soul Gazing" and recommends limiting sessions to a maximum of five minutes until you are well-grounded in the technique.

7. If you can't find a partner interested in practicing this with you, you can gaze at your own face reflected in a large mirror propped securely in front of you.

Appendix B
A Sample Living Will

1. This example is closely based on a widely circulated model that first appeared in an article by Sessela Bok, M.D., in the *New England Journal of Medicine* and was re-published with permission to duplicate in "Questions of Life and Death," *MemoScope* 15, no. 3 (Summer 1985). Although this sample is not intended to serve as a legal document, some states have now passed legislation recognizing such documents as binding. Check with an attorney familiar with the laws in your state. Even where "living wills" have no *legal* status, expressing your desires in this way will nevertheless inform your family and final caretakers of your beliefs and preferences about the role of medical intervention during your last days.

About the Author

Genia Pauli Haddon, D.Min., Ph.D. is the founder of Haelix, a center for wholeness and transformation of consciousness in Scotland, Connecticut. She lectures widely on spirituality and personal development.

The scope of Dr. Haddon's trainings and certifications embraces a spectrum of spiritual disciplines. She is ordained to ministry in a mainline Protestant denomination, and served as a parish minister and pastoral counselor prior to retiring from formal ministry in 1991. She has studied with Yogi Amrit Desai, completing both basic and advanced trainings for certification as a Kripalu yoga teacher, and serves on the program staff at *Kripalu Center for Yoga and Health*. In 1978 and 1980, she studied briefly at the *C.G.Jung Institute* in Zurich, holds doctorates in analytical psychology and counseling, and has fifteen years' experience as a depth psychotherapist. At *The Monroe Institute*, center for researching human consciousness, she has trained with Robert A. Monroe, creator of Hemi-Sync, and is fully certified by the Institute to train others. A practitioner of neo-shamanic healing methods, her shamanic training includes courses at the international *Foundation for Shamanic Studies*, most notably with anthropologist Michael Harner. She holds an appointment at *The Union Institute* as Adjunct Professor for the Ph.D. program in spirituality and psychology.

Dr. Haddon is "over fifty," and "post-menopausal." Her own spiritual development has required several crises, experiences on which she draws in helping others during spiritual emergence. Some key milestones are a "born again" conversion to Christianity, a six-month suicidal depression, and more than a thousand hours of intense Jungian psychoanalysis. She and her life partner, Ren, have been together more than thirty years. They have two adult children. Leisure enjoyments include country walks, gardening, and building mortarless walls of natural fieldstone.

❖

Index

257

F

FSH, 130-32
Fate, 150, 156
Father (God-Masc.), 67,
99-100, 106-109, 112,
120, 124, 141, 162,
178, 180, 199-200
Father (in human family),
50-51, 172
Fathers (founders), 9,
51,52, 70
Fear, 23, 39, 48, 66
of Crone, 143-144, 148
of Death, 148, 153
of God, 99
of Menopause, 148,
of Thirteen, 149
of Yang womb, 57, 158
Feminine, femininity, 15-
19, 21, 26, 30, 55
Exertive/yang:
and coming Age, 74,
80-97
and yang-masc., 157
and yin-fem., 45, 168
anger and, 49, 55
as primary identity, 58
and religion, 66, 227-
31, 236-37
childhood experiences of,
46-47
contrast yang-masc.,
26, 47-48, 59
contrast yin-fem., 45, 55
described, 23-24
developing, 31, 47, 49-
50, 53-56, 59
exaggeration of, 48
fear of, 32, 46-48, 158
repressing, 43-45, 48,
59, 167
substituting yin-fem.,
51
substituting phallic,
49-52, 55, 58-59
Gestative/yin:
and Matrical Age, 74,
76-79, 95-96
and religion, 65, 220-
25, 233
contrast yang-fem., 55,
74

contrast yin-masc., 26,
35,
described, 19, 22-23
developing, 57
exaggeration of, 52,
57-58, 163, 166, 172,
174
rejecting, 58
substitute for yang-
fem., 45
Fetus, 16, 81
Full moon, 116, 118-19,
125, 130, 132-33, 136,
176-78, 194-95,

G

"Gail," 56-58
Gandhi, Mahatma, 125
Genes, 81-82, 88-90
Gilligan, Carol, 14
"Glorious Things of Thee
Are Spoken," 226, 234
"Go to Dark Gethsemane,"
229, 236
Goal(s), 10, 18, 23, 47-48,
59, 103, 170, 203
God:
is One, 10, 68-69, 99,
109, 200, 202, 221,
227, 230
name not to be spoken,
101
names are metaphors,
99-100
new names of, 100, 107
See also Deity; and various names/titles
God-Feminine, 17, 77,
130, 133, 142, 146,
148, 175-76, 179-80,
182, 185, 189-95, 197-
99, 202-204
See also various names
and titles
God image(s), 25, 99, 107,
133, 163, 170, 176,
198, 200
God-Masculine, 130, 148,
153, 168, 175, 192,
194, 197, 201
See also various names
and titles

God-Mother, 150-52, 155-
56, 159, 161, 172,
175, 236
Goddess, 15, 112, 147-
148, 155, 157-58, 181-
82, 188-89, 193-95,
203
See also various name
and titles
Good Friday, 66
Great Goddess, 44, 109
Great Mother (God-Fem.),
172, 188
Great Woman (God-Fem.),
188, 200
Grief, 111-12, 120, 143,
155
Gynogen, 136

H

H-Y antigen, 87
Hades (God-Masc.), 120,
122-25
Hair
facial, 143-45, 206
on chest, 59
on legs, 44, 52-53
Hathor (God-Fem.), 102
Hecate (God-Fem.), 53,
118, 120, 125
Helios (God-Masc.), 120,
125
"Henry," 37-40
"Her Many Names," 185
Hera, 108
Hermes (God-Masc.), 120,
122,
Heroine, hero, 150, 161-
64, 169-70, 174, 196
Herod, 128
Hierarchy, hierarchical,
10-11, 51, 65, 75, 77,
93, 123-26, 140, 217
Hologram, 209-10
Holy Spirit (God-Fem.),
108-109, 112, 178-79,
195-96, 198-99, 207,
235
Homosexual, 39
Hormone(s), 85, 88, 130-
33, 135-36, 142-45,
206

U

Unconscious(ness), 9, 13, 25, 35, 75, 154, 166, 174
Underworld, 109-11, 113, 120, 137, 190
Unisex ideal, 15
Uroboros, 101, 103
Uterus, 16, 131-33, 170, 206
See also Womb

V

Vagina, 19, 22, 68, 118, 130-32, 135, 144, 206
Venus (God-Fem.), 108
Vessel, 19, 33-34, 99, 140
Vesta (God-Fem.), 108
Victor(ious), 10, 65, 122-23, 128, 160, 162-63, 168, 170
"Vincent," "Vince," 40-42
Virgin (God-Fem.), 176
Virgin-Mother (God-Fem.), 118, 141

W

Waning (moon), 116-17, 119, 121-22, 132-33, 176-77
Waxing (moon), 116-19, 121, 132-33, 176-77
"We Are the World," 96
Web, 57, 166
Whole(s), 75, 77, 92-95, 113, 170, 181

Wisdom, 49, 52, 57, 107, 114, 125, 127, 134, 138, 140-41, 179, 195-96
Witch, 30, 45, 114, 137-38, 155, 163
Wither(ing), 114, 121-22, 153-54
Womb, 9, 43, 46, 50, 54, 59, 76, 160, 163, 170, 176, 181, 192
Divine, 67, 109, 118, 122-24, 125-29, 141, 153, 156, 180, 193-94, 198-99, 207, 222, 226, 230-31, 236
conversion to, 108-28
exertive, 23-24, 26, 50-51, 54, 63, 75, 121-22, 125, 127, 129, 131, 141, 158-59, 166-67, 169, 173, 200, 204, 227
gestative, 19, 22-24, 26, 49-50, 57, 63, 127, 129, 134-35, 141, 153, 166, 189, 200
Women's Movement, 12, 49, 72-73, 97, 104
Worship(ing), 61-71, 99, 176, 178, 182, 197
four services, 217-37

X

X chromosome, 83, 85, 88-90, 133

evolution of, 89-90
in males, 97-98
X^mX^p pattern, 103, 91-92, 95, 97, 157, 170
XX pattern, 75, 83-85, 87-88, 206
XY pattern, 75, 83-85, 87-89, 98, 206

Y

Y chromosome, 83, 85-86, 88-89, 91, 97-98, 162, 170
evolution of, 89-90
Yahweh (God-Masc.), 106, 195, 224
Yang, 18-19
and dark Goddess, 119
and light/good, 118
cyclicity with yin, 133-34
definition, 20-21
Yin, 18-19
and dark/evil, 118
and Mother Goddess, 119
contrast masculine yin, feminine yin, 35, 48-49
cyclicity with yang, 133-34
definition, 20-21, 29

Z

Zeus (God-Masc.), 108, 120, 122-24, 139

SUPPORTING YOUR SPIRITUAL LIFE

Practicing Sacramental Awareness   AUDIO CASSETTE
by Genia Pauli Haddon

Clear, gentle guidance for practicing sacramental awareness, as described in Haddon's *Uniting Sex, Self, & Spirit*. Genia's narration is accompanied by the spell-binding tones of the Tamboura, an ancient stringed instrument designed to recreate the eternal sound of OM. SIDE 1 (27 min.) leads you through a consciousness exercise focusing on your own hands. SIDE 2 (28 min.) introduces the practice of sacramental gazing, to be done with a partner or your own reflection in a mirror.

#SA-14/1.5 - 55 Min. cassette
$14.95 + $1.50 shipping
ISBN 1-881311-14-7

The Art of Living   CARDS
by Haelix

Ancient yogic wisdom for living today. Each card presents an inspiring Affirmation in the language of the deep Self, with teachings on the reverse side to engage the finite mind with profound insights about how to actualize these values in your own daily life, plus ways to orient yourself within the six stages of spiritual evolution. Choose a card each day as the template through which to embrace spiritual living with greater depth and focus. TEN PALM-SIZED CARDS SAY IT ALL. Packaged in a richly patterned wallet-folder with velcro closure.

#A-L10/1 - 5¹/4" x 2³/4" Inspirational Cards
$10.95 + $1 shipping
ISBN 1-881311-21-X

Yoga for Round Bodies, 1 & 2   VHS VIDEOS
with Certified Kripalu Yoga Teachers
Linda DeMarco & Genia Pauli Haddon

You can enjoy the physical and subtle benefits of KRIPALU YOGA right now, just as you are! Classic postures modified to fit the unique needs of the ample figure, are taught by two round-bodied teachers. Each volume contains three half-hour sessions. Fun, Gentle, Easy to Do. Features music by Steve Roach.

Recommended by *New Age Journal!*

"Gifted teachers....A first quality production" —*Big Beautiful Woman*

"Emphasizes meditative movement. Helpful." —*Yoga Journal*

"Warmth & humor shine through. Highly recommended."—*Kripalu Yoga Teachers Newsletter*

#Y4-29/3 - VHS Videos, each vol. approx. 1-1/2 hours
$29.95 each + $3 shipping
Vol.1-ISBN 1-881311-05-8   Vol.2-ISBN 1-881311-06-6

TO ORDER-Send check or money order for products and shipping to:
PLUS Publications, Box 265 Suite 93, Scotland, CT 06264
-Connecticut purchasers, add State Sales Tax • Prices subject to change without notice-

Uniting Sex, Self, & Spirit   QUALITY PAPERBACK
by Genia Pauli Haddon, D.Min. Ph.D.
Foreword by Georg Feuerstein

Let the body be your guide to new consciousness and deeper spirituality in a changing Age. Our own bodies, male and female, reveal four distinct templates shaping our every experience of both the seen and unseen dimensions of the Universe. Understanding these four metaphors can radically change your relationships to other people, to the Earth, to the Divine, and to yourself. Fresh solutions to hard everyday problems may suddenly seem obvious as you look at life through the lens of the body metaphors. Living with these new perspectives, you'll grow to appreciate your personal role in the cultural, spiritual, archetypal shift now underway as a New Age dawns. "Visionary...Powerful...Eloquent...Passionate...Integrative... bold..." -Georg Feuerstein.   "Fascinating...Iluminating...Liberating..."-Christine Downing. "The wisdom here is ageless..."-James David Audlin, Regional Chief, Free Cherokee Nation.

#SSS-15/2.5 - 6" X 9", 271 pages; Indexed
$15.95 + $1 shipping
ISBN 1-881311-13-9

Tamboura with Hemi-Sync™ for Meditating   STEREO AUDIO TAPE
by Haelix, with Hemi-Sync by The Monroe Institute

Ancient and modern technologies blend seamlessly in this unique resource to support spiritual work in altered states such as meditating, "journeying," and trance-state healing. The tamboura is a Vedic stringed instrument tuned to recreate the sound of the eternal OM. Hemi-Sync is specially formulated combinations of sounds, carefully blended and sequenced to synchronize electrical patterns in the two hemispheres of the brain and gently entrain brainwave patterns to match specific states of consciousness. Developed at The Monroe Institute, world renowned center for research on human consciousness, this safe, effective technology has been use-tested by more than 50,000 people. Unobtrusively woven through the rich reverberations of the tamboura, Hemi-Sync signals draw you smoothly into meditative states. SIDE 1 is calibrated to invite relaxation and stimulate dream-like imagery. SIDE 2 takes you into deep meditation.

#T/HS-14/1.5 - 30 min. each side
$14.95 + $1.50 shipping
ISBN 1-881311-15-5

One God, Many Names: Praise Him! Praise Her!   SPIRAL BOUND
Edited by Genia Pauli Haddon, D.Min.

A collection of more than twenty inspirational songs and hymns for rejoicing in the Divine One through both masculine and feminine imageries. New words to familiar hymns bring better balance. Several all-new compositions give expression to feminine nuances of Christian faith.

#FMH-6/1 - 5¹/2" x 8¹/2", 24 pages
$6.95 + $1 shipping
ISBN 1-881311-07-4

TO ORDER-Send check or money order for products and shipping to:
PLUS Publications, Box 265 Suite 93, Scotland, CT 06264
-Connecticut purchasers, add State Sales Tax • Prices subject to change without notice-

⇨ ⇨ MORE ⇨

Celebrating the Word Made Flesh:
Sacred Music of Christmas   SPIRAL BOUND
Edited by Genia Pauli Haddon, D.Min.

The revised Christmas songs in this book express the mystery of God-*with*-us, celebrating the intimate presence (rather than the superior distance) of the Divine. Think of these modified carols not as corrections, but as complements to the traditional songs of the season you love so well. May they deepen and enhance your musical celebration of the Christmas miracle.

#XS-5/1 - 5¹/2" x 8¹/2", 20 pages
$5.95 + $1 shipping
ISBN 1-881311-08-2

Family Advent Services:
for Families with Children age 3-8   SPIRAL BOUND
by Warren D. Haddon, M.S. and Genia Pauli Haddon, D.Min.

Sensitively designed to enthrall your children as *they* help re-create the Christmas story week by week, using Creche figures, candles, and such props as flashlights and blindfolds to enact key meanings. Encourages reverent regard for the Earth by calling attention to the role of stars, animals, and the very stones in welcoming the Christ-child. Written in simple language, without gender bias. Features extra-large print for the simple prayers, brief scriptures, and original holiday songs set to familiar tunes such as "Twinkle, Twinkle Little Star" and "Frere Jacque." Detailed guidance for creating five family programs, one for each of the four weeks of Advent, plus one for Christmas Eve or Christmas Night.

#ADV-8/2 - 5¹/2" x 8¹/2" , 50 pages
$8.95 + $2 shipping
ISBN 1-881311-12-0

Discovering Hemi-Sync™   AUDIO CASSETTE & BOOKLET
from Haelix and The Monroe Institute

Learn how whole-brain audio technology created by Robert A. Monroe, author of *Journeys Out of the Body*, can open doors to fuller consciousness, deeper meditative states, self-healing, and transpersonal guidance. Experience total relaxation as you listen to tones that synchronize the two halves of the brain and entrain its wave-patterns to match those typical for the relaxed state. Audio Cassette plus easy to understand booklet by Certified Hemi-Sync Trainer Genia Pauli Haddon, Ph.D. introduces this safe, powerful technology. Hemi-Sync tapes are regularly $14.95. With this SPECIAL OFFER, you get *both* the tape and booklet for just $12.95!

#HS+B-12/2 - approx. 40 Min. ea. side; both sides alike
$12.95 + $2 shipping
ISBN 1-881311-09-0

PLUS Publications is a Division of HAELIX.
ALL HAELIX PRODUCTS ARE GUARANTEED.

TO ORDER-Send check or money order for products and shipping to:
PLUS Publications, Box 265 Suite 93, Scotland, CT 06264
-Connecticut purchasers, add State Sales Tax • Prices subject to change without notice-